NEW STUDIES IN

C000193736

Slave of Christ

Titles in this series:

NEW STUDIES IN BIBLICAL THEOLOGY 8

Series editor: D. A. Carson

Slave of Christ

A NEW TESTAMENT METAPHOR FOR TOTAL DEVOTION TO CHRIST

Murray J. Harris

APOLLOS

APOLLOS (an imprint of Inter-Varsity Press),
38 De Montfort Street, Leicester LE1 7GP, England

© Murray J. Harris 1999

Murray J. Harris has asserted his right under the Copyright, Designs and Patents Act,
1988, to be identified as Author of this work.

First published 1999

British Library Cataloguing in Publication Data
A catalogue record for this book is available from the British Library.

ISBN 0–85111–517–9

Set in Times New Roman
Typeset in Great Britain
Printed in Great Britain by Creative Print and Design Group (Wales), Ebbw Vale

To my dear wife, Jennifer,
a modern-day Dorcas

Contents

Series preface

New Studies in Biblical Theology is a series of monographs that address key issues in the discipline of biblical theology. Contributions to the series focus on one or more of three areas: 1. the nature and status of biblical theology, including its relations with other disciplines (*e.g.*, historical theology, exegesis, systematic theology, historical criticism, narrative theology); 2. the articulation and exposition of the structure of thought of a particular biblical writer or corpus; and 3. the delineation of a biblical theme across all or part of the biblical corpora.

Above all, these monographs are creative attempts to help thinking Christians understand their Bibles better. The series aims simultaneously to instruct and to edify, to interact with the current literature, and to point the way ahead. In God's universe, mind and heart should not be divorced: in this series we will try not to separate what God has joined together. While the notes interact with the best of the scholarly literature, the text is uncluttered with untransliterated Greek and Hebrew, and tries to avoid too much technical jargon. The volumes are written within the framework of confessional evangelicalism, but there is always an attempt at thoughtful engagement with the sweep of the relevant literature.

This volume by Professor Murray Harris combines the meticulous scholarship for which he is known, and the careful unpacking of a biblical theme that is widely neglected. Doubtless the West's involvement in slavery in centuries past has contributed to our reluctance to perceive what Professor Harris has made obvious: very often when our English translations speak of 'servant', the Greek writers are thinking of a slave. But serious Christians will not be satisfied with a cloak of euphemisms. They will want to grasp, so far as they are able, what the biblical writers were saying to their first readers. Professor Harris's study probes not only the linguistic matters but the historical, legal and social contexts that defined slavery in the first century – and he does this in service to his careful and probing delineation of what it means to be a 'slave of Christ'.

Perhaps I may add a personal note. It was with profound regret that his colleagues at Trinity Evangelical Divinity School bade farewell to Murray and his wife Jennifer when they left us to return to New Zealand. We are grateful to God for the sustaining grace that links us together in the gospel across the thousands of miles – not least in a valuable work like this one.

D. A. Carson
Trinity Evangelical Divinity School

Author's preface

This book is an expanded form of the Annual Moore College Lectures given in August 1997 in Sydney, Australia, at Moore Theological College. I am most grateful to the Principal, Rev. Dr Peter F. Jensen, for his generous invitation to contribute to the life of the College in this way, and to the Vice Principal, Rev. Dr Peter T. O'Brien and his wife, Mary, for their warm hospitality during those pleasant two weeks. With its highly talented faculty and graduates, this college has rightly gained a worldwide reputation not simply as a bastion of historic Christianity, but in particular as a shining exemplar of 'informed conservatism' as they have consistently embodied the distinctives of evangelicalism —a focus on the centrality of Jesus Christ and in particular his substitutionary death; on the entire trust-worthiness of Scripture and its ultimate authority in all matters of faith and conduct; on the need for conversion and the primacy of the evangelistic task; and on the defence of the essentials of the faith. For this contribution to contemporary Christianity, the whole Christian world stands in their debt. *In multos annos!*

I am very grateful to Professor Donald A. Carson for his invitation to contribute to this series; to Julie Aldridge for her cheerful and efficient work in typing the manuscript; to Jeremy Hultin and Sam Lamerson for bibliographical aid; and to my daughter, Jessie Jane, for typing the indexes.

I am delighted to be able to dedicate this book to my wife of three and a half decades, who has often, with justification, been called a modern-day Dorcas (see chapter 9). Her artistic handiwork in fabrics adorns a multitude of homes across the world and her quilted banners may be found in churches or chapels in Hungary, Kenya, Illinois, Minnesota and Utah.

Unless otherwise indicated, the translations of ancient texts are my own.

Murray J. Harris

11

Abbreviations

Ancient sources: standard abbreviations are used; authors and titles are given in full in the 'Index of other ancient authors and writings' on p. 222.

ABD
: D. N. Freedman (ed.), *The Anchor Bible Dictionary*, 6 vols. London and New York: Doubleday, 1992.

AER
: *American Ecclesiastical Review.*

AJP
: *American Journal of Philology.*

AV
: The Authorized (King James) Version of the Bible, 1611.

BAGD
: W. Bauer, *A Greek–English Lexicon of the New Testament and Other Early Christian Literature.* Eng. tr. adapted by W. F. Arndt & F. W. Gingrich; 2nd ed. rev. and augmented by F. W. Gingrich and F. W. Danker. Chicago: Chicago University Press, 1979.

Berkeley
: *The Holy Bible: The Berkeley Version in Modern English*, 1959.

BETS
: *Bulletin of the Evangelical Theological Society.*

BR
: *Bible Review.*

BT
: *The Bible Today.*

BZ
: *Biblische Zeitschrift.*

Cassirer
: H. W. Cassirer, *God's New Covenant: A New Testament Translation*, 1989.

CEV
: Contemporary English Version of the Bible, 1995.

CIL
: *Corpus Inscriptionum Latinarum.*

Conybeare & Howson
: W. J Conybeare & J. S. Howson, *The Life and Epistles of St. Paul*, 2nd ed. London: Longmans, 1898.

CTJ
: *Calvin Theological Journal.*

EGT
: W. R. Nicoll (ed.), *The Expositor's Greek Testament*, 5 vols. Reprinted Grand Rapids: Eerdmans, 1970 (= 1st ed., 1907–10).

EQ	*The Evangelical Quarterly.*
EVV	English versions.
GNB	The Good News Bible, 1976.
Goodspeed	E. J. Goodspeed, *The New Testament: An American Translation.* Chicago: University of Chicago Press, 1923.
IDB	G. A. Buttrick *et al.* (eds.), *The Interpreter's Dictionary of the Bible,* 5 vols. New York: Abingdon, 1962–76.
ILS	*Inscriptiones Latinae Selectae,* ed. H. Dessau.
*ISBE*2	G. W. Bromiley *et al.* (eds.), *The International Standard Bible Encyclopedia,* 4 vols., 2nd ed. Grand Rapids: Eerdmans, 1979–88.
JB	The Jerusalem Bible, 1966.
JBL	*Journal of Biblical Literature.*
JBR	*Journal of Bible and Religion.*
JHS	*Journal of Hellenic Studies.*
JJS	*Journal of Jewish Studies*
JR	*Journal of Religion.*
JRS	*Journal of Roman Studies.*
JTS	*Journal of Theological Studies.*
LN	J. P. Louw & E. A. Nida, *Greek–English Lexicon of the New Testament Based on Semantic Domains,* 2 vols., 2nd ed. New York: United Bible Societies, 1989.
LSJ	H. G. Liddell & R. Scott, *A Greek–English Lexicon,* 9th ed. by H. S Jones *et al.,* 2 vols. Oxford: Clarendon, 1940; supplement, 1968.
LXX	Septuagint (Gk. version of the OT).
mg.	margin.
Moffatt	J. Moffatt, *The Moffatt Translation of the Bible.* London: Hodder, 1935.
Montgomery	H. B. Montgomery, *The Centenary Translation: The New Testament in Modern English.* Philadelphia: Judson, 1929.
MS	*Milltown Studies.*
MS(S)	manuscript(s).
n(n).	note(s).
NAB1	New American Bible, 1970.
NAB2	New American Bible: Revised New Testament, 1988.
NASB	New American Standard Bible, 1977.
NEB	New English Bible, 1970.
NIDNTT	C. Brown (ed.), *The New International Dictionary of*

	New Testament Theology, 3 vols. Exeter: Paternoster; Grand Rapids: Zondervan, 1975–78.
NIV	New International Version of the Bible, 1984.
NIVI	New International Version of the Bible, inclusive language edition, 1996.
NJB	New Jerusalem Bible, 1985.
NLT	New Living Translation of the Bible, 1996.
NovT	*Novum Testamentum.*
NRSV	New Revised Standard Version of the Bible, 1990.
NTS	*New Testament Studies.*
OED	*The Oxford English Dictionary.* Oxford: Clarendon, 1961 reprint (= 1933).
PAPS	*Proceedings of the American Philosophical Society.*
Phillips	J. B. Phillips, *The New Testament in Modern English.* London: Bles, 1958.
RB	*Revue Biblique.*
RE	*Review and Expositor.*
REB	Revised English Bible, 1990.
RSV	Revised Standard Version of the Bible, 1952.
RV	Revised Version (New Testament), 1881.
SB	H. L. Strack & P. Billerbeck, *Kommentar zum Neuen Testament aus Talmud und Midrash*, 4 vols. Munich: Beck, 1922–28.
s. v.	*sub verbo* (Lat.), under the word.
TCNT	Twentieth Century New Testament, 1904.
TDNT	G. Kittel & G. Friedrich (eds.), *Theological Dictionary of the New Testament*, 9 vols. Grand Rapids: Eerdmans, 1964–74.
TLS	*Times Literary Supplement.*
TLZ	*Theologische Literaturzeitung.*
Weymouth	R. F. Weymouth, *The New Testament in Modern Speech*, 3rd ed. London: Clarke, 1909.
Williams	C. B. Williams, *The New Testament: A Translation in the Language of the People.* Chicago: Moody, 1950.
ZNW	*Zeitschrift für die neutestamentliche Wissenschaft.*
ZPEB	M. C. Tenney & S. Barabas (eds.), *The Zondervan Pictorial Encyclopedia of the Bible*, 5 vols. Grand Rapids: Zondervan, 1975.

Ὁι δοῦλοι, ὑπακούετε τοῖς κατὰ σάρκα κυρίοις
... ὡς δοῦλοι Χριστοῦ.

Slaves, obey your earthly masters ... as slaves of Christ.
Ephesians 6:5–6

Ὁ ἐλεύθερος κληθεὶς δοῦλός ἐστιν Χριστοῦ.

The person who was free when called is a slave of Christ.
1 Corinthians 7:22

Chapter One

Introduction

Reasons for this study

There have been several experiences that generated my special interest in the topic of slavery in the New Testament. For many years I included in a course on New Testament Greek exegesis a segment that discussed the theory of translation and examined how various translation theories are reflected in the twenty major translations of the New Testament. To discover that only one of these major English translations consistently renders the term *doulos* by 'slave' – E. J. Goodspeed's *The New Testament: An American Translation* (1923) – came as a surprise, since this is the most distinctive Greek term for 'slave', there being at least six other New Testament Greek words that may appropriately be rendered 'servant'. What accounts for this strange phenomenon? A universal abhorrence of slavery in any form? An uneasy conscience about the persistence of slavery into modern times? A concern about the emotional connotations that attach to the word 'slave' (visions of Kunta Kinta in *Roots*)? A conviction that there cannot be a positive metaphorical use of *doulos*?

The second reason for my fascination with this topic has been my involvement with the New International Version (NIV) translation since its inception in the early 1970s. Then, until my return to New Zealand, I was privileged to serve for twelve years (1984–96) on the Committee on Bible Translation, the central committee ultimately responsible for this translation, in their ongoing systematic review of the text. As a result of my raising this issue of how *doulos* should be translated, I was asked to prepare a report on the matter, with special attention to the NIV renderings of the word. This alerted me to the complexity of the issues and prompted me to consider in more detail the metaphorical use of *doulos* in the New Testament. In what sense should Christians regard themselves as the slaves of Christ or God?

But quite apart from these issues of translation, my attention has been drawn to this topic in a variety of other ways. In October 1987, at the annual Global Ministries Institute at Trinity Evangelical Divinity School, our speaker was Dr Josef Tson, a Romanian pastor who had been arrested and imprisoned in 1974 and 1977, then exiled in 1981. He forcefully expressed his preference to be introduced simply as 'a slave of Jesus Christ'. 'There aren't many people', he observed, 'who are willing to introduce me as a slave. They substitute the word "servant" for "slave". In twentieth-century Christianity we have replaced the expression "total surrender" with the word "commitment", and "slave" with "servant". But there is an important difference. A servant gives service to someone, but a slave belongs to someone. We commit ourselves to do something, but when we surrender ourselves to someone, we give ourselves up.'

Then in 1990 there appeared a book entitled *Slavery as Salvation: The Metaphor of Slavery in Pauline Christianity* by Dale B. Martin. It was a revision of his Yale doctoral dissertation written under the supervision of Professor Wayne Meeks. Martin seeks to discover how the metaphor of slavery to God or Christ 'was able to function as a positive soteriological image for early Christians even in a Greco-Roman, urban environment' (1990: 137; *cf.* xiv). Focusing on the language of 1 Corinthians 9, Martin argues that when Paul portrays himself (in 1 Cor. 9:16–18) as Christ's slave steward (*oikonomos*; *cf.* 'slave of Christ' in Rom. 1:1; Gal. 1:10; Phil. 1:1), he is indicating not only his authority and power but his high standing as an 'upwardly mobile' slave who reflects the status of Christ his master. With the other self-designation, 'slave of all' (1 Cor. 9:19–23), Paul deliberately lowers himself in status after the 'enslaved leader' pattern of political rhetoric (*viz.* leadership from below) and in imitation of Christ's *kenōsis*, in order to 'gain' those of lower status and to afford an example to the socially elite among his converts in the interests of Christian unity and upbuilding. 'Precisely because the social institution of slavery carried different connotations in different contexts, references to slavery could represent self-abasement as well as upward mobility and access to high status' (132; *cf.* 58). It seems that the validity of this sociological approach needs to be assessed against the data of all the Pauline epistles, as well as all the New Testament. (Martin's views are elaborated and discussed at various places in the following chapters, but especially in chapter 7.)

My colleague from Tyndale House (Cambridge, UK) days, Dr David Wenham, has been for many years investigating various aspects of the relation between Jesus and Paul. His *magnum opus* on this theme, *Paul: Follower of Jesus or Founder of Christianity?* (1995), arrives at the simple but significant conclusion that 'Paul saw himself as the slave of Jesus Christ, not the founder of Christianity' (410).

These, then, are the main reasons for my particular fascination with this topic in recent years. My hope and prayer are that my effort to draw attention to this metaphor of slavery will not only revive interest in a neglected theme in New Testament theology but also promote wholehearted devotion to the Lord Christ.[1]

The metaphor of slavery

Since my primary focus is on the metaphorical use of slavery as one picture of the Christian's relationship to Christ or God, it will be appropriate to make some comments on the nature of metaphor and to list all the New Testament passages where the phrases 'slave(s) of God' (*doulos/douloi theou*) or 'slave(s) of Christ' (*doulos/douloi Christou*) are found.[2]

A metaphor is a figure of speech that describes one entity or realm of experience in terms borrowed from another. It incorporates features that may be recognized as apt in reference to the entity being described and other features that are clearly inapplicable. For example, if we say, 'The moon was a gleaming coin', the points of aptness relate to shape (circular), appearance (shining) and perhaps size (small in relation to its immediate surroundings).[3] But it is also obvious that, unlike a coin, the moon is not (for example) connected

[1] Unfortunately the book by I. A. H. Combes, *The Metaphor of Slavery in the Writings of the Early Church* (Sheffield: Sheffield Academic Press, 1998), appeared too late to be consulted.

[2] On religious metaphor, see the illuminating comments of Crabtree 1991: 11–17. Russell (1972: 469) has argued that 'the title "slave", in the New Testament as in the Old, is the expression of the fundamental spiritual attitude of man the contingent, the sinner, before God the absolute and merciful', so that, paradoxically, although 'the title slave is termed a metaphor in its religious use, it would be more exact to say that it has its true realism in describing the relationship of God to man and that its sociological use is actually the metaphorical one' (*cf.* 455). Russell maintained the same position, although less decisively, in his earlier work that was based on his doctoral dissertation (1968: 16–17, 34 n. 21, 88). But this approach seems to assume that the basic connotation of slavery is dependence and that in some sense physical slavery is legitimate in that it reflects the essential condition of humans before God.

[3] Beekman & Callow (1974: 127) identify the three elements of a metaphor as: '(1) the *topic*, that is, the item which is illustrated by the image; (2) the *image*, that is, the "metaphorical" part of the figure; (3) the *point of similarity*, which explains in what particular aspect the image and topic are similar'.

with commerce or created by humans. The open-ended potency of metaphor derives from its suggestiveness and the surprise it creates in the listener or reader regarding the point or points of aptness. In the present work it is assumed that the metaphor of slavery was capable of multiple connotations, given the extraordinary complexity and variety of slavery in the first century.

But how are we to determine which aspects of the metaphor are apt and which inappropriate? When a writer uses slave terminology in reference to the human–divine relationship, there is an indirect appeal to a set of common ideas that are popularly associated with the notion of slavery. Our concern must be to identify the system of common-alities that are attached to slave terminology in the first century AD. For this one must look to (a) the customary depiction of slaves and slavery in literature of the general period; and more importantly (b) the connotations of slave terminology in the New Testament itself and in the Greek Old Testament (the LXX), the seed-bed of most New Testament concepts. Possible connotations revealed by (a) become restricted under (b) to those that aptly describe the human–divine relationship – ideas such as exclusive ownership by the master, total availability for service to the master, and complete dependence on the master. Other ideas come to be seen as inapplicable to that relationship – for instance, enforced obedience, loss of freedom, and cringing subservience.

In his work Martin undertakes a wide-ranging study of the Greco-Roman background of the metaphor of slavery to a god and provides exemplary documentation, yet it remains true, as he himself says, that his focus is on 'one function of one metaphor as seen primarily in one text (*viz.* 1 Cor. 9)' (1990, xiv). My study of backgrounds, Jewish, Greek and Roman, is relatively meagre – nevertheless, I trust, adequate – but my focus is much broader, namely, on the multiple functions of the one metaphor of slavery as seen in all the relevant New Testament texts.

The expression 'slave(s) of God'[4]

*In the plural (*douloi theou*)*

Acts 2:18   Even on *my slaves, both men and women*, I will pour out my Spirit in those days, and they will prophesy.

[4] I have included passages where, instead of *theou*, we find *mou* ('my'), *sou* ('your'), or *autou* ('his'), or *kyriou* ('Lord's').

Acts 4:29	Now, Lord, consider their threats and enable *your slaves* to speak your word with full boldness.[5]
Acts 16:17	While she [a female slave who had a spirit of divination] followed Paul and us, she would shout out, 'These men are *slaves of the Most High God*, who are telling you the way to be saved.'
1 Pet. 2:16	Live as free persons, but do not use your freedom as a pretext for evil; rather, live as *slaves of God* [in reference to all Christians].
Rev. 1:1a	The revelation of Jesus Christ, which God gave him to show *his slaves* what must soon take place.[6]
Rev. 7:3	Do not damage the land or the sea or the trees until we have put a seal on the foreheads of *the slaves of our God* [of the 144,000, Rev. 7:4].
Rev. 10:7	But at the time when the seventh angel is about to blow his trumpet, the hidden purpose of God will be accomplished, just as he announced to *his slaves the prophets.*
Rev. 11:8	The nations were angry, but your wrath has come, and the time for judging the dead and for rewarding *your slaves the prophets*, and your saints, those who reverence your name.[7]
Rev. 19:2	He [God] has judged the great prostitute who corrupted the earth by her licentiousness. He has avenged on her the blood of *his slaves* [in reference to Christian martyrs].
Rev. 19:5	Then a voice came from the throne, saying: 'Praise our God, all you *his slaves*, you who fear him, both small and great'.

[5] That *kyrios* ('Lord') here refers to God, not Christ, is clear from v. 26 (which distinguishes 'the Lord' from 'his Anointed') and v. 27 (which speaks of 'your holy servant Jesus').

[6] In Rev. 1:1a and 22:6 the primary reference in 'his slaves' may be to Christian prophets but Christians in general are probably included (*cf.* Rev. 1:3; 22:16).

[7] In Rev. 11:18 there could be three categories of persons enumerated: God's slaves the prophets, his saints, and those who reverence his name (thus Swete 1909: 144, who sees the latter group as 'the unbaptized adherents of the Church, enquirers and catechumens'). Others find a single category (*cf.* Rev. 19:5): 'your slaves, that is, the prophets and the saints, even those who reverence your name', where *tois prophetais kai tois hagiois* is in epexegetic apposition to *tois doulois*, and the *kai* before *tois phoboumenois to onoma sou* is epexegetic (thus Beckwith 1967: 609f.). Alternatively, and preferably, *kai* could be epexegetic of *tois hagiois* alone: 'your slaves the prophets, and the saints, those who reverence your name' (so Moffatt 1970: 420).

Rev. 22:3   Nothing accursed will be found there any more. But the
             throne of God and of the Lamb will be in the city, and
             his slaves will serve him.[8]

Rev. 22:6   And he [the angel] said to me, 'These words are
             trustworthy and true. The Lord, the God of the spirits of
             the prophets, has sent his angels to show *his slaves* what
             must soon take place.'[9]

Also here we could list a use of *syndoulos* ('fellow-slave').

Rev. 6:11   They [Christian martyrs] were each given a white robe
             and were told to rest a little longer until the number was
             completed both of their *fellow-slaves* and of their
             brothers and sisters who were to be killed as they
             themselves had been.

In the singular *(*doulos theou*)*

Luke 1:38   'Here am I, *the slave* (*doulē*) of the Lord,' Mary
             answered. 'May it be to me as you have said.'

Luke 1:48   For he [God] has looked with favour on the humble
             state of *his slave* (*doulē*).

Luke 2:29   Lord, as you have promised, you are now dismissing
             your slave in peace [of Simeon].

Titus 1:1   Paul, *a slave of God* and an apostle of Jesus Christ.

Jas. 1:1   James, *a slave of God* and of the Lord Jesus Christ.

Rev. 1:1b   The revelation of Jesus Christ, which God gave him to
             show his slaves what must soon take place. He made it
             known by sending his angel to *his slave* John.

Rev. 15:3   And they [those who had been victorious over the beast,
             Rev. 15:2] sang the song of Moses, the slave of God,
             and the song of the Lamb.

Two uses of *syndoulos* belong in this category:

---

[8] This verse could equally appropriately be listed under 'slaves of Christ', for the singulars 'his slaves' (*hoi douloi autou*) and 'him' (*autō*) could refer to 'the Lamb', the nearest antecedent. More probably, however, the reference is to both God and the Lamb, conceived of as forming an inviolate unity, just as in Rev. 11:15 the one kingdom belongs to 'our Lord' and 'his Christ', in Rev. 21:22 the one temple in the heavenly city is 'the Lord God Almighty and the Lamb', and in Rev. 22:1 the one throne belongs to 'God and the Lamb'.

[9] See n. 6 above.

Rev. 19:10   Then I fell down at his feet to worship him [the angel], but he said to me, 'You must not do this! I am a *fellow-slave* with you and your brothers and sisters who hold the testimony of Jesus. Worship God! For the testimony of Jesus is the spirit of prophecy.'

Rev. 22:9   But he [the angel] said to me, 'You must not do this! I am a *fellow-slave* with you and your fellow prophets, and with those who keep the words of this book. Worship God!'[10]

There are also four or five places where God is the object of a verb denoting slavery: *douleuō* ('serve as a slave') in Matthew 6:24; Luke 16:13; 1 Thessalonians 1:9; and probably Romans 7:6 (*cf.* 7:4); and *douloō* ('enslave') in Romans 6:22. Those who serve God as a slave, or are enslaved to God, are, by implication, 'God's slaves'.

The expression 'slave(s) of Christ'[11]

In the plural (douloi Christou)

Eph. 6:6   Obey them [your earthly masters], not only when their eye is on you and in order to win their favour, but as *slaves of Christ*, doing the will of God from your heart.

Phil. 1:1   Paul and Timothy, *slaves of Christ Jesus*.

Rev. 2:20   But I have this against you [Christians of Thyatira]: you tolerate that woman Jezebel, who calls herself a prophet and by her teaching is beguiling *my slaves* into sexual immorality and the eating of food sacrificed to idols.

In the singular (doulos Christou)

Rom. 1:1   Paul, *a slave of Christ Jesus*, called to be an apostle and set apart for the gospel of God.

Gal. 1:10   Am I now trying to win human approval, or God's approval? Or am I trying to please people? If I were still trying to please people, I would not be *a slave of Christ.*

1 Cor. 7:22   Whoever was a slave when called by the Lord is a freed

---

[10] In Rev. 19:10; 22:9 the angel is a 'fellow-slave' with human believers since all serve the same God (*cf.* Heb. 1:7, 14). Nowhere is an angel described as an angel 'of Jesus' or 'of Christ'.

[11] Included here are passages where, instead of 'Christ', we find 'Christ Jesus', 'the Lord [Jesus]', 'the Lord Jesus Christ', or *emos* ('my').

person belonging to the Lord; similarly, whoever was free when called is *a slave of Christ.*

Col. 4:12   Epaphras, who is one of you and *a slave of Christ Jesus*, sends his greetings.

2 Tim. 2:24 And *the Lord's slave* must not be quarrelsome but kind to everyone, able to teach, not resentful.[12]

Jas. 1:1   James, *a slave* of God and *of the Lord Jesus Christ.*

2 Pet. 1:1   Simeon Peter, *a slave* and apostle *of Jesus Christ.*

Jude 1   Jude, *a slave of Jesus Christ* and a brother of James.

To this latter category could be added two uses of *syndoulos* ('fellow-slave'):[13]

Col. 1:7   You learned this from Epaphras, our dear *fellow-slave*, who is a faithful minister of Christ on our behalf.

Col. 4:7   Tychicus will let you know about all my circumstances. He is a dear brother, a trustworthy helper and *fellow-slave* in the Lord.

Finally, on five or six occasions, the verb *douleuō* ('serve as a slave') has Christ as its object, implying that those who serve this way are 'slaves of Christ': Acts 20:19; Romans 12:11; 14:18; 16:18; Ephesians 6:7; and probably Philippians 2:22 (*cf.* 2:21).[14]

---

[12] It is probable that *kyrios* here refers to the Lord Jesus, since v. 22 speaks of 'those who call on the Lord', an expression which in Pauline usage describes 'those who call on the name of our Lord Jesus Christ' (1 Cor. 1:2). Note also the association of *kyrios* (= Christ) with *doulos* in 1 Cor. 7:22.

[13] These two cases probably belong under 'slaves of Christ', given the reference to Christ (Col. 1:7) or to the Lord (Jesus) (Col. 4:7) later in the verse.

[14] Behind Rom. 14:4 may lie the concept of Christians as the *oiketai* ('[household] slaves') of Christ the *kyrios*: 'Who are you to judge someone else's slave [*allotrion oiketēn*]? It is before his own master [*tō idiō kyriō*] that he stands or falls.'

Chapter Two

Slavery in the Roman Empire in the first century AD

Definitions of slavery vary from the relatively simple to the highly technical, from the legal to the sociological. In Justinian's *Digest* of Roman law (AD 533),[1] slavery is defined as 'an institution of the law of nations by which, contrary to nature, a person is subjected to an alien dominion'.[2] 'The law of the nations' refers to the law observed by all peoples. In Roman law slavery was contrary to the natural order because all people were born free and because slavery resulted from war. Then, writing from a sociological perspective, O. Patterson (1982: 13) describes slavery as 'the permanent, violent domination of natally alienated and generally dishonored persons'. According to Patterson, in both ancient and modern times slavery was essentially a relation of human 'parasitism', in which domination characterized the master and social death was the plight of the slave. In his emphasis on the slave's alienation, Patterson follows the distinguished Cambridge classicist, M. I. Finley, an authority on slavery in the Greco-Roman world, who observes that 'the slave was always a deracinated outsider' (Finley 1980: 75), originating from outside the particular society and being denied kinship.[3]

For our purposes we may define a slave (whether literal or figurative) as someone whose person and service belong wholly to another.[4] On this view slavery involves (a) absolute ownership and

---

[1] The *Digest* is a compilation of Roman law based on jurists' opinions, prepared at the instigation of the Byzantine Roman Emperor Justinian who ruled AD 527–565. Although the *Digest* was promulgated in the sixth century (AD 533), it incorporates much earlier – even pre-Christian – material which it is impossible to date precisely.

[2] *Digest* 1. 5. 4. 1 (= Florentinus, *Institutions*, Book 9); *cf.* 12. 6. 64; Justinian's, *Institutes* 1. 3. 2.

[3] On the distinction between chattel slavery (reflected in the two definitions given), serfdom and debt-bondage, see Fisher 1993: 3–6. The basic difference between chattel slavery and indentured servitude is that the latter is entered by contractual agreement and for a specific period.

[4] *Cf.* Aristotle, *Pol.* 1. 2. 6: 'Whereas a master is merely a slave's master and does not

control on the part of the master and the total subjection of the slave;[5] and (b) the absence of the slave's freedom to choose his action or movement.[6] Absent from this definition is any reference to how slavery was entered and how the service was rendered − whether involuntarily or voluntarily. For although most slaves did not choose to be slaves and gave their services out of necessity, some people sold themselves into slavery and others served willingly. Also absent is any reference to the duration of the servitude. For although the slave was usually the property of the master for life, the master could choose to set the slave free. Nor does the definition refer to the violence, social alienation and dishonour that were often but not always associated with slavery in the Greco-Roman world.

Historians who wish to give a balanced account of slavery in that world face several severe limitations.[7] Records of ancient Greek and Roman slavery come from the pens of adult male citizens, free men or freedmen, and most references are incidental and anecdotal. Systematic treatments of slavery as an institution, as well as slave autobiographies, are conspicuously absent. 'Members of the Greek and Roman citizen elite who wrote works of philosophy or literature were not interested in preserving "objective" information about slavery for later historians: they were using their idea of what slavery meant in order to communicate with other citizens. They were not thinking about slavery so much as using the concept "slavery" to think with' (Wiedemann 1987: 11).[8] K. Hopkins (1981: 122 n. 50) notes that the longest treatment of slavery in classical literature is

---

himself belong to his slave, a slave is not merely a slave of his master but also wholly belongs to his master.' My proposed definition would not apply to Jewish (as opposed to non-Jewish) slaves, since, as Tuente (1978: 593) points out, their person remained inviolable.

[5] In Roman legal terms, the slave-owner had both *dominium* ('absolute ownership', as opposed to *possessio*, 'possession', which could be partial or total, temporary or permanent) and *potestas* ('absolute power') in relation to the slave.

[6] Although I shall use gender-neutral language throughout this book wherever appropriate, in speaking of the two parties in slavery I shall refer to 'master' or 'slave' as 'he' as a matter of convenience, recognizing, of course, that there were 'mistresses' and female slaves. See further Appendix 2 on the terminology of slavery.

[7] For a brief history of the study of slavery, see Vogt 1972: 97–111; Bartchy 1973: 29–35. On the primary source material for the study of slavery in the Greco-Roman world and the limitations of the available evidence, see Harrill 1995: 18–30.

[8] Wiedemann also observes that 'from the fifth century BC on, many of the instances when Greeks talk of *douleia* ["slavery"] and, later, Romans of *servitus* ["slavery"] are not about the social institution of slavery at all, but about the metaphor of political slavery: the absence of freedom' (1987: 13–14).

found in Dio Chrysostom (*c*. AD 40–111) (*Orationes* 14–15), an orator from Bithynia, and runs to only fifteen pages. But with these qualifications noted, such glimpses of slave conditions as may be gleaned from the extant literature accord in detail with autobiographical accounts from modern times (Hopkins 1981: 119 n. 44, 123), so that we need not imagine that we are far astray in our efforts to reconstruct slave life in the first century.

When we consider the background of 'slavery' in New Testament times, we must distinguish physical slavery from metaphorical. Literal or physical slavery involves the outward relationship of two persons, where the master 'owns' the slave's person and service. This chapter and the next (*viz.* chapters 2 and 3) are concerned with this external form. On the other hand, metaphorical or spiritual slavery relates to an inward relationship, where a person is under the sway of another person (*e.g.*, 'a slave of Christ') or even of some thing (*e.g.*, 'a slave to duty', 'a slave of fashion'). This internal form of slavery is the focus of the remainder of the book (*viz.* chapters 4–9).

But there is a further distinction that must be carefully drawn when discussing the backdrop to New Testament slavery – the distinction between conceptual and historical backgrounds. Since Christianity began as a conventicle of Judaism, the first Christians were Jews, although the church rapidly incorporated a large Gentile element. So we should expect that the New Testament view of slavery, whether literal or figurative slavery, will reflect Jewish and more generally Ancient Near Eastern ideas. But Greek and Roman conceptions must also play a part. All the New Testament was written in Greek, the common language of the Hellenistic age, so that the New Testament terminology of slavery comes with heavy Greek freight. As for the Roman conceptual component, the Roman laws of slavery have been called 'the most characteristic part of the most characteristic intellectual product of Rome' (Buckland 1969: v). Throughout the chapters that follow, all three conceptual backgrounds – Jewish, Greek and Roman – will be considered as they are relevant. With regard to the historical circumstances of physical slavery in the first century AD, we will give brief attention to the Jewish and Greek situations, but the Roman setting will be our main concern, for the simple reason that even Jewish and Greek slaves and masters throughout the Mediterranean were ultimately subject to Roman law, whatever variations of practice applied within their own culture.[9]

---

[9] While we cannot assume that in the first century AD Roman law was applied equally

It is to these latter issues that we now turn.

Jewish slavery[10]

The economy of ancient Israel was not based on slave labour in either the city or the country, but rather on free labour. Where slaves were used, they were involved mainly in unskilled household tasks; that is, they were generally 'domestics'. But particularly during the reigns of David and Solomon, we find slaves of the state engaged in forced labour (*e.g.*, 2 Sam. 12:31). Also, there were temple slaves who performed menial maintenance tasks (*cf.* Ezek. 44:7–9).

Slaves were acquired in a variety of ways: through capture, birth to slave parents, purchase, default on debt, the sale of minors, or inheritance. As in the case of Ancient Near Eastern legislation generally, the Old Testament distinguishes clearly between free citizens and slaves; but equally clearly it distinguishes non-Jewish from Jewish slaves. Whereas non-Jewish slaves were regarded and treated as chattels or movable property (Lev. 25:44–46), Jewish slaves who had voluntarily sold themselves into slavery to escape poverty were to be viewed and treated as hired hands, not as slaves (Lev. 25:35–43).[11] Apparently their master had rights over their work, but not over their person, which remained inviolable because all Jews were part of a nation that had been rescued from slavery in Egypt and had thus become the slaves of Yahweh (Lev. 25:42–43).

In comparison with other Ancient Near Eastern societies, Israel's regulations governing slavery (principally in Exod. 21, Lev. 25 and Deut. 15) are more humane.[12]

---

uniformly in Rome and the provinces, we should not imagine that local practice ever subverted Roman law. The coinage of the Greek term *pekoulion*, a transliteration of the Latin word *peculium* (a slave's accumulated property or wealth, used to purchase freedom) is evidence of the influence of Roman manumission practices. Lyall (1984) argues that where Paul, the Roman citizen, refers to secular law, it is Roman law that he has in mind, so that metaphors relating to slavery, adoption and inheritance find their background in Roman rather than Jewish or Greek law, although he concedes that the metaphor of redemption is best understood in relation to biblical and Jewish law. See also Lyall 1970: 73–79.

[10] On this topic, see in particular Mendelsohn 1949, *passim*; and, more briefly, de Vaux 1965: 80–90.

[11] This assumes that the expression 'the slave is his property' (lit. 'silver', 'money', *kesep̄*) (Exod. 21:21) refers only to non-Jewish slaves (*cf.* 'inherited property' in Lev. 25:46) or actually means 'the slave is his by right of purchase' (NJB).

[12] Similarly Philo, *Virt.* 121–123, 125; *Spec. Leg.* 2. 79–82.

1. Since slaves were regarded as part – albeit an inferior part – of the master's family, they participated in Sabbath rest (Exod. 20:10; 23:12; Deut. 5:14) and the religious feasts (Exod. 12:43–44; Deut. 16:11, 14).

2. Jewish slaves had to be released after six years (Exod. 21:2–4; Deut. 15:12; but see also Jer. 34:8–17), unless they chose to remain as slaves in perpetuity (Exod. 21:5–6; Deut. 15:16–17). When released, the slave was to be given generous provisions, adequate to lead to self-sufficiency (Deut. 15:13–14).

3. If a slave – Jewish or non-Jewish – was permanently injured by his master, he or she was to be set free in compensation for the injury (Exod. 21:26–27). In other Ancient Near Eastern cultures, such an injury required only monetary compensation, and then only for someone else's slave.

4. As we have already seen, impoverished Israelites who sold themselves to a master had to be treated as paid workers, not slaves (Lev. 25:39–40).

5. Manumission might take place not only after six years' service or as a result of permanent maiming (see above), but also in the Jubilee Year (Lev. 25:54), or through redemption – either when a clan member, acting as a 'kinsman-redeemer' (gōʾēl, Exod. 21:8; Lev. 25:48–49), bought an individual out of slavery, or when the slave, having accumulated property or wealth (e.g., 2 Sam. 16:4), purchased his own freedom (Lev. 25:49).

6. Foreign slaves fleeing from their masters or Hebrew slaves who had escaped from their foreign masters were to be granted asylum in Israel (Deut. 23:15–16).

7. Slaves in Israel bore no external indication of their servile status, such as branding with the name of the ruler (as in Egypt) or the wearing of tablets around the neck or wrist or ankle (as apparently in Babylonia). The one exception was the slave who chose to remain with his master at the end of his six years of servitude and whose ear was then pierced with an awl (presumably for some form of tag) (Exod. 21:5–6; Deut. 15:16–17). But this mark symbolized his attachment to the family (de Vaux 1965: 84), rather than his servitude.

8. Twice in Leviticus 25 (vv. 43 and 46) we read the injunction that slave-owners were not to rule over their fellow-Israelites 'ruthlessly'. It comes as no surprise, therefore, to learn that friendship and trust often developed between master and slave. For instance, Eliezer was designated Abraham's heir (Gen. 15:2–4), and Gehazi was Elisha's adviser (2 Kgs. 4:12–13; 8:4–5).

This humanization of slavery was explicitly related to Israel's own history: 'Remember that you were slaves in Egypt and that Yahweh your God brought you out of there with a mighty hand and an outstretched arm' (Deut. 5:15; *cf.* 15:15; Lev. 25:55).

Like its Ancient Near Eastern neighbours, Israel took slavery for granted as an unalterable fact of life. Neither free persons nor slaves themselves agitated for its abolition. But two Old Testament passages are harbingers of things to come – the abolition of distinction between slave and free. On the coming Day of the Lord, God would pour out his Spirit on all people, 'even on the slaves, men and women' (Joel 2:28–29, NJB [Joel 3:1–2, LXX]). Then there is the grounding of human equality in the creatorial order, found in Job 31:13–15; every person, including the slave, was created by God:

> If I ever denied justice to my male and female slaves when they brought a complaint against me, [14]what will I do when God confronts me? What will I answer if he intervenes? [15]Did not he who made me in the womb make them? Did not the same God create us both in the womb?

In spite of the Talmudic tradition that the enslavement of fellow-Israelites ceased from the period of the Second Temple (*Git.* 65a; *Ar.* 29a), we know that there were Jewish slaves in Palestine in the first century AD. Archaeologists have discovered in Jerusalem a stone dating from that time on which both Jewish and non-Jewish slaves were displayed for auction (Jeremias 1969: 36, 51, 110f., 312).[13] And there is no reason to believe that the relevant Old Testament regulations were not observed by Palestinian or Diaspora Jews in the first century,[14] although, as Jeremiah 34:8–17 indicates with regard to the Sabbath-year manumission, there were probably always deviations from the biblical norms. But, as J. Jeremias (1969: 312) asserts, the position of Jewish slaves in Palestine 'was regulated in accordance with the humane Old Testament prescriptions'.

Greek slavery

At all stages of their history the Greeks cherished freedom as a

---

[13] For rabbinic directives about Jewish slaves, see SB 4. 698–716.

[14] See, *e.g.*, Philo, *Virt.* 122–123, on the sabbath-year manumission; *Spec. Leg.* 3. 184, regarding manumission for permanent maiming; and *Quaest. in Gen.* 3. 50, on the circumcision of slaves (Gen. 17:12–13).

priceless treasure and regarded its possession as the distinguishing characteristic of the citizen. To be a citizen was to be free – free to act and move as one chooses, without subservience to an alien will. To such freedom, slavery was diametrically opposed, since it involved the forfeiture of autonomy, subjection to another person's will. According to Plato the only slavery that was legitimate was to the laws, for they embodied the goal of ideal human life in the city-state.[15]

Greek writers were acutely conscious of the contradiction or irreconcilable tension between human freedom arising from birth and human enslavement validated by law, and between treating a slave as private property and regarding him as a human being. Aristotle, for example, after affirming that 'the slave is a living tool and the tool a lifeless slave',[16] continues: 'As a slave, then, one cannot be friends with him; but as a man, one can' (*Eth. Nic.* 8. 11).[17] Another important recognition of Greek writers was that the nearer the condition of the slave came to that of the free person, the more economically advantageous slavery became. Yet never was the conclusion drawn that slavery ought to be abolished.

There is no codification or summary of Greek law such as is found for Roman law in the work of Gaius (second century AD) and Justinian (sixth century AD). Each Greek city-state had its own set of laws, including laws about slavery. But, not unfairly, we may generalize by saying that slavery among the Greeks was primarily industrial rather than agricultural, involving mainly skilled workers in

---

[15] *Leg.* 3. 698c, 700a; 4. 715d (cited by Rengstorf 1964: 262 and Kleinknecht 1967 1030). In classical times it was rare for a person's devotion to a god to be expressed in terms of slavery (see Rengstorf 1964: 264f.). However, 'in Hellenistic mystery religions which come from the Orient the initiate is considered to be the "slave" of the mystery divinity, to whom the initiate's entire life henceforth is to be dedicated' (Dibelius 1976: 65, citing Apuleius, *Met.* 11. 6.

[16] This statement of Aristotle has often been misunderstood. We need to turn to his *Politics* to discover what he meant by 'tool' or 'instrument' (*organon*). 'A slave is a living article of property', an article of property being 'a tool needed to live' (*Pol.* 1. 2. 4), something giving assistance regarding the necessities of life (1. 2. 14). 'The slave is a tool that assists action' (1. 2. 6). For Aristotle, then, a 'tool' is simply something needed to get a job done and is not in itself a derogatory term. 'Some tools are lifeless and others are living. For example, the rudder is a lifeless tool for a ship's helmsman, whereas the look-out man is a living tool' (1. 2. 4).

[17] Aristotle's analysis of the nature and functions of a slave is threefold (*Pol.* 1. 2. 7): 'First, a human being who by nature [with strong and stooped body] belongs not to himself but to another person – such a one is by nature a slave. Second, a human being belongs to another if he is an article of property as well as being a human being. Third, an article of property is a tool used to assist some action and is separable from its owner.'

the cities rather than manual labourers in the country (see Garlan 1988). Many of these skilled workers lived where they chose, apart from their owners (as *hoi chōris oikountes*, 'those who live apart'), pursued their own trades as 'earners of wages' (*hoi misthophorountes* or *ta misthophorounta sōmata*) and gave their owners a percentage of their income. But it was their owners who drew up the terms of the contract for their services. W. L. Westermann (1974: 20, citing Aeschines, *Tim.* 97) refers to the case of an Athenian politician named Timarchus, some of whose slaves were 'leather-cutters' (perhaps shoe-makers). Their services were leased by Timarchus to a shopkeeper who paid three obols per day for each slave, two obols going to Timarchus and one to the slave.

In his major work on Greco-Roman slavery, Westermann (1955) describes several tendencies in the Hellenistic period (roughly 300 BC – AD 300). One was the rejection by theorists of Aristotle's defence of slavery, a defence which appealed to the supposed natural division of humankind based on racial inferiorities and superiorities; some people exhibit a natural aptitude for servitude (*Pol.* 1. 2. 7). The Stoics, for example, stressed the freedom of all persons by nature, the equality of all, and the origin of slavery in human avarice. The real slave was the person devoid of wisdom.[18] Another tendency was the levelling of status distinctions between slave and free. There were social organizations or benefit clubs (*eranoi*) with exclusively slave membership, and other societies and cult shrines open to both enslaved and free persons (Westermann 1955: 41). Or again, we find an increasing clarity in distinguishing the separate category of freedmen (*exeleutheroi* or *apeleutheroi*) and correspondingly a rise in the laws relating exclusively to them (42f.). Finally, 'the general impression left by the sources ... is that the slave system of the Hellenistic period was not of an oppressive or extremely brutal type, either in the area of the Aegean Sea and the Greek homeland or in the conquered countries of the near East' (41).

Perhaps the most accurate indication of the view of freedom and slavery held by Greeks in the Hellenistic age may be derived from the more than 1,000 inscriptions, dating from 200 BC to AD 74 and found at Delphi in northern Greece, that record slave manumissions. Four liberties of the freedman, denied to him previously, are often mentioned in these inscriptions. From these four aspects of freedom

---

[18] There are important reviews of Westermann's book by P. A. Brunt in *JRS* 48 (1958), 164–170; and by R. E. Smith in *JHS* 77 (1957), 338–339.

Westermann (1974: 26f.) legitimately infers the main personal restrictions that marked full slave status:

1. Whereas the freedman can be his own representative in legal matters, the slave must be represented by his master or someone appointed by him.

2. Whereas the freedman is not subject to seizure as property, the slave, particularly the fugitive slave, is subject to seizure and arrest.

3. Whereas the freedman may do what he desires, the slave must do what his master orders.

4. Whereas the freedman may go or live where he chooses, the slave cannot go or live where he wishes.

Freedom, that is, involves being one's own master, protection against attack or summary arrest, freedom of action, and freedom of movement. The free person or the freedman acts as he chooses (*hēkōn*, 'willingly') the slave, however, acts under orders (*akōn*, 'unwillingly').

These elements of Greek freedom were divisible, for although a freedman could be legally free in the first sense, he could be under an 'obligation to continue in service' to his former owner (the *paramonē* contract), an obligation that in fact was a restriction on action or movement. So a person could be part free and part slave. For example, the slave who was a skilled tradesman and lived apart from his owner was a 'half slave' (*hēmidoulos*), legally a slave but in reality enjoying freedom of movement and perhaps also of action (Westermann 1974: 27–30). Given this divisibility of freedom, it is not surprising to learn of 'debtor slaves, who are free' or of 'free slaves of the unprivileged classes' (31; and see Westermann 1938). Westermann concludes that 'there was an astonishing fluidity of status in both directions, from slavery to freedom as from freedom to slavery. This it is which, in large measure, explains the absence of slave revolts in the Greek classical period' (1974: 31).

Roman slavery

There can be little doubt that 'Rome evolved the most complex slave system of all the peoples of the premodern world' (Patterson 1982: 88). The slave was so ubiquitous in Roman society that the standard text on the Roman law of slavery in the imperial period begins with the observation that 'there is scarcely a problem which can present itself, in any branch of law, the solution of which may not be affected by the fact that one of the parties to the transaction is a slave, and, outside the region of procedure, there are few branches of the law in which the slave does not prominently appear' (Buckland 1969: v).[19]

Estimating ancient population numbers is not a precise science, but it would appear that at the end of the first century BC there were some two million slaves in Italy out of a total population of five to six million (see Hopkins 1978: 99–102). In Rome itself this 1:3 ratio of slave to free may have been higher; indeed, some have argued that the majority of those living in Rome at that time were of servile extraction – slaves, ex-slaves, or their descendants.[20] If the slave–free ratio throughout the Empire was 1:5 (Rollins 1976: 830), and the population of the Empire at the time of Augustus was 50–60 million (Hopkins 1978: 102, following K. J. Beloch), there may have been ten to twelve million slaves under Roman jurisdiction. It was the opinion of Westermann that 'the numbers of slaves to be found in any group of [Christian] converts would presumably approximate the proportion of slaves to free, which existed in the particular town or city of each Christian congregation' (1955: 150).[21]

At all stages of Roman history, the number of slaves in a household reflected the owner's wealth and status. A poor citizen might have as few as one or two slaves, a senator as many as 400 or more,[22] while the *familia Caesaris*, 'Caesar's household' (Phil. 4:22), was a network of some 20,000 slaves and freedmen, who cared for the administrative details of the Empire.

The prices of slaves varied, of course, according to supply and demand, and according to the slave's level of education and skill. In the Hellenistic period 500–600 denarii was a normal price for an unskilled male adult, but a skilled worker such as a vinedresser could cost as much as 2,000 denarii (Jones 1974: 9f.). A denarius was a labourer's average daily pay. It is therefore clear that slaves were not inexpensive. To be seen in public with an entourage of slaves was to display one's wealth.

[19] Finley (1974: 70) notes that Buckland's observation is true also for Greek law.

[20] P. A. Brunt, *Italian Manpower* (Oxford: Clarendon, 1971), 377, 386 (cited by Hopkins, 1978: 116 n. 32). But the generalization is fair that in ancient as well as in modern times, the slave population of any particular area was no more than one third of the population (Patterson 1982: 353).

[21] In a strongly Romanized colony such as Corinth slaves probably made up between one-fifth and one-third of the total population (of approximately 200,000). So also in the Corinthian congregation (*cf.* 1 Cor. 1:11, 16, 26–28). Bartchy (1973: 58f.) suggests that slaves and ex-slaves accounted for as much as two-thirds of the Corinthian population in the first century AD.

[22] See, *e.g.*, Tacitus, *Ann.* 14. 43. 4 (regarding L. Pedanius Secundus).

We should not imagine that slaves were confined to menial tasks. They served in a wide variety of roles. In fact, one scholar has drawn up a list of over 120 different duties and occupations![23] For example, some served as employees of a city or of the state, being salaried executives with heavy responsibilities. Others were employed in business as managers of shops or of ships. Others worked the land as farm labourers, often in chain gangs in the case of condemned criminals, and sometimes in appalling conditions. Or again, many worked in city households, as cooks or cleaners, as tutors or doctors, or as sexual partners. With regard to this variety of role and status, S. S. Bartchy (1992: 61, 68)[24] appropriately notes that 'the only thing that slaves in the first century AD had completely in common was the fact of their enslavement', 'the fact that each of them had an owner'. Given the ubiquity of slaves and the bewildering variety of their roles, it is not surprising that slaves were not readily identifiable, either by outward appearance or by race or by speech or by occupation. Many, if not most, of the tasks assigned to slaves were also performed by free persons.

This range of tasks undertaken by slaves falls into two broad, distinct categories (*cf.* Justinian's *Digest* 32, 99): rural and agricultural on the one hand, including any work outside the city, such as manning the galleys or toiling in the mines; urban and administrative on the other hand, including household, municipal and imperial slavery. Rural slavery was often disagreeable; urban slavery, not infrequently quite tolerable, especially if master and slave worked side by side. A personal relationship between master and slave was more likely to be established with urban slaves who saw their master regularly than with rural slaves who rarely saw their master but worked under the supervision of an overseer who was usually a fellow-slave. In fact, dismissal from an urban to a rural *familia* was sometimes viewed as a punishment. Rural slaves did not in any sense share in the status of their master, but urban slaves often gained a certain distinction, apart from their particular role, from being the slave of a master who had social status and wealth. This was most apparent in the case of 'Caesar's household'. To be an imperial slave was to be in the employ of the most powerful figure of the time and

---

[23] J. Marquardt, *Das Privatleben der Römer*, 2nd ed. (Leipzig: Hirzel, 1886), 139–159, as cited by Coleman-Norton 1951: 164 n. 42. On the variety of slaves' occupations, see Bradley 1994: 57–80; Martin 1990: 11–22, 166–173, 187–188.

[24] See the important review of Bartchy's book in Harrill 1995: 94–102.

so carried with it a sense of prestige, if not privilege. But even within this *familia* there were clearly defined gradations of status.[25]

Another way in which ancient writers classified slaves was according to their responsibility, whether managerial or menial.[26] Most slaves held menial posts as household servants or agricultural workers, but a minority held managerial positions of trust in the city or country, frequently indistinguishable from positions held by free persons. These 'socially mobile' slaves often enjoyed a higher standard of living than many free citizens. The Roman writer Suetonius notes that the grammarian Gaius Melissus preferred to be the slave of Maecenas, the leading literary patron under Augustus, than to be free, although he was later granted his freedom (*Grammarians* 5. 21, cited by Martin 1990: 194 n. 164).

Slaves, then, did not form a single, homogeneous class. At one end of the spectrum were the 'penal slaves' (*servi poenae*) condemned for life to the mines; at the other, 'Caesar's slaves' (*Caesaris servi*), the attendants of the emperor. In between these extremes were those slaves who themselves owned slaves. A *servus vicarius* (lit. 'a slave taking the place [of another slave]') was an under-slave bought and kept by another slave to assist him in his work. A first-century inscription from Rome speaks of a financier of the emperor Tiberius who had sixteen under-slaves (*vicarii*):

> To Musicus Scurranus [slave] of Tiberius Caesar Augustus, superintendent of the Gallic Treasury for the province of Lyon: [Dedicated] to him, as he well deserved, by those of his under-slaves who were with him at Rome when he died (*ILS* 1514 [= *CIL* 6. 5197], cited by Wiedemann 1981: 123f.).

Perhaps the most notable first-century example of 'a slave who made good' was Marcus Antonius Pallas, who accumulated great wealth, and, as a freedman, became Claudius's financial secretary with slaves of his own (see Oost 1958). Among slaves who were not

---

[25] In his authoritative work on the *familia Caesaris*, Weaver (1992: *e.g.* 199, 295) has demonstrated that there was marked social differentiation not only between those who constituted this 'household' and those slaves and freedmen outside this *familia*, but also with the *familia* itself. There were five distinct status groups: the emperor's freedmen, his immediate slaves, the freedmen of the emperor's freedmen, the slaves of the emperor's freedmen, and the slaves of the emperor's slaves.

[26] For instance, the *Oeconomica* of Pseudo-Aristotle distinguishes the 'manager' or 'supervisor' (*epitropos*) from the 'worker' (*ergatēs*) (1. 1344a). See also Garnsey 1982: 105.

part of the imperial *familia*, the most famous was probably Epictetus (c. AD 55–135), the Stoic philosopher whose lectures and *Manual*, published posthumously, greatly influenced the emperor Marcus Aurelius.

In Roman law, slaves were 'chattels' (*mancipia*), 'mortal objects' (*res mortales*) (Justinian's *Digest* 21. 1. 23. 3). A Roman could buy, rent or sell a slave, as he would a piece of property. An owner's right to use and dispose of his slave as he wished was called *dominium*, 'the right of absolute ownership'. Varro, the Roman politician and polymath, described a slave as 'a kind of talking tool' (*instrumenti genus vocale*; *De Re Rust.* 1. 17. 1). Owners of an estate would classify slaves as 'articulate equipment' as opposed to oxen which were 'inarticulate equipment'.

This concept of the slave as 'property' (*mancipium*) and the term 'slave' (*servus*) itself were both regularly traced by the Romans to a military origin. Slaves were *mancipia* because they were those captured by force of arms (*manu capiantur*; Justinian's *Digest* 1. 5. 4). A *servus* was someone 'kept safe' or 'preserved' (*servare*), that is, not slain, in war. 'Slaves (*servi*) gain their name because generals have a custom of selling their captives, thus saving (*servare*) them instead of killing them' (*Digest* 1. 5. 4).

Being a mere object (*res*), not a subject, in the eyes of the law, the slave was 'rightless'. He lacked the right of recourse to the law for protection[27] and could not be called as a free witness.[28] Nor could a slave own property, make a contract that was legally binding, hold public office or serve in the army. Only when a slave was freed and became a citizen did he gain the right to become a property-owner, to act as his own legal representative, to hold office, and to serve in the army.[29] So a slave was effectively marginalized and rendered powerless.

Yet we must recognize that although legally slaves were objects, devoid of rights, in practice their personhood was not denied.[30] They

---

[27] However, when Greek slaves were mistreated they could take refuge in a temple and be given a formal legal hearing if their accusations against their master could be substantiated.

[28] It was assumed that only if a slave's testimony had been extracted by torture would it be reliable. See references in Balsdon 1969: 108, 378.

[29] When, faced with a manpower crisis at a time of national emergency, the Greeks and Romans employed slaves as rowers or legionaries, it was only after they had been manumitted or promised freedom for fighting well (Wiedemann 1981: 44–45).

[30] 'There does not seem to be a single text in the whole Corpus Iuris Civilis, or in the Codex Theodosianus, or in the surviving classical legal literature which denies person-

were permitted carefully circumscribed privileges. First, there was common-law cohabitation (*contubernium*, lit. 'tent-companionship'), which was clearly distinguished from legal marriage (*conubium*). But a child born to a female slave belonged to her owner, irrespective of the status of the father. Second, slaves could be members of various religious, social or funerary clubs or 'associations' (*collegia*), albeit with their masters' authorization (Buckland 1969: 74f.; Barrow 1968: 164–168; Bömer 1957–63). Third, it was customary for masters to allow their slaves access to property or money (*peculium*) that they could use as working capital 'borrowed' from the master. This 'private purse', a symbol of slaves' sought-after independence, was technically always owned by the master but in practice it could be used at the slave's discretion, ultimately to purchase his freedom.[31] Fourth, one trace of the recognition that a slave was a person like any other, before the gods, was the fact that prior to manumission he was usually compelled to take an oath, placing him under a religious obligation, when free, to adhere to the promise of *operae* ('works'), a work commitment to his former master, now his patron (Buckland 1969: 73f.). Fifth, 'they could attend the theatre, the gladiatorial games, and the races and might, upon occasion, share in municipal banquets' (Westermann 1955: 108). Further indications of a slave's personhood in Roman practice are his criminal liability and his capacity to become a Roman citizen through formal manumission and to act for his master contractually (Szakats 1975: 39).

There were two main ways in which slaves gained relief from their situation: they could run away or their master could set them free, that is, he could 'manumit' them.[32] In one case the slave took the initiative; in the other, the master. These two means of relief, absconding and manumission, must be considered in more detail.

Runaway slaves created a massive problem in the late Republic and early Principate (see Bellen 1971). During the civil wars, Augustus returned 30,000 runaway slaves to their masters for suitable punishment (*Res Gestae* 25) – punishment that ranged from death by

---

ality to a slave' (Buckland 1969: 4). Consequently, manumission cannot be regarded as the acquisition of personality on the part of the slave (*cf.* Buckland 1969: 715).

[31] Under the Empire such a purchase of freedom was protected by law, so that the emancipated slave could appeal to the Prefect in Rome or the governor in the provinces if he wished to instigate proceedings against his owner on whose good faith he had relied (*Digest* 40. 1. 5).

[32] The English term 'manumit' comes from the Latin *manu* ('by the hand') and *emittere* ('send on one's way'), referring to the master's gesture on setting a slave free.

crucifixion, to branding on the forehead with the letter F or the three letters FVG, standing for the word FVGITIVVS, 'runaway (slave)' (see further Coleman-Norton 1951: 176). Under Roman law it was an offence to harbour a runaway (Justinian's *Digest* 11. 3. 1. 2), but T. Mommsen[33] has argued convincingly that the relevant law (*lex Fabia de plagiariis*) did not extend to the provinces, so that Paul was not legally obliged to return the runaway slave Onesimus to Philemon, his owner[34] (whether or not Philemon was a Roman citizen). However that be, when a slave ran away, a master had reason for anxiety, for slaves were a costly investment (see above) and the apprehension of a runaway involved costs such as the employment of a slave-catcher,[35] not to speak of the reduced resale value of a slave with a history of absconding and a master's concern that other slaves in the household or on the estate may have co-operated in enabling the escape.

The frequency of slaves' efforts to run away illustrates the fact that a slave's chief desire was to gain his freedom. Epictetus, once himself a slave, put it simply: 'it is the slave's prayer that he be set free immediately' (*Diss.*, 4. 1. 33).[36] Indeed, if there was no prospect of freedom, as was the case for criminals working in the mines or on the rural estates, the lot of slaves was intolerable (*cf.* Cicero, *Rab. Perd.* 5. 15). But most urban slaves gained their freedom through manumission by their thirties at the latest (Lampe 1992b: 22).[37] Expressed another way, the urban slave would serve his master between ten and twenty years before manumission.

It is not difficult to identify a slave's motives for seeking to merit or gain manumission. This would end the humiliation of being under the will and at the mercy of another human being. It would begin to re-establish his self-esteem as he acquired relative independence – freedom of choice with regard to employment and movement. He

[33] *Römisches Strafrecht* (Leipzig: Dunker & Humbolt, 1899), 780, cited by Coleman-Norton 1951: 173).

[34] This is the conclusion of Coleman-Norton 1951: 174.

[35] 'The search for slaves in *fuga* became under the Empire an organized business conducted by private *fugitivarii* ['slave-catchers'] who delivered the apprehended runaways either directly to the owners or to the nearest municipal magistrate' (Westermann 1955: 107).

[36] Yet Epictetus was well aware that the emancipated slave, suddenly without the necessities of life that had previously been supplied by his master, could find himself in a more miserable state than slavery (*Diss.* 4. 1. 35–37).

[37] Lampe cites G. Alföldy, 'Die Freilassung von Sklaven und die Struktur der Sklaverei in der römischen Kaiserzeit', in *Sozial- und Wirtschaftsgeschichte der römischen Kaiserzeit*, ed. H. Schneider (Darmstadt: Wissenschaftliche Buchgesellschaft, 1981), 359. But see the further judicious comments of Hopkins 1978: 127 n. 63.

would be free from seizure as property and from involuntary sale back into slavery. If his master was a Roman citizen and he was manumitted formally, he would gain Roman citizenship (de Visscher 1946)[38] and with it the right of legal marriage (*matrimonium*) and access to the courts and to public office. Emancipation would also enable him to begin a family line of free persons and citizens who could own property. And sometimes manumission led to marriage to the owner's daughter or son, or even to the owner himself.

Motivation for a slave-owner's act of manumission was varied and usually many-sided, but while gratitude for a slave's past faithful service sometimes prompted a master to act, self-interest of some sort was generally the governing factor. It may be the desire to marry the slave or to formalize a sexual relationship by marriage, the wish to gain a reputation for benevolence and magnanimity, or the hope of promoting eager compliance among slaves prior to their manumission.[39] From the viewpoint of Roman society itself, manumission aimed at, or had the result of, integrating outsiders into society,[40] enlarging the number of potential soldiers, and increasing the political power of the wealthy whose freedmen would vote for their patron.

There is plentiful evidence that during the last century BC and the first century AD, hundreds of thousands of slaves gained their freedom. We can gather the extent of manumission by examining statements about the 5% tax that was levied on freed slaves and deposited in the sacred treasury. From such data for the period 81–49 BC, T. Frank deduced that half a million slaves were freed during that time.[41] If this tax was designed 'to discourage manumission and preserve the native Roman character of society, then it must be pronounced a dismal failure' (Duff 1958: 30). In any case, many masters avoided paying this tax by means of informal as opposed to

---

[38] Acquisition of citizenship was not a corollary of manumission in Greece (see Bartchy 1973: 91 n. 345).

[39] *Cf.* Dionysius of Halicarnassus, *Ant. Roma.* 4. 24. 1–6.

[40] 'Rome, alone of all cities of antiquity, has the honour of having redeemed her outcasts by opening her doors to them' (Carcopino 1940: 59). Wiedemann (1981: 3), too, notes the sense in which 'slavery can be interpreted as a process rather than a permanent condition – a temporary phase by which an outsider is allocated a place within a society which has no natural obligations of kinship or guest-friendship towards him'. Martin (1990: 32) goes one step further: 'Slavery was arguably the most important channel through which outsiders entered the mainstream of Roman power structures.'

[41] *AJP* 53 (1932) 360, cited by Rupprecht 1975: 458.

formal manumission.[42] Augustus met this threat to the distinctiveness of Roman civilization by the *lex Fufia Caninia* of 2 BC, which on a sliding scale limited the number of slaves that a master could free in his will. For example, if 100–500 slaves were owned, the limit was one-fifth, and the upper limit was set at 100.

But manumission never brought absolute freedom, for in Roman society a manumitted slave entered a client–patron relationship with his former master, a relationship which involved particular duties prescribed by the patron. Such patronage was ubiquitous. As E. Ferguson (1987: 45) observes, 'Everyone from slave to aristocrat felt bound to display respect to someone more powerful than himself, up to the emperor.'

Scholars are disagreed about the general lot of slaves in the Roman Empire in the first century AD. Clearly the treatment of slaves varied greatly, depending on many variables, such as the nature of the slave's work, how he was acquired by his owner, where he worked (the city or the country,[43] in a family setting or on a plantation), whether there was the hope of manumission, and the temperament of the master.

At one extreme we know of cases where masters showed kindness to their slaves. Pliny the Younger is a notable example. When one of his highly gifted slaves, called Zosimus, contracted tuberculosis, Pliny sent him to Egypt to recuperate and later to the farm of his friend Valerius Paulinus. 'Nature has so made us that nothing serves to incite and inflame our love for something as does the fear of losing it – a sentiment I have experienced regarding Zosimus more than once' (*Ep.* 5. 19). Also, Pliny permitted his slaves to make 'a kind of will which I observe as carefully as if it were valid in law' (*Ep.* 8. 16), although legally slaves could not own or bequeath property. Then there is the general admonition of the Stoic philosopher Seneca, who, in one of his *Moral Letters*, bids masters cultivate their slaves' respect, not their fear: 'The person who shows respect also shows love, and love and fear cannot be mingled. So I judge you to be entirely right in not wishing to be feared by your slaves, and in lashing them merely with words; only dumb animals are admonished by the whip' (*Ep.* 47. 18–19).

---

[42] The distinction between formal and informal manumission will be discussed in chapter 4.

[43] Note the oft-quoted statement of Carcopino (1940: 56): 'With few exceptions, slavery in Rome was neither eternal nor, while it lasted, intolerable.'

At the opposite extreme, since slavery was based on coercion, it was often true that fear and mutual hostility governed the master–slave relationship. The Roman historian Tacitus expressed a widespread sentiment: 'Now that we have within our households nations with different customs and foreign cults or none, you will never coerce such a mixture of humanity except by fear' (*Ann.* 14. 44).[44] This mutual hostility is epitomized in the common Roman proverb, 'There are as many enemies as there are slaves' (*totidem hostes esse quot servos*; Seneca, *Ep.* 47. 5).[45] And so we read of horrendous punishments inflicted on slaves, such as crucifixion, the breaking of bones, amputations, hot tar, restraining collars and the rack.

Now on the premise that ancient sources generally mention only what is exceptional practice, it could be argued that such punishments were uncommon. If slaves were expensive commodities, would masters maim or kill them for minor infractions? We may grant that the punishments mentioned above were probably extreme. But there must be limits to our suspicion of the sources,[46] for 'Roman literature abounds with examples of incidental cruelty to individual domestic slaves' (Hopkins 1978: 118).[47] Without fear of contradiction we may say that the flogging of slaves was simply routine. In the comedies of the Roman satirist Plautus, the slave is by definition 'he who is whipworthy'.[48]

There can be no doubt that there was an improvement in the west of the Roman Empire with regard to the treatment of slaves, both legally and practically, during the first three centuries AD; in the eastern provinces slavery had always been more humane.[49] This amelioration of slave conditions came about partly as a result of the rising number

[44] Philo spoke of 'the fear of the master' (*ho despotikos phobos*) (*Spec. Leg.* 1. 128), and Paul refers to 'the spirit of a slave, that fills you once more with fear' (Rom. 8:15).

[45] See also Macrobius, *Saturnalia* 1. 11. 13. When, in AD 61, the City Prefect, Pedanius Secundus, was murdered by a slave, all 400 of his household slaves were executed, on the assumption that a slave could not have acted alone in the murder, so that all the slaves were culpable accessories. 'A crime has many antecedent symptoms' (Tacitus, *Ann.* 14. 44).

[46] It seems arbitrary, for instance, to suggest that the advice of Cato the Elder that old or sick slaves should be sold, together with worn-out oxen, an old wagon and old iron tools (*Agr.* 2. 7), was irregular and did not reflect the practice of agricultural slaveowners.

[47] See Hopkins' whole discussion (1978: 118–123) and also Westermann 1955: 105–106.

[48] See further Segal 1987: 138–140; and on the depiction of slaves in Roman satire in general, see Ramage *et al.* 1974: 32, 38, 61, 82, 106, 122f.

[49] For details, see Westermann 1955: 102–117; and, more briefly, Carcopino 1940: 57f.; Balsdon 1969: 109.

of slaves born in their master's house and therefore to greater responsibility and privilege within the family, but also it was partly due to a growing public antipathy towards the arbitrary power of the *paterfamilias* ('head of a family' or 'proprietor of an estate') and to the increasing humanitarianism among the general populace.[50] However, humanitarian gestures by legislation or by individual masters were almost always prompted by self-interest, *viz.* the desire to preserve the value of the slave for the greatest possible return on the investment.

It is impossible to ignore the negative stigmatic associations of slavery during the Roman Republic and Empire (see Bradley 1994: 144f., 176–180). The name 'slave' (*servus*) was regarded as a term of disgrace and insult (see Vogt 1972: 94).[51] When Tacitus describes crucifixion as 'a punishment belonging to slaves' (*servile supplicium*; *Hist.* 4. 11), he means that the worst form of death is appropriate and reserved for the lowest grade of human beings. This is a pointed testimony to what T. E. J. Wiedemann (1987: 25) aptly calls 'the conceptual inferiority of slaves'. Also, slavery was seen, especially in legal texts, as tantamount to death,[52] while the members of one private club of slaves spoke of themselves as 'comrades in death [*commorientes*]' (Barrow 1968: 168). So we must demur at D. Tidball's (1984: 115) contention that 'by the time of Paul it [slavery] was not a severe and cruel institution', and G. Corcoran's (1980a: 3) view that 'slavery as Jesus and his audience knew it was essentially benign and accepted as normal'.[53] 'Accepted as normal' – yes. 'Essentially benign' – no.

The final evaluation of Hopkins (1978: 121, 123) may stand:

> The viciousness of Roman slavery, the exploitation, cruelty and mutual hostility are worth stressing because modern accounts often focus instead on those elements in Roman philosophy, literature and law which point to the humanitarian

---

[50] With the arrival of the *pax Romana* in the aftermath of Augustus's victory at the battle of Actium (31 BC), the main source of slaves, *viz.* war captives, largely dried up, so that the price of slaves gradually increased. With this came greater humanitarianism towards slaves.

[51] Martin (1990: xxi, 30) has minimized the dishonour or shame that actually attached to slavery, in his effort to highlight the honour felt by the small but significant number of 'middle-level, managerial slaves' who were 'upwardly mobile'.

[52] Justinian's *Digest* 35. 1. 59. 2; 49. 15. 18; 50. 17. 209, cited by Bradley 1994: 25.

[53] Corcoran (1980b: 76) asserts that the harsh side of slavery 'emerges only rarely' in the New Testament, citing Matt. 18:25; Rom. 6:17, 19, 20; Gal. 4:3, 8, 9, 25.

treatment of slaves, and to the willing loyalty of some slaves to
their masters ... The mitigation of slavery by philosophical
belief and imperial decree probably made little impression on
the routine corruption implicit in a elite culture which took the
massed subservience of slaves for granted.

Ancient and modern slavery

Now that we have completed our sketch of Jewish, Greek and Roman
slavery in the first century AD, let us briefly consider a wider issue.
How did ancient slavery differ from modern slavery? Or more
specifically, what distinguished Greco-Roman slavery from New
World slavery?[54]

In the first century, slaves were not distinguishable from free
persons by race, by speech or by clothing; they were sometimes more
highly educated than their owners and held responsible professional
positions; some persons sold themselves into slavery for economic or
social advantage; they could reasonably hope to be emancipated after
ten to twenty years of service or by their thirties at the latest; they
were not denied the right of public assembly and were not socially
segregated (at least in the cities); they could accumulate savings to
buy their freedom; their natural inferiority was not assumed.

Do these two types of slavery, then, have anything in common?
Finley (1976: 819) has argued that 'although the existence of slaves is
virtually ubiquitous, throughout the ages in all parts of the globe,
slavery as an institution essential to a society, to its production and to
its lifestyle, was to be found only in classical Greece and classical
Rome, and in the modern era in Brazil, the Caribbean and the
southern states of the United States'. For Finley, the essential
ingredient that distinguished these five instances of societies that
were based on slavery from other societies where slavery was present
was the slave's alienation from family and tribe, including communal
religion, so that his focus of attachment became his master; his
identity became inseparable from his master. A similar verdict was
reached by Wiedemann (1987: 3), another specialist in Greco-Roman
slavery: 'What makes slavery unique as an unequal relationship, is
that it denies the slave any existence as a person independent from
that which his master chooses to grant him.' At the heart of slavery,

[54] See the useful chart in Dodd 1996: 87–89.

ancient or modern, are the ideas of total dependence, the forfeiture of autonomy and the sense of belonging wholly to another. A slave lacked the power of refusal,[55] in the sense that he knew that if he refused to obey his master, he would suffer dire consequences. His was the frustration not only of powerlessness, but also of relative hopelessness, for even in the first-century setting, manumission was never guaranteed and even a promise of emancipation could be revoked by the arbitrary decision of the master.

I conclude this sketch of first-century slavery by noting that whereas in many parts of the English-speaking world slavery is part of our history, in the Mediterranean lands of the first century, slavery was part of their life. This difference is a ground, I submit, not for the purging of the language of slavery from the New Testament, but for its preservation. That is, if the language of slavery is offensive, the offence would have been considerably greater for those who lived in societies where slavery was intrinsic than for us for whom slavery is simply an unpleasant and embarrassing memory.

---

[55] When Seneca (*De Ben.* 3. 19. 1) says that 'a slave does not have the power to refuse', he is citing an opinion he does not accept (*cf.* 'Even if I accept these premisses ...' 3. 19. 2), for he is showing that in conferring a 'benefit' on his master, a slave has done something he could have chosen *not* to do (3. 19. 1–4).

Chapter Three

The New Testament attitude towards physical slavery

Do the references to literal slavery in the New Testament lead us to conclude that the early Christians endorsed slavery? Or does the evidence suggest that while the early church recognized and accepted slavery as a fundamental strand in the fabric of society, it did not endorse it as a social system?

Slaves and slave-owning

Slaves figure in no fewer than thirteen of the parables of Jesus:

1. Weeds (Matt. 13:24–30)
2. Unmerciful slave (Matt. 18:23–35)
3. Vineyard workers (Matt. 20:1–13)
4. Wicked tenants (Matt. 21:33–44; Mark 12:1–11; Luke 20:9–16)
5. Wedding banquet (Matt. 22:1–14; Luke 14:16–24)
6. Overseer (Matt. 24:45–51; Luke 12:42–48)
7. Talents (Matt. 25:14–30; Luke 19:11–27)
8. Doorkeeper (Mark 13:32–37)
9. Waiting slaves (Luke 12:35–38)
10. Barren fig tree (Luke 13:6–9)
11. Prodigal son (Luke 15:11–32)
12. Shrewd manager (Luke 16:1–8)
13. Obedient slave (Luke 17:7–10)

These parables accurately reflect the circumstances under which slavery operated in the first century. One slave could be the master of another slave (Luke 12:42, 45) in the sense of being responsible to the master for the conduct of other slaves; a slave could carry out several duties, working both outside and indoors (Luke 17:7–8); a slave could collect dues on behalf of his master (Matt. 21:34); sometimes a master would entrust his slaves with money to invest (Matt. 18:23–

24; 25:14–30; Luke 16:1–8); some slaves abused their master's trust (Luke 12:45–46); a slave's faithfulness was measured by his obedience to commands and adherence to duty (Luke 12:42–43);[1] some slaves were day-labourers, negotiating a daily rate (Matt. 20:1–2, 8); a slave could summon guests to a wedding (Matt. 22:3–4, 8–10); if a slave was unable to repay a debt, he and his family could be sold (Matt. 18:25) or he could be imprisoned (Matt. 18:28–30); a master could dispense summary punishment as *paterfamilias* (Matt. 24:51). The one (intentional) divergence from customary practice, reflected in the parables, was that the reward given for loyal service was not manumission but increased responsibility (Matt. 24:46–47; 25:21, 23). There is also the picture of a master waiting on his own slaves (Luke 12:37), but this unheard-of reversal of roles was for dramatic effect: watchfulness will be richly rewarded.

In none of the parables is it suggested that slavery as such is iniquitous; on the other hand, nowhere is slavery explicitly sanctioned. Rather, it is simply accepted as an inevitable part of the social and economic *status quo*. Yet conduct inappropriate for a slave is censured. So, for example, mistreatment of fellow-slaves and carousing during the master's absence are severely punished (Luke 12:45–46).[2]

In addition to the parables, we find references to slaves in several incidents in the gospels and Acts. In these cases, too, there is no moralizing about slavery as a social institution:

1. The healing of the centurion's slave (Matt. 8:5–13; Luke 7:1–10)
2. The healing of the official's son (John 4:46–53)
3. The arrest of Jesus (Matt. 26:50–51; Mark 14:46–47; Luke 22:49–51; John 18:10)
4. The denial of Peter (Matt. 26:69–75; Mark 14:66–72; Luke 22:54–62; John 18:15–18)
5. Cornelius and Peter (Acts 10:7, 17–23)
6. Peter's escape from prison (Acts 12:13)

Whereas in Jesus' parables most slaves appear as agricultural

---

[1] But Beavis (1992: 54) rightly observes that slaves are sometimes portrayed as 'moral agents, capable of making ethical choices over and above simple obedience to their masters' (*cf.* Matt. 18:31; Luke 13:8–9).

[2] The even-handedness of masters seems always to be assumed (*e.g.*, Matt. 18:23–27, 31–34), as do their absolute prerogatives (*e.g.*, Matt. 20:1–16).

workers, in the letters of the New Testament, which are generally addressed to Christians living in cities, we must presuppose urban rather than rural slavery. But in both cases the slaves normally belonged to extended households, whether they were called *douloi* ('slaves'), *oiketai* ('household slaves') or 'those who belong to the family of *X*' (*e.g.*, Rom. 16:10–11) or '*X*'s people' (*e.g.*, 1 Cor. 1:11). Specific directives are given to slaves in four Pauline epistles (Eph. 6:5–8; Col. 3:22–25; 1 Tim. 6:1–2; Titus 2:9–10) and in 1 Peter (2:18–21), and to masters in three Pauline epistles (Eph. 6:9; Col. 4:1; Philem. 8–22). In every case in the Pauline epistles it is implied that both the slaves and their masters are Christians.[3] But in 1 Peter 2:18 the possibility that slaves would have surly, harsh or ill-tempered masters (*skolioi*) – presumed to be non-Christians – is envisaged. And in 1 Timothy 6:2 the very expression 'those [slaves] who have believing masters' leads us to suppose that some slaves did not. In fact, the previous verse (1 Tim. 6:1), with its encouragement to Christian slaves not to bring the name of God and apostolic teaching into disrepute, suggests that non-Christian masters in particular are in view in verse 1. Whatever a Christian slave's situation – whether serving under a Christian master or a non-Christian – it is everywhere assumed that a person could be a slave-owner and also a Christian, and that he or she could own non-Christian slaves, as in the case of Philemon before Onesimus's flight and conversion. If the early Christians uniformly regarded slavery as an unmitigated evil, it is difficult to believe that slave-owning would not be castigated in some New Testament document.

The 'slave–free' contrast

On four occasions in Paul's letters (1 Cor. 12:13; Gal. 3:28; Eph. 6:8; Col. 3:11) and three times in the Apocalypse (Rev. 6:15; 13:16; 19:18), we find the 'slave–free' (*doulos–eleutheros*) antithesis.[4] In the Roman world (in the form *servus–libertus*), as in the Greek world, this antithesis was a standard way of classifying human beings – as basic a way as 'male–female' or 'young–old'. Although this social distinction is not explicit in all strands of the New Testament, there is no reason to believe that all the early Christians did not recognize the

---

[3] Rhoda, who is described as a 'female slave' or 'servant girl' (*paidiskē*), would also be an example of a Christian slave belonging to a Christian, in this case Mary of Jerusalem (Acts 12:15).

[4] In Rev. 13:16; 19:18 we find the reverse order: 'free–slave' (*eleutheros–doulos*).

distinction as existing and in that sense accept it. But so far from supporting the distinction in principle on either theological or pragmatic grounds, Paul argues that with regard to status and privilege before God the distinction is invalid, for all believers, whether slave or free, are one in Christ (1 Cor. 12:13; Gal. 3:28; Col. 3:11) and on an impartial basis will be recompensed for doing good (Eph. 6:8). No longer did Paul see the 'slave–free' or the 'Jewish–Gentile' or the 'male–female' antithesis as of fundamental importance in any categorizing of humanity. Their place was taken by the 'in Christ'– 'separated from Christ' antithesis (Eph. 2:12–13; *cf.* Rom. 9:3). From the time of his conversion Paul ceased to view humans from a purely natural standpoint (2 Cor. 5:16). As a person newly constituted by being in Christ (2 Cor. 5:17), he not only saw Christ as God's promised Messiah but also viewed humans in the light of the cross as being either united to Christ by faith or devoid of a knowledge of Christ.

Further evidence that the early believers rejected the validity of the 'slave–free' antithesis as a primary way of classifying humankind may be seen in the numerous 'one another' commands found in the New Testament. Christians are enjoined to love one another,[5] serve one another (Gal. 5:13), accept one another (Rom. 15:7), be hospitable to one another (1 Pet. 4:9), greet one another with a holy kiss,[6] be devoted to one another (Rom. 12:10), honour one another (Rom. 12:10), live in harmony with one another (Rom. 12:16; 1 Pet. 3:8), bear with one another (Eph. 4:2; Col. 3:13), be kind and compassionate to one another (Eph. 4:32), carry one another's burdens (Gal. 6:2), forgive one another (Eph. 4:32; Col. 3:13), build one another up (1 Thess. 5:11), admonish one another (Col. 3:16), and encourage one another (1 Thess. 4:18; 5:11; Heb. 3:13; 10:25). In each of these cases, 'one another' implies 'without distinction on the basis of social status or personal preference'. Nor should one overlook Paul's directive to 'mingle readily with people of low status' (Rom. 12:16),[7] where the primary reference is probably to slaves but also included all those who are outcasts because of social status. The apostle is

---

[5] John 13:34–35; 15:12, 17; Rom. 13:8; 1 Pet. 1:22; 1 John 3:11, 23; 4:7, 11–12; 2 John 5.

[6] Rom. 16:16; 1 Cor. 16:20; 2 Cor. 13:12; 1 Pet. 5:14.

[7] Although the expression *tois tapeinois* is parallel to *ta hypsēla*, it need not be construed as neuter (since *ta hypsēla phronountes* is equivalent to *hypsēlophronountes*, *cf.* 1 Tim. 6:17; thus Cranfield 1979: 644), but is probably masculine (as elsewhere in the NT) or a personalized use of the neuter (as in 1 Cor. 1:27): 'the humble', 'people of low standing', 'the lowly', 'people held in low regard'.

encouraging all Christians to have unself-conscious interaction with those people who are commonly regarded as valueless and unimportant.

Imagery drawn from slavery

We may glean a clue to the New Testament view of physical slavery from the nature of its imagery that is drawn from slavery. If there is only positive imagery, it would be possible to infer that the New Testament sanctions slavery.[8] But if the negative connotations of slavery are also present, it would be difficult to conclude that slavery is endorsed as a system.

The New Testament does not hesitate to use slavery imagery in a positive sense to depict the Christian life as a whole or in some specific aspect. Thus Christians are called the slaves of God (*e.g.*, 1 Pet. 2:16) or of Christ (1 Cor. 7:22; Eph. 6:6) or of one another (2 Cor. 4:5; *cf.* Gal. 5:13), referring, in general, to their total availability and devotion to a person. They are also enjoined to show a character trait that was commonly associated with slaves, *viz.* the humble service of others. In 1 Peter 5, after giving directions to the 'elders' or 'shepherds' (vv. 1–4) and to 'the younger ones' (v. 5a), Peter calls on all church members to exhibit mutual humility: 'In your relations with one another, all put on humility as an apron' (v. 5b). The verb used here, 'put on (as an apron)' (*enkomboomai*), is very picturesque and is found only here in the New Testament. Slaves and the poor used to wear a tunic with only one sleeve (*exōmis*), that left one shoulder bare.[9] Over this tunic slaves would wear an apron (*enkombōma*) that kept the tunic clean.[10] So Peter's addressees are being told to put on the apron of humility in the same way that slaves would tie an apron over their one-sleeved tunic as they began their work.[11]

---

[8] Vogt (1972: 95f.), for example, asserts that in Jesus' use of the concept of slavery as a picture of the God–man relationship within the kingdom of God there is a sanctioning of slavery as an institution. A similar sentiment regarding Paul is expressed by Corcoran (1980a: 24): 'By modelling the relationship between Christ and the Christian on that existing between master and slave, he [Paul] showed clearly that he did not see the institution as something evil in itself.'

[9] The *exōmis* is sometimes called the *chitōn heteromaskalos*, an 'undergarment with one hole for the arm', that is, an undergarment that comes over only one shoulder.

[10] Pollux, *On.* 4. 119. An *enkombōma* was any article of dress tied on with a knot (*kombos*).

[11] This is not the same as saying that they were to display the humility that marks the slave. It is the apron that is the slave's, not the humility.

1 Peter is replete with allusions to incidents in the gospels in which Peter himself figures prominently. So it is not fanciful to find in this distinctive verb in 1 Peter 5:5 a reminiscence of John 13:2–5. There we are told that Jesus took off his outer clothes,[12] wrapped a long towel (*lention*) around his tunic (v. 4), and washed his disciples' feet, wiping them with the linen cloth. This action of wrapping a garment around one's waist in preparation for service was pre-eminently and characteristically a slave's action (*cf.* Luke 12:37; 17:18).[13] Is it not significant that the point of this acted parable is precisely the same as 1 Peter 5:5 – the need for mutual humility (see John 13:12–15) – and that Jesus immediately says, 'A slave (*doulos*) is not greater than his master (*kyrios*)' (John 13:16)?

But negative ideas that are associated with slavery are also found in the New Testament. To 'be a slave' to a person or thing in a negative sense is to be under the control of that person or thing as a helpless victim.[14] Certain people are said to be slaves, or to be in bondage, to sin (John 8:34; Rom. 6:16–17, 20), to depravity (2 Pet. 2:19), to elemental spirits or forces (*ta stoicheia*) (Gal. 4:3, 9), to passions and pleasures (Titus 3:3), to false gods (Gal. 4:8), to drink (Titus 2:3), to the fear of death (Heb. 2:15), to the law (Gal. 5:1; *cf.* 4:24), and to other persons (1 Cor. 7:23). Also, creation is described as being in bondage to decay until it gains the glorious freedom of God's children (Rom. 8:21). Finally, a link between slavery and fear is made in Romans 8:15, where Paul contrasts 'a Spirit/spirit of slavery' (*pneuma douleias*) and 'the Spirit of adoption' (*pneuma huiothesias*). The second use of *pneuma* clearly refers to the Holy Spirit who effects the adoption of believers as God's sons. In the first case, if *pneuma* refers to an attitude or disposition (*cf.* Hos. 4:12, 'a spirit of harlotry'), the sense will be 'You did not receive a spirit that marks the state of slavery and leads you back into fear' (*palin eis phobon*), or 'You did not receive the spirit of a slave, to fill you once more with fear' (TCNT). Alternatively, if the two uses of *pneuma* have an identical reference (*viz.* the Holy Spirit), Paul is saying 'The Spirit

---

[12] The plural *ta himatia* may be generalizing (thus 'his outer robe') or may be a true plural ('his outer clothes', *viz.* his robe and tunic), indicating that Jesus stripped to only his loin-cloth.

[13] Footwashing was usually regarded as beneath the dignity of Jewish slaves (*Mekilta* on Exod. 21:2). The midrash on Gen. 21:14 indicates that when Abraham banished Hagar, his wife's slave, he wrapped Hagar's shawl around her waist 'so that people would know that she was a slave' (SB 2. 557).

[14] In all the examples that follow, the *doul-* root is found.

you received does not bring you into slavery and back into fear, but brings about your adoption as sons.'

Since the New Testament draws both positive and negative images from slavery, we conclude that it neither endorses slavery (given the negative imagery) nor rejects slavery (given the positive imagery).

Aspects of slavery repudiated

The New Testament firmly rejects two aspects of the practice of slavery. The first is the exploitation of the slave for monetary gain. At Philippi Paul and his companions encountered a slave girl (*paidiskē*) who had 'a spirit of divination' (*pneuma pythōna*, Acts 16:16), that is, a spirit that enabled her to predict the future. By her fortune-telling she earned large profits for her owners (16:16), who were intent on protecting this source of revenue and their property rights (as they regarded them) (*cf.* 16:19). When she persisted in following Paul and his company, shrieking, 'These men are slaves (*douloi*) of the Most High God, who are telling you the way to be saved', Paul exorcised the spirit in the name of Jesus Christ, and it immediately left her (16:17–18). Although Paul's action precipitated his arrest and imprisonment along with Silas (16:19–24), Luke's report of the episode does not suggest the inappropriateness of Paul's action, but rather the opposite; the abuse of a slave was to be repudiated. This is also clear, by implication, from those passages where slave-owners are directed to treat their slaves justly and fairly (Col. 4:1) and to refrain from threats (Eph. 6:9).

Second, the kidnapping of persons for slavery and trafficking in slaves are strongly censured. In a list of persons and practices that are castigated by the commandments of the law and are opposed to wholesome teaching as embodied in the gospel (1 Tim. 1:9–11), we find mention made of 'man-stealers'. The Greek word *andrapodistēs* refers to someone who sells slaves ('slave-dealer'), and in particular to someone who kidnaps people for sale as slaves ('kidnappers').[15] Paul is alluding to the eighth commandment, 'You shall not steal' (Ex. 20:15), which applies to persons as well as to things.[16] Exodus

---

[15] The term *andrapodistēs* is formed from *andrapodon*, lit. 'a man-footed object', used of a war captive who was sold as a slave (LSJ, 128 *s. v.*) which itself is constructed on the model of *tetrapodon*, 'a four-footed creature'. See Spicq 1978: 201–204.

[16] In Paul's catalogue of vice, 'those who ill-treat their fathers or mothers' alludes to the fifth commandment (Exod. 20:12); 'murderers', to the sixth (Exod. 20:13); 'immoral persons' and 'homosexuals', to the seventh (Exod. 20:14); and 'liars' and 'perjurers', to

21:16 prescribes the death penalty for the kidnapper (*cf.* Deut. 24:7). That is, while both Testaments assume the practice of slavery, both repudiate kidnapping and dealing in slaves.

New attitudes inculcated

Voices of protest against the exploitation of slaves and against slave-trading were not uncommon in antiquity. But what makes the New Testament distinctive in its first-century setting is its directives to Christian masters *and* slaves, where the emphasis rests on obligations to be fulfilled rather than on rights to be asserted.[17]

First, with regard to *slaves*. They are elevated to a parity of status with masters in the divine economy. Their personal dignity is thus established. Significantly, in the pre-Christian social codes slaves are not included as addressees, because they were regarded either as non-persons or as persons without the social responsibilities of the free. Evidence for this Christian dignifying of slaves is as follows:

1. In the catalogues of domestic duties, commonly known as *Haustafeln* ('household tables'), slaves are the recipients of apostolic directives,[18] equally with their masters.[19] They are addressed as persons capable of moral decision.[20]

2. As with masters (Col. 4:1), so with slaves, the motivation for right conduct is Christological: slaves are to act 'out of reverence for the Lord' (Col. 3:22), viewing their action 'as a service rendered to

---

the ninth (Exod. 20:16). In rabbinic exegesis the eighth commandment was often related to slave-dealing (see SB 1. 810–813).

[17] It is important to recognize that Paul is referring to *Christian* masters when he says that slaves are to obey their masters 'in everything' (*kata panta*, Col. 3:22; *cf.* Titus 2:9). This removes the sting from Davies's rhetorical question: 'How could young male and female slaves who might be required to provide their masters with sexual services "work with liveliness, serving the Lord"?' (1995: 343, citing Petronius, *Sat.* 75. 11; Horace, *Sat.* 1. 2. 116–119). Note also Seneca's comment that slaves 'are not compelled to obey us in everything – they would not carry out orders contrary to the interests of the state, and they would not become accomplices in any crime' (*Ben.* 3. 20).

[18] Eph. 6:5–8; Col. 3:22–25; 1 Tim. 6:1–2; Titus 2:9–10; 1 Pet. 2:18–21. The detailed treatment of the slave–master relation, with the focus on the slave's responsibilities, in Col. 3:22 – 4:1 may have been prompted by the recent flight of Onesimus from Philemon at Colossae.

[19] Eph. 6:9; Col. 4:1. 1 Peter contains no directions to Christian masters either because they were relatively few in number in the regions addressed or because Peter assumed that Christian masters would treat their slaves humanely.

[20] The very possibility that slaves may suffer 'unjustly' (1 Pet. 2:19) indicates that they are being regarded as persons with rights.

the Lord' (Col. 3:23).[21] Obedience to earthly masters is obedience to
Christ (Eph. 6:5). Service to an earthly master is service to Christ. To
carry out the directives of an earthly master is to do the will of God:
'[Obey them ...] as slaves of Christ, doing the will of God enthusiastically, and rendering a slave's service wholeheartedly, as one
actually serving the Lord and not merely men' (Eph. 6:6b–7). The
motive for the slave's wholehearted, obedient service is not to be
cringing servility before an earthly master, but reverential fear before
the heavenly Lord. For Peter the slave's conduct is to be governed not
only by total reverence for God (*en panti phobō*, 1 Pet. 2:18) but also
by full awareness of God's presence and his will for believers (*dia
syneidēsin theou*, 1 Pet. 2:19). But Peter goes one step further. The
slave who patiently endures suffering that results from doing good
enjoys God's approval (v. 20) and is following the example of Christ
(v. 21), who, during his suffering and death, refused to retaliate or
issue threats but instead entrusted himself and his cause to God who
judges justly (vv. 22–23). That is, by reacting appropriately to unjust
suffering at the hands of his master, the Christian is pursuing the
imitation of Christ – a dignified calling indeed!

3. Like their masters, slaves will be duly requited for wrongdoing
(Col. 3:25), and in the court of the heavenly Master no favouritism is
shown in dispensing rewards and punishments or in treating masters
and slaves. 'The wrongdoer will be repaid for the wrong he did, and
there is no favouritism' (Col. 3:25b).[22] Certainly Paul does not
glamorize slavery, as though, however a slave acted, he could do no
wrong. Also, from Paul's later injunctions to slaves in the pastoral
epistles, we infer that slaves were liable to be refractory, to be guilty
of pilfering (Titus 2:9–10), and to be disrespectful (1 Tim. 6:2).

4. Those who are 'in Christ', that is, 'in the body of Christ' and 'in
personal fellowship with the risen Christ',[23] be they slaves or masters,
enjoy an identical status before God: 'There is neither Jew nor Greek,
slave nor free, male nor female, for you are all one by being in Christ
Jesus' (Gal. 3:28). This same theme of oneness in Christ and the

[21] The word *hōs* ('as') in the phrase 'as to the Lord' (Col. 3:23) does not introduce an
unreal or hypothetical situation (as it does in 3:22, with the negative implied), 'as if it
were for the Lord' (JB). Rather, it expresses subjective motivation, 'with the thought that
you are actually doing it for the Lord'. See further Harris 1991: 184.
[22] In this verse the primary reference is probably to the slave guilty of dishonest action
(since the verse comes at the end of Paul's directions to slaves), but it is possible that the
master who metes out injustice (*cf.* Col. 4:1) to his slaves is principally in mind. In the
wider context both slaves and masters may well be in view (*cf.* Eph. 6:8).
[23] See the discussion of Paul's 'in Christ' formula in Harris 1978: 3. 1192.

consequent insignificance of traditional distinctions is found in 1 Corinthians 12:13, 'For in one Spirit we were all baptized into one body – whether Jews or Greek, slave or free – and we were all given the one Spirit to drink;' and in Colossians 3:11, 'Here [in this new humanity, the church] no distinction exists between Greek and Jew, circumcised and uncircumcised, barbarian, Scythian, slave, and free person, but Christ is everything and in all of you.'

5. Slaves and masters have one and the same heavenly Master to whom both equally are accountable (Eph. 6:9; Col. 4:1). When Paul qualifies the reference to masters (*kyrioi*) by 'earthly' or 'human' (*kata sarka*), he is implying that only in the earthly or human realm are slave-owners 'masters' (Eph. 6:5; Col. 3:22).

6. Whereas slaves were denied parity of status with free persons both by law and in practice, within the church they were accepted, along with their masters and all persons of free birth, as candidates for baptism and as participants in the Lord's Supper and Christian fellowship in general. Even offices in the church were open to them.

7. The Christian concept of 'brotherhood' elevates all to an identical status, that of membership in God's family where there are no favourite sons or daughters. Anti-Christian polemic might point out that the term 'brother' was used by members of funerary and social guilds (see Westermann 1955: 151), but the depth and intensity of Christian brotherhood were certainly distinctive, for it was the product of an intimate relationship with God as Father.

Second, with regard to *masters*. Paul insists that they will be held accountable to their own heavenly Master for their treatment of their slaves. They are therefore to give their slaves just and even-handed treatment: 'Masters, treat your slaves justly and fairly,[24] because you know that you, like your slaves (*kai hymeis*, "you too") have a Master – one in heaven' (Col. 4:1).[25] In Ephesians 6:9 Paul adds that masters

---

[24] The middle voice (*parechesthe*, 'treat') emphasizes the necessary involvement and initiative of the masters: they should act voluntarily from their own resources (Zerwick 1988: 453–454). Alternatively, the middle may point to the reciprocal duty of the slave-owners: 'exhibit on your part' (Lightfoot 1900: 228). The article is repeated with the second substantive (*tēn isotēta*) not only because of the change in gender from neuter (*to dikaion*) to feminine, but also to point to specific instances of fairness, acts that are equitable rather than equity as an abstract principle. Paul is not demanding social equality through the emancipation of slaves, but rather even-handedness of treatment.

[25] This explicit Christological motivation for masters' actions towards slaves stands in stark contrast to the advice given by the first-century Roman agricultural writer, Columella, whose advocacy of the kindly treatment of slaves was prompted by the desire for economic productivity. 'Sick slaves were to be given medical attention so that they

are not to issue intimidating threats, presumably as a means of ensuring compliance with commands.

Paul's letter to Philemon

The fullest picture the New Testament affords of the early Christian attitude towards slavery is found in Paul's letter to Philemon. Not that this short letter is a disquisition on slavery. G. A. Deissmann (1903: 3–59, esp. 44f.) was right to see this document as epitomizing the difference between the informal 'letter', personal, artless and occasional, and the formal 'epistle', impersonal, artistic and timeless. Nevertheless, while not being a philosophical treatise on slavery, the letter clearly reflects Christian attitudes towards slavery and so must be considered in some detail.

Onesimus was a slave of Philemon in Colossae (*cf.* Col. 4:9). He had not only run away from his master (Philem. 15–16) but had also absconded with some of Philemon's money or possessions (vv. 18–19). Attracted by the anonymity and excitement of a large metropolis, he travelled furtively to Rome, where somehow he met the imprisoned Paul, possibly through Epaphras.[26] Paul led Onesimus to faith in Christ (v. 10) and soon discovered him to be an able and willing helper as well as a Christian companion (vv. 11–13, 16–17). Other considerations apart, Paul would have kept Onesimus at his side (v. 13), but he felt compelled to send him back to Colossae, so that Philemon, the legal owner of Onesimus (v. 16), might himself have the opportunity of receiving him back as a Christian brother (v. 16) and of releasing him for further service to Paul (vv. 14, 20–21).[27]

---

[26] But Lampe has argued that Onesimus was not technically a *fugitivus* ('runaway slave') – since he intended to return to his master – but rather sought Paul out as a friend of his master (*amicus domini*) so that Paul could act as mediator in the grievance (*cf.* Philem. 18–19) between Philemon and Onesimus (1985: 135–137; 1992b: 5. 21, followed by Rapske 1991).

[27] The directive of Deut. 23:15–16 that a runaway slave should not be returned to his master can hardly mean that any fugitive slave – Hebrew or alien – should be granted asylum. 'If this law literally applied to any slave who had run away from his master, it certainly was unrealistic, for if put to practical use, it would have resulted in the immediate abolition of slavery' (Mendelsohn 1962: 4. 389). Rather, the intent was either that foreign slaves should receive asylum in Israel or that Hebrew slaves should not be returned to foreign owners.

Accordingly, Onesimus returned to Philemon with this letter (v. 12) in the company of Tychicus, the bearer of Colossians and Ephesians (Col. 4:7–9; Eph. 6:21–22).[28]

After the introductory greeting (vv. 1–3) and his thanksgiving and intercession for Philemon (vv. 4–7), Paul issues a general appeal on behalf on Onesimus, an appeal for Philemon to accept Onesimus on his return (vv. 8–16). Then follows the heart of the letter (vv. 17–20), *viz.* three specific requests Paul makes regarding Onesimus, each expressed by an imperative. First, Philemon was to welcome (*proslabou*) Onesimus as he would Paul. Such welcoming would imply not only the forgiveness of Onesimus but also his reinstatement in the household of Philemon (v. 17). Second, Philemon was to charge (*elloga*) to Paul's account any loss or debt incurred by him because of Onesimus's actions (vv. 18–19).[29] Third, Philemon was to refresh (*anapauson*) Paul's heart (v. 20b) by affording him some 'benefit' (v. 20a), *viz.* Philemon's warm reception of Onesimus back into his household, and possibly also the cancelling of Onesimus's debt now debited to Paul's account (v. 19) and the release of Onesimus for further service to and with Paul (v. 21).

The paradoxical nature of this whole situation should not be overlooked. Here is Paul, a highly educated Roman citizen, pleading the cause of a runaway slave whose life was potentially forfeit because of his flight and his theft. This indicates that Paul believed that the same brotherly love that would be shown to a free person should be expressed to a slave. It is of interest that although Paul is confident that Philemon would comply with his basic request (v. 21a) and accept and forgive Onesimus, he leaves him free, beyond this, to follow the dictates of his Christian conscience in determining how his love should be expressed (vv. 5, 7). So it is with pastoral tact that Paul does not actually define the 'more than I am asking' which he knows Philemon will do (v. 21b). That additional element could be the manumission of Onesimus for Christian service either at Colossae

---

[28] In this paragraph and in what follows on Philemon, I am drawing on material scattered throughout my 'exegetical guide' (Harris: 1991).

[29] After saying to Philemon, 'I will repay you myself', Paul adds (v. 19b) '– not to mention that you owe me your very self'. This addition to Paul's promissory note in v. 19a shows that he is not really envisaging a precise monetary debt or an actual legal obligation. He is saying, in effect: 'If "debts" are under review, you owe infinitely more to me than Onesimus does to you! I have not "charged" you who are my son in the faith; you should not "charge" Onesimus who is now your Christian brother. But if you choose to, I will pay on his behalf.'

or at Rome with Paul (*cf.* Ollrog 1979: 102–106, 122).[30] J. B. Lightfoot (1900: 321) comments: 'The word "emancipation" seems to be trembling on his [Paul's] lips, and yet he does not once utter it.'[31] Indeed, when Paul says in verse 15, 'it may be that he was separated from you for a short time precisely so that you might have him back permanently', he is entertaining the possibility that Philemon will retain Onesimus as a slave. Nowhere in the letter does Paul demand the release of Onesimus or even assume that Philemon will set him free. Clearly, the apostle accepts slavery as an existing social condition and as a legal fact (he returns Onesimus to his rightful owner[32] with a promissory note to cover any indebtedness), so that we may say, minimally, that Paul did not object to slave ownership within Christian ranks. Yet he indirectly undermines the institution of slavery by setting the master–slave relation on a new footing when he highlights Onesimus's status as a dearly loved Christian brother. If Philemon decided to retain the services of Onesimus, it would be 'no longer merely as a slave but as more than a slave – as a dear brother' (v. 16a). That is, the outward master–slave relation would remain unaltered, but a new inward relation would apply – that of Christian brotherhood.[33]

Did Paul ever advocate manumission? This brings us to the hotly contested verse, 1 Corinthians 7:21. This seventh chapter of 1 Corinthians deals principally with marriage and divorce against the backdrop of certain Corinthian ascetics who apparently advocated sexual abstinence (*cf.* vv. 1–5) and the annulment of marriages (*cf.*

[30] In proposing that a slave become his co-worker (Philem. 13, 20–21), Paul is illustrating the truth of his own maxim that in Christ there is neither slave nor free (Gal. 3:28).

[31] Mueller (1964: 312) believes that in Philem. 16 Paul is 'discreetly suggesting' that Philemon should emancipate Onesimus.

[32] Since Philemon was probably a provincial, Paul may not have been legally obligated to return Onesimus, who had apparently sought refuge with Paul. See the discussion in Coleman-Norton 1951: 173–174.

[33] Bruce (1977: 401): 'What this letter [Philemon] does is to bring us into an atmosphere in which the institution [of slavery] could only wilt and die.' Petersen (1985: 269) argues (unconvincingly in my view) that 'because they *are* in Christ, Onesimus cannot *be* both Philemon's slave and his brother, and Philemon cannot *be* both Onesimus's master and his brother.' Philemon faces a conflict of identities. 'It is logically and socially impossible to relate to one and the same person as both one's inferior and as one's equal ... Because Onesimus is no longer a slave but a brother, both in the flesh and in the Lord [Philem. 16], his *being* a brother to Philemon means that he cannot also *be* a slave to Philemon in any domain' (289). 'Paul's line of argument strongly suggests that the only acceptable action would be for Philemon to free his slave' (290).

vv. 10–11). In the paragraph 7:17–24 Paul three times enunciates the guiding principle, 'Everyone should remain in the situation assigned to them at the time of their calling' (*cf.* vv. 17, 20, 24). Two illustrations of the principle are given: circumcision (vv. 18–20) and slavery (vv. 21–24). In verse 21 Paul asks, 'Were you a slave when you were called?'[34] To anyone who could answer, 'Yes, I was', he then says, 'Don't let it trouble you (*mē soi meletō*)!' This stock phrase, applied by Stoic philosophers to the irrelevance of one's external situation to the soul's freedom, is used by Paul to highlight the primacy of God's call in Christ and the Christian's relationship to the Lord (*cf.* v. 22) over any earthly relationship, so that even the state of slavery is irrelevant to the keeping of God's commands (*cf.* v. 19) (*cf.* Bellen, 1971: 148). On this view, the 'for' (*gar*) of verse 22 introduces the reason that concern about servitude is misplaced: 'For the person who was a slave when called by the Lord is the Lord's freed person; similarly, the person who was free when called is Christ's slave.'[35] This makes verse 21b a parenthetical exception to the principle, 'remain as you were when called': 'But if you are actually able (*kai dynasai*) to gain your freedom,[36] seize it all the more.' A slave was not free to choose or reject manumission; Bartchy (1973: 106, 109) is right to insist on this point[37] that has sometimes been overlooked by those commentators and translators who construe the verse to mean, 'Even if you are able to become free, instead use [your slavery for the glory of God].'[38] No, a slave did not have the

[34] This rendering of *doulos eklēthēs* (as in NEB, REB, NAB; similarly RSV, NRSV) is to be preferred over 'Were you called to be a slave?' as Russell (1968: 44f.) proposes.

[35] Paul's injunction, 'Don't worry about it!' (1 Cor. 7:21a), *viz.* the fact that you were a slave when you received the call to become a Christian, should not be read as a heartless rebuff from a free person, but as realistic consolation grounded in the spiritual truth of v. 22a – that the Christian slave is in reality the Lord's freedman.

[36] This 'becoming free' (*eleutheros genesthai*, 1 Cor. 7:22b) is by manumission, not by flight or by seeking and gaining asylum (as Bartchy 1973: 109–110 rightly sees).

[37] Bartchy's point stands in spite of the protestations of Harrill (1995: 100; *cf.* 6, 88–90), who, while showing that 'slaves did not always accept offers of freedom, notably when a nondomestic party proposed to put up the cost', seems to overlook the fact that a master never forfeited his inalienable right to sell or to keep a particular slave, whatever the preference of the slave.

[38] That is, if the decision to manumit a slave was wholly the owner's, Paul's injunction in 1 Cor. 7:21 cannot mean that even if a slave gained an opportunity to be set free, he should continue to serve as a slave. See the sketch of the history of the interpretation of this verse in Harrill 1995: 74–108, and Bartchy 1973: 1–25, especially his chart on pp. 6–7. Bartchy's own translation reads: 'But if, indeed, you become manumitted, by all means [as a freedman] live according to [God's calling]' (183; *cf.* 157–159). The most detailed recent treatment of the verse is found in Harrill 1995: 108–127; *cf.* 8, 85, 194.

option of choosing freedom, but if his master suggested that he could purchase his freedom by using his *peculium* (money or property accumulated by the slave at the master's pleasure), then the slave should eagerly grasp the opportunity to gain his freedom.[39]

Concluding observations

How, then, may we sum up the New Testament attitude towards physical slavery?

To begin with, let us not overlook the obvious fact that Christianity did not create enslavement but inherited a deeply entrenched system of slavery.[40] Along with almost all other contemporary religious movements, Christianity accepted slavery as an inevitable part of the social and economic *status quo*,[41] without questioning or trying to justify its existence.[42] If we may generalize, ancient writers about

---

He examined seventeen uses of the *mallon* + *chraomai* combination in ancient Greek literature (along with *P. Oxy.* 16. 1865), and discovered that the adverb *mallon* has an adversative sense ('instead') when two different (as opposed to similar) situations are envisaged – as in 1 Cor. 7:21b, *viz.* slavery and the offer of manumission. 'But if you can indeed become free, use instead [freedom]' (118, 194). The other passage that is the focus of Harrill's attention is Ignatius, *Poly.* 4:3: 'They [Christian slaves] should not desire to be set free with money from the [church's] common fund, lest they be found to be slaves of lust.' According to Harrill, Ignatius is not rejecting privately funded manumission but is addressing an abuse of corporate manumission, *viz.* payment for manumission out of the community's common chest (8–9, 128, 158–195).

[39] So also Coleman-Norton 1951: 162. This view assumes that *tē eleutheria* (rather than *tē douleia* or *tē klēsei*), the nearest conceptual antecedent, should be understood with the imperative *chrēsai*. For a balanced defence of this view, see Fee 1987: 315–318, which now may be supplemented by Llewelyn 1992: 67–70, who usefully analyses ellipses in conditional sentences and examples of the *ei ... mallon* construction in the NT. His own rendering of the sentence is: 'But if ever you are able to become free, avail yourself of it all the more' (70).

[40] For an enlightening analysis of 'Debates and Issues in the Study of Slaves and Slavery', see Yavetz 1988: 115–162.

[41] It seems that in the first century AD only two religious groups repudiated slavery in principle: the Essenes of Judea, who included the Dead Sea Covenanters, and the Therapeutai, a community of pious Jews in Egypt. The Essenes rejected slavery on the ground that it tempted people to be unjust (Josephus, *Ant.* 18. 21) – presumably by their taking advantage of slaves and by their meting out unjust punishment – and corrupted the principle of equality and destroyed the law of the natural brotherhood of all persons (Philo, *Omn. Prob. Lib.* 79). For their part, the Therapeutai denounced slavery on the ground that it was 'absolutely and wholly contrary to nature', in that nature had created all people free, yet covetous slave-owners had imposed a yoke of inequality on their slaves (Philo, *Vit. Cont.* 70).

[42] Interestingly, however, the Roman jurists regularly traced the word *servus* ('slave') to the word *servatus* (Justinian's *Digest*, 1. 5. 2). In battle, the defeated foe was often

slavery, assuming the inevitability and indeed necessity of slavery for the well-being of society, focused their attention not on the slave's gaining or regaining of physical independence but on the need for spiritual freedom in the midst of physical servitude. Although the body may be enslaved, the spirit or mind remains free, while the spirit of many free people is enslaved to passion.[43] But this was not the emphasis of Christianity. For the early Christians, whether slave or free, both body and spirit belonged to the Lord (1 Cor. 6:15, 17) and slavery to him constituted true freedom.[44]

Even slaves did not envision a slaveless society. None of the slave revolts during the period 140–70 BC, ending with the fall of Spartacus in 71 BC, aimed at the abolition of slavery as an institution, but only at the securing of freedom for the slaves actually involved in the rebellion. Indeed, when rebel slaves were successful in gaining their freedom, they promptly embraced the ideals and pursuits of their former owners and so perpetuated the *status quo*! 'It did not occur to slaves any more than to anyone else in antiquity that social equality might be a viable political programme' (Wiedemann 1981: 12f.). Bartchy (1973: 87) makes the same point vividly: 'If someone in Greece or Rome in the middle of the first century AD had cried, "Slaves of the world unite!" he would have attracted only the curious.'

But the New Testament acceptance of the *status quo* should not be equated with endorsement of the *status quo* with respect to slavery. Toleration is not the same as approval. Apostolic directives about the conditions of slavery should not be read as approval of slavery as an institution. Moreover, the silence of the New Testament writers with regard to any explicit approval of slavery should not be converted into what one writer calls 'the clear teaching of Scripture [in endorsing slavery]' (Giles 1994: 4). This suggested distinction between acceptance and endorsement, between toleration and approval, is not a case of scholastic casuistry or semantic gymnastics. And this for three reasons.

First, there are other New Testament instances of practices that were tolerated but not endorsed. Two may be mentioned.[45]

---

not killed but 'preserved (alive)' (*servatus*) as the property of the beneficent victor. The captive, now a slave, had been 'saved' from death and from starvation.

[43] See, *e.g.*, Seneca, *Ben.* 3. 20; Epictetus, *Diss.* 4. 1.

[44] This latter point will be developed in chapter 4.

[45] One could surmise that Paul tolerated the circumcision of the sons of Jewish

1. As a result of the Jerusalem Council of AD 49 (Acts 15:1–35), a letter was prepared by the Jerusalem leaders and sent to Antioch by the hands of Judas and Silas (vv. 22–34). One item in the codicil (vv. 20, 29) to the decree itself (vv. 19, 28) was the injunction to Gentile believers to 'abstain from food sacrificed to idols' (*eidōlothyta*, v. 29). Later (about AD 50), as Paul and Silas revisited the cities of South Galatia on Paul's second 'missionary journey', they 'delivered the decisions reached by the apostles and elders in Jerusalem for the people to obey' (Acts 16:4). Yet some five years later, when writing to the church at Corinth, Paul discusses the same issue of 'food offered to idols' (*eidōlothyta*, 1 Cor. 8:1) and says, 'Eat anything sold in the meat market without raising questions of conscience' (1 Cor. 10:25). However this paradox is explained,[46] Paul apparently tolerated the injunction to abstain when he was promulgating the Jerusalem decree in AD 50 in Syria, Cilicia and South Galatia (Acts 15:41 – 16:4) but his directions to another of his Gentile churches in AD 55 show that he did not endorse this item of the codicil in that new setting. That is, he accepted the eating of 'food that had been offered to idols' as necessary at a particular time and in a particular circumstance without being able to endorse it in principle.

2. The practice of divorce affords another instance of this 'permitted but not approved' principle.[47] Like slavery, divorce was accepted by almost all as a fact of life in the first century AD. In Jewish circles there was difference of opinion about the permissible ground(s) for divorce, but the legitimacy of divorce as such was not questioned.[48]

---

believers (*cf.* Acts 16:3; 21:20–21) but would not have endorsed the practice in general (*cf.* Gal. 5:2; 6:15–16). But it is impossible to prove this conjecture.

[46] Paul probably regarded the codicil of the decree as being of local and temporary validity, rather than being universal and permanent in applicability. As Bruce (1988: 305; *cf.* 298) observes, the apostolic decree was addressed 'to the Gentile believers in Antioch, Syria and Cilicia' (Acts 15:23), that is, Antioch and her daughter churches; but the churches of South Galatia (*cf.* Acts 16:1–4), evangelized from Antioch, might have been included by implication.

[47] This analogy was first suggested to me by Colin Chapman during the Moore Lectures, but is also mentioned by Knight 1992: 86. Two exclusively OT analogies would be the practice of polygamy and the establishment of the monarchy. See Daube 1959.

[48] The dispute related to the meaning of the phrase 'some indecency' or 'something indecent' (Heb. *'erwat dābār*; LXX *aschēmon pragma*, 'a scandalous matter') in Deut. 24:1. The school of Shammai, stressing the word *'erwat* ('indecency'), interpreted the expression as referring to adultery, while the more liberal school of Hillel, emphasizing the word *dābār* ('some'), understood it as any misdemeanour or as marital incompatibility in general.

Deuteronomy 24:1, 3 directed that a husband who wished to divorce his wife must give her a 'certificate of divorce', a provision that was intended to curb divorce and to protect the wife from a hasty or capricious divorce and from a charge of adultery in the event of her remarriage, since this legal document stated both the fact and ground of the divorce (*cf.* Is. 50:1; Jer. 3:8; Hos. 2:2). In Matthew's account of the dispute between the Pharisees and Jesus concerning divorce (Matt. 19:1–9), the Pharisees claim that Moses had 'commanded' (*eneteilato*) the husband to give his wife a certificate of divorce and send her away (v. 7). Jesus responds that Moses had merely 'permitted' (*epetrepsen*) divorce;[49] the Mosaic legislation did not reflect the original divine ideal of permanent 'one-flesh-ness' (Gen. 2:24) but was a non-normative concession to human 'hardness of heart' (v. 8; *cf.* vv. 4–6).[50] Matthew's two 'exceptive clauses' (Matt. 5:32; 19:9)[51] – no divorce 'except for marital unfaithfulness' (NIV) – show that in the early church divorce continued to be permitted, but only on the ground of adultery. We may therefore say that according to the New Testament divorce is tolerated but not endorsed.[52]

In the second place, so far from approving of slavery as it was currently regarded and practised, Peter and Paul elevated the status of slaves by addressing them as persons and as moral agents who were responsible, and ought to be responsive, to their earthly masters as well as to their heavenly Lord. Paul seeks the amelioration of the slave's conditions of work when he encourages masters to reward slaves suitably for honest work, to desist from threatening them (Eph. 6:8–9), and to give them just and equitable treatment (Col. 4:1).[53]

---

[49] On the relation between the Matthean and Markan accounts at this point, see Gundry 1982: 380.

[50] This 'hard-heartedness' (*sklērokardia*, Matt. 19:8) could refer to stubborn resistance to God's commandment regarding marriage (Gen. 2:24) or to the refusal of the 'innocent' party to forgive the repentant 'guilty' party (*cf.* Luke 17:3).

[51] On these two verses see Harris 1978: 3. 1195.

[52] But neither of these two proposed analogies is exact, for Paul did reject abstention from *eidōlothyta* (1 Cor. 10:25) and both Testaments do repudiate divorce as contrary to the original divine plan for an exclusive, lifelong commitment between husband and wife (Mal. 2:16; Mark 10:6–8; 1 Cor. 7:10–11), whereas the NT nowhere denounces slavery as such.

[53] But this is not to endorse Theissen's (1982: 107) analysis of the dominant ethos of primitive Christianity as 'love-patriarchalism' which 'takes social differences for granted but ameliorates them through an obligation of respect and love, an obligation imposed upon those who are socially stronger. From the weaker are required subordination, fidelity and esteem.' But Pauline and NT ethics call for mutual love, respect and submission among all believers (*e.g.*, Rom. 13:8; Eph. 5:21; 1 Pet. 2:17; 5:5), irrespective of social status. And in Paul 'the strong' and 'the weak' should be defined in terms not of social

Now it is true that most of Paul's commands are directed to slaves, not to masters; but when slaves, with a new motivation for their service, complied with their master's wishes, they were indirectly improving their own work conditions.[54]

Third, quite apart from this Christian 'humanizing' of slavery,[55] the New Testament represents a direct challenge to the fundamental pillar on which slavery was built – the belief that the 'slave–free' division was natural and necessary in both principle and practice within any well-ordered society. Against this belief stands the repeated Pauline assertion that '[in Christ] there is neither Jew nor Greek, there is neither slave nor free, there is no "male and female"; for you are all one in Christ Jesus' (Gal. 3:28; *cf.* 1 Cor. 12:13; Col. 3:10–11).[56] Distinctions based on social status (slave–free), as also on race (Jew–Greek) and sex (male–female), have become invalid in the church because of spiritual unity in Christ. 'This [parity of status] could mean, for example, that someone who was a slave in the outside world might be entrusted with spiritual leadership in the church, and if the owner of the slave was a member of the same church, he would submit to the spiritual leadership' (Bruce 1982: 188f.).

To conclude this chapter, some tentative observations are in order on the vexed question of why the New Testament writers did not launch a 'frontal attack' on slavery as a social institution that was generally based on coercion and undermined personal dignity. It was not until the second half of the eighteenth century that slavery as an institution was considered morally reprehensible. Previously, its inevitability had been assumed or at least its existence tolerated. The *treatment* of slaves was the only point of intersection between slavery

---

standing but of maturity of conscience with respect to the exercise of Christian freedom.

[54] Bradley (1994: 150f.), however, vigorously demurs. For slaves Christianity brought change – for the worse. Paul's injunctions to slaves, including the 'novel refinement' that to follow the master's wishes was to behave as the Master wished, had the effect of reinforcing the legitimacy of slavery as an institution.

[55] *Cf.* Osiek 1984: 155: 'The key to the ancient Christian attitude toward slavery is humanization in Christ within a social structure that is accepted as non-negotiable.' Interestingly, above the title of Osiek's article ('Slavery in the New Testament World') appears the aphorism, 'What the New Testament never questioned, yet transformed' (151).

[56] *Cf.* Bellen 1971: 147: 'The teaching that "in Christ Jesus" the distinction between slave and free loses its validity, was suited to bring Christianity into opposition to the system of slavery.' Similarly Tidball 1984: 115: 'Paul did, in fact, challenge the institution of slavery but his challenge was directed to its inner meaning rather than its external existence' (*cf.* 108).

and morality in the ancient world. Abuses within the institution of slavery were condemned, but not the institution itself. But there are, indeed, some scholars who castigate the early Christians for their failure to recognize the social implications of a gospel that presupposes the inherent dignity of human beings as made in God's image, and that declares the irrelevance of social distinctions in Christ.[57]

Slavery in the ancient world was an extraordinarily complex phenomenon, so that, correspondingly, it is *a priori* unlikely that the 'failure' of the New Testament writers to call for the abolition of slavery can be attributed to a single cause. But many such single causes have been proposed: the expectation of an imminent parousia; the early church's conviction that evangelism took precedence over agitation for civil rights; a fear of governmental recrimination against the infant church; the desire to ensure that the church's image was not tarnished and its mission thus frustrated by charges that it encouraged either insurrection among slaves or the offering of asylum for runaway slaves; a preoccupation exclusively with the relation of Christian slaves to Christian masters.

It would seem more satisfactory to account for the absence of any condemnation of slavery and call for its abolition among the New Testament writers by appealing to a combination of possible explanations, which may be conveniently grouped under three headings.

Historical

1. There existed a mechanism for emancipation in the legal process of manumission which became increasingly common in the Late Republic and early Empire. As we have noted (chapter 2, p. 40 and n. 41), it is estimated that half a million slaves were emancipated during the years 81–49 BC.

2. Slave revolts had proved failures, most notably the slave war

---

[57] See especially Schulz 1972, and comments on Schulz's view by Harrill (1995: 91–93). For a more recent powerful denigration of the 'callous indifference to the evils of slavery' shown by the authors of the NT epistles, see Davies 1995: 338–347 (quotation from 346). For example: the letter of Philemon endorses the social institution of slavery and 'suggests' that Christian slave-owners should not manumit their slaves (342); there is 'no suggestion that Christian communities should redeem their slaves, not even out of a concern for the slave's ability to practice [*sic*] his or her religion and avoid idolatry (contrast Jos. *Ant.* 16. 1–2)' (342); there is no reference to the Jubilee year emancipation of slaves (Lev. 25) (342) or to Exod. 21:26–27 (344); in 1 Tim. 6:1 ('Let slaves under the yoke regard their own masters as *worthy* of all honour'), 'slaves are being told, unreasonably, to abandon any moral insight they might have' (345).

under Spartacus of 73–71 BC, which ended with the crucifixion of 6,000 slaves along the length of the road from Capua to Rome (Appian, *Bell. Civ.* 1. 14. 120). To have fomented a slave revolt would not only have proved futile[58] but would have ensured deterioration of the condition of slaves as ruthless recompense was meted out to them. In any case, history had shown that slaves, when freed, simply adopted the attitudes and ways of their former masters, so that slavery itself was not eradicated. More importantly, social revolution is nowhere countenanced in the New Testament, especially where (as in Rom. 13:1–7 and 1 Pet. 2:13–17) the relation of Christians to the state or society at large is discussed.

Sociological

1. The insignificant social status of the leaders of early Christianity meant that they lacked a platform from which to launch societal change – if that had been part of their purpose.

2. To try to effect the abolition of slavery was not only unrealistic;[59] the sudden emancipation of slaves, even if possible, would have produced unmitigated social chaos, with a vast mass of persons suddenly unemployed and without the means of self-support.

3. Any public attack on slavery would have laid the early Christians open to the charge that their religious teaching was merely a front for social revolution. Their evangelistic mission would thereby have been seriously compromised.

Religious

If Christianity is viewed as basically a movement of social reform, then this silence regarding slavery is indeed surprising, if not culpable. But Christianity in its essence is concerned with the

---

58 'A large-scale rebellion is impossible to organize and carry through except under very unusual circumstances. The right combination appeared but once in ancient history, during two generations of the late Roman Republic, when there were great concentrations of slaves in Italy and Sicily, many of them almost completely unattended and unguarded, many others professional fighters (gladiators), and when the whole society was in turmoil, with a very marked breakdown of social and moral values' (Finley 1974: 66).

59 Barclay (1991: 183f.) argues that if Christian slave-owners manumitted all their slaves, local churches would be hard pressed to continue meeting in homes, since assistance from slaves would have been essential to maintain a house of sufficient size to host a local assembly of Christians. But Davies (1995: 341f. n. 70) rightly observes that paid servants could have been hired and that Christians did not have to meet in the houses of slave-owners or in houses at all.

transformation of character and conduct rather than with the reformation of societal structures. Its primary focus is on individual ethics within the Christian community rather than on corporate ethics within society at large, on interpersonal relationships rather than on social reformation through institutional change. The principal change sought is in the individual,[60] and the secondary in society, through transformed individuals. With regard to Paul and slavery, R. N. Longenecker (1971: 84) suggests that the apostle's approach 'was to work from a "Christ consciousness" in the individual to a "Christian consciousness" in society'.[61]

If, then, these are some of the reasons for Christianity's apparent lack of action in the first century with regard to the overthrow of slavery, what may we say concerning its role in the decline and ultimate abolition of slavery?[62] The point is vigorously debated.[63] Whatever other influences contributed to the demise of slavery,[64] it should not be questioned that in undermining the discriminatory hierarchy of social relations that is at the heart of slavery, Christianity sounded the death-knell of slavery; or, to change the metaphor, it laid the explosive charge, or one of the explosive charges, that would ultimately – although sadly, belatedly – lead to detonation, and the destruction of slavery.[65]

---

[60] Although Paul does not say so explicitly, he would probably not be averse to saying about slavery what he says about circumcision: 'In Christ Jesus neither physical slavery nor physical freedom is of any (spiritual) importance; the only thing that counts is a new creation' (cf. Gal. 6:15). Yet one can empathize with Westermann's (1955: 151) telling remark that 'a paradox existed between the Christian teaching of sympathy for the poor and wretched and the apathetic attitude toward the slave institution as such'.

[61] Mueller (1964: 313) observes that when Christians were reminded of 'their liberty, equality, and union in Christ a peaceful revolution would take place: a transformation of hearts which would bring about a social change in its train'.

[62] The answer to the modern question, 'Is slavery to be condemned from a Christian viewpoint?' all depends on one's definition of slavery. If it involves the absolute possession or inhuman use of one human being by another, the answer must be 'Yes'. But if slavery is understood as indentured service or remunerated labour that one person gives to another, the answer may be 'No'.

[63] See the earlier standard work by Wallon (1879); Allard (1914); and the more recent works by Gülzow (1969); Davis (1966) and Sowell (1994). On the attitudes to slavery among the church fathers, see Rupprecht 1974: 261–277.

[64] From an economic point of view, slavery ultimately declined in the ancient world, and was replaced by serfdom, because of its economic inefficiency. It was based on coercive power, not a desire to realize maximum profit, and returns on initial capital outlay were slight and delayed.

[65] On the issue of why it took so long for Christian principles to contribute or lead to the abolition of slavery, see Westermann 1955: 151, 161–162.

Chapter Four

Slavery and freedom

In the previous two chapters we have discussed slavery in its literal or physical aspect in three first-century AD Mediterranean societies and in the writings of the New Testament. This discussion forms the necessary backdrop for the remainder of our investigation, the figurative use in the New Testament of the *doulos* ('slave') family of words and in particular of slavery as one way of describing the believer's relation to Christ.

When the New Testament writers use the term *doulos* and related words of themselves and other Christians, there are four main connotations associated with this word group: freedom, lordship, ownership and privilege. Hence the titles of this and the next three chapters.

Freedom *and* slavery

It seems to be universally true that people regard slavery and freedom as mutually exclusive opposites. That person is free who is not a slave. That person is a slave who has no freedom. These two concepts seem naturally to be defined in contrast to each other.[1] For example, the Pharisees remonstrate with Jesus, 'We are descendants of Abraham and have never been in slavery to anyone. What, then, do you mean by saying, "You will be set free"?' (John 8:33). Similarly, the Roman jurist, Gaius, writing in the late second century AD, affirms that in Roman law the main distinction between persons is that between free and slave (*Inst.* 1. 9).[2]

Among the Greeks freedom in the broadest sense involved four

---

[1] But Finley (1974: 72) draws attention to a paradox in Greek history: 'The cities in which individual freedom reached its highest expression – most obviously Athens – were cities in which chattel slavery flourished ... One aspect of Greek history ... is the advance, hand in hand, of freedom *and* slavery.'

[2] But Roman jurists also distinguished between free persons who were born free (*ingenui*) and free persons who had been set free (*libertini*).

specific elements – the right to represent oneself legally, protection against attack or summary arrest, freedom of action, and freedom of movement.[3] Greek thinkers tended to match freedom with wisdom, and slavery with ignorance: 'only the wise person is free' (*monos ho sophos eleutheros*). But politically speaking, the free person was the citizen who enjoyed full rights in the city-state, the *polis*, which was regarded as the community of the free. The slave, on the other hand, lacked all the rights of citizenry. From another perspective, however, slavery was the norm for the ancient classification of persons: the slave (*doulos*, Lat. *servus*) was the property of another person, subject to an alien will, while someone without such a relation, whose autonomy was intact, was a free person (*eleutheros*, Lat. *liber*),[4] and a person who was no longer in such a relation of dependence was a freed slave (*apeleutheros* or *exeleutheros*, Lat. *libertus* or *libertinus*) (*cf.* Acts 6:9).

Such distinctions may have applied in theory, but in practice the lines of distinction between the free person and the slave were blurred.[5] For instance, in Roman society a slave was not distinguishable from a citizen by colour, dress or speech, and a slave could occupy a more responsible position than a poor citizen. Or again, from a financial standpoint, the average free labourer in Rome fared no better than many slaves. Working six days a week, such a man earned a wage of one denarius a day (*cf.* Matt. 20:2), or about 313 denarii a year, of which some 280 or so would be spent on necessities of food, clothing and shelter. A slave, however, received these basic necessities free of charge and might expect 5 denarii a month in addition.[6] That is, some slaves would be better off by about 27 denarii a year, roughly a month's salary for a free labourer!

Now it is true that the New Testament often refers to this traditional

---

[3] See chapter 2, 'Greek slavery', pp. 30–33.

[4] 'It is the mark of a free man that he does not live under the restraint of another (or, at another's beck and call) [*pros allon*]' (Aristotle, *Rhet.* 1. 9. 31–32).

[5] 'In spite of the Roman law's insistence on sharply distinguishing between slave and free, the evidence suggests that in social, cultural and economic terms there was something much more like a "continuum" of statuses, quite apart from labour conditions in which the free worker might be worse off than the slave' (Crook 1967: 58, cited by Bartchy 1973: 40). During the Roman civil wars social mobility was common, so that the distinction between free person, ex-slaves and slaves became blurred. Augustus addressed this situation – which was a grave concern among the free (*e.g.*, Pliny the Elder, *Hist. Nat.* 33. 8. 33) – by the *lex Aelia Sentia* of AD 4, which, in formulating many regulations regarding manumission, distinguished three categories of freed persons, *viz.* citizens, Latins, and subjects (*dediticii*).

[6] See Frank 1935: 2. 266–283 (cited by Rupprecht 1975: 5. 460).

dual classification of persons, 'slave' (*doulos*) and 'free' (*eleutheros*) (*e.g.*, Gal. 3:28; Col. 3:11; Rev. 19:18).[7] But are freedom and slavery presented there as irreconcilable opposites or as concepts that are not mutually exclusive?

Freedom *from* slavery

We have seen that for the majority of slaves, being set free was their dominant goal. The only exceptions were condemned criminals who would end their days labouring in the mines or quarries or on the galleys, and slaves who were sick or aged or unskilled and knew that they would never prosper under newly acquired independence.

In Roman society, manumission – the act of freeing a slave – took place formally or informally.[8] In the first century AD formal manumission (*manumissio iusta*, 'rightful manumission') occurred in two ways.[9] 'Manumission by [the touch of] the rod' (*manumissio vindicta*) was normally performed before the praetor or some other state official. In this simulated lawsuit concerning property, a 'proclaimer of freedom' (*assertor libertatis*) represented the slave, since the latter had no legal rights. Using a rod (*vindicta*), the symbol of property, this proclaimer touched the slave and declared that he was really a free person wrongfully enslaved. Since the master entered no objection, the praetor then issued his verdict in the lawsuit, *viz.* that the slave was indeed free. There followed a strange ritual whose significance is unclear. The master gave the slave a slap on the head. Some suggest that the purpose of this slap was to prevent the slave from improper pride in his newly gained freedom, or to reinforce his awareness of the dramatic event that had just taken place. But more plausible is the theory that the slap was a symbol of the final insult the master could ever inflict; the freedman was for ever free from the insults of slavery.

The second and most common type of formal manumission was 'manumission by will' (*manumissio testamento*), by which the master gave a directive that certain slaves were to be freed at the time of his

---

[7] See chapter 3, 'The "slave–free" contrast', pp. 49–51.

[8] 'In ancient usage, a Roman householder "emancipated" (*emancipo*) a son or daughter from his *patria potestas*, but "manumitted" (*manumitto*) a slave' (Harrill 1995: 4). The following information is drawn from Duff 1958: 21–26.

[9] During the Republic there was a third method – 'manumission by the census' (*manumissio censu*), through which masters had the censors add the names of slaves to the register of Roman citizens at the quinquennial registration (Duff 1958: 24).

death. To qualify for emancipation under this provision, the slave had to be the property of the master both when the testator made his will and when he died. To be valid, the reference to manumission in the will had to couched in the form of a command: '*X* is to be set free,' or 'I direct that *X* be set free.' Occasionally the person set free was simultaneously appointed an heir.

When a slave was set free by one of these 'lawful' or 'legitimate' methods of manumission, he normally became a Roman citizen (Dionysius of Halicarnassus, *Ant. Rom.* 4. 24. 4). What was conferred in manumission was 'liberty with citizenship' (Buckland 1969: 714). This sudden and dramatic change of status was a remarkable phenomenon. Overnight, and by the wave of the hand, so to speak, a rank outsider became a genuine insider.

Informal manumission (*manumissio minus iusta*) took place in three ways: through a letter (*per epistulam*) in which the master granted freedom to his slave; by inviting the slave to sit with him at his table (*per mensam*), as a mark of his slave's elevation to freedom; or through a declaration of the slave's liberty made by the master in the presence of friends (*coram amicos*) who served as a family council of witnesses. Informal manumission was popular because it was simple, not involving officialdom, and because it avoided the 5% tax levied on the person who initiated the actual manumission proceedings, whether the master or the slave. Slaves set free by informal manumission had no citizenship rights and only a *de facto* freedom under the protection of the praetor. But sometimes this type of manumission was later followed by the formal ceremony before a magistrate who touched the slave 'with the rod' (*vindicta*) which led to full citizenship (Pliny, *Ep.* 7. 16).

By whatever method a slave became liberated, he was never totally free under Roman law. He was permanently obliged to render certain services (*operae*) to his former master, now his patron (*patronus*), tasks related to his former employment and performed on a specified number of days each month or year. The ex-slave, now a client, might be expected to give gifts (*munera*) to his patron, must be willing to administer his patron's affairs and act as his son's guardian, and was required to show 'due respect' (*obsequium*), which involved a commitment always to act in his patron's interest and which included care for a physically or financially ailing patron.[10] In fact, if a freed

[10] See Justinian's *Digest* 37. 14. 19; 38. 1. 1–3. On these matters, see Duff 1958: 36–49, and especially Waldstein 1986.

person failed to support his destitute patron or was guilty of contemptuous conduct against him, he could be formally charged with ingratitude (Barrow 1968 191f.).

Manumission among the Greeks differed in four main ways from Roman practice:

1. It increasingly became a public act, announced before some public assembly and with legally constituted witnesses who in effect became guarantors of the freedman's liberty.

2. Manumission was often carried out near an altar or under the auspices of a god and the supervision of temple priests who sometimes inscribed in a public place the terms of the manumission contract, circumstances that afforded a certain protection of the freedman's rights. (On these two points see further Bartchy 1973: 94–96.)

3. When a master entered into a *paramonē* agreement with his slave upon his emancipation, the freedman was obliged to 'stay with' (*paramenein*) his master for a specific number of years, obeying his orders and paying an annual fee (in effect his redemption price).[11] But when the specified period ended, the ex-slave became completely free and neither party was under obligation of any kind.

4. Manumission brought varying degrees of freedom, but not citizenship.[12]

If we examine the concept of freedom in the New Testament we discover several distinctives. To begin with, the New Testament words denoting 'freedom' (*eleutheria* and cognates) never signify political freedom, in the sense of liberation or independence from people who are political overlords. Rather, freedom is seen as spiritual. It refers to the act of emancipation or of being emancipated, especially from bondage to sin (*e.g.*, Rom. 6:18, 22; 8:2), or to the resulting state of emancipation (*e.g.*, Gal. 5:13; 1 Pet. 2:16). These two aspects are combined in two places: 'If the Son sets you free [the act], you will be truly free [the state]' (John 8:36); 'For freedom [the state] Christ has set us free [the act]' (Gal. 5:1).

Moreover, unlike the Greeks, for whom freedom involved the ability to choose the course of one's life and the use of one's energies, New Testament writers located freedom (as a state) in an

[11] At this point Jewish practice was unlike both Roman and Greek procedure, for in Jewish law manumission severed all ties between the former slave and his master.

[12] In a cosmopolitan city like Corinth, that was simultaneously Greek and Roman in the first century AD, 'owners of slaves ... could manumit their slaves by means of a variety of procedures – formal or informal, public or private, religious or secular' (Bartchy 1973: 96).

acknowledged dependence on God (*e.g.*, Heb. 4:16; 1 Pet. 5:7) and a voluntary surrender to his will (*e.g.*, 1 Pet. 5:6). When James speaks of 'the law that gives freedom' (Jas. 1:25; 2:12), he is referring to the divine law enshrined in the gospel that requires neighbour-love: 'You shall love your neighbour as yourself' (Lev. 19:18, cited in Jas. 2:8 where it is called 'the royal law'). Obedience to this law emancipates people from self-pleasing (*cf.* Jas. 1:27; 2:1–13).

Another distinctive of the New Testament view is the close relation between freedom and Christ, between freedom and the Spirit, and between freedom and the future. It is Jesus, the proclaimer and embodiment of divine truth (John 1:14; 8:31–32: 14:6), the unique Son of God (John 5:19–23), who sets free the slaves of sin: 'If the Son sets you free, you will be truly free' (John 8:36). Paul, for his part, can speak of 'our freedom, which we have by being in Christ Jesus' (Gal. 2:4). If freedom is effected by the person and work of Christ, it becomes a reality in the experience of the believer through the presence of the Spirit. 'The principle of the life-giving Spirit has, through [the work of] Christ Jesus, set you free from the principle of sin and death' (Rom. 8:2). Then at the close of a passage (2 Cor. 3:12–18) that contrasts two ministries (one characterized by death, the other by the Spirit) and two covenants (the old and the new), Paul makes the generalization, 'Where the Spirit is, there is freedom' (2 Cor. 3:17). In the immediate context, this freedom may be freedom from the veil of ignorance or hardheartedness (2 Cor. 3:14–15), or freedom from the old covenant (2 Cor. 3:14), or the law and its effects (2 Cor. 3:6), or the freedom of direct and permanent access into the divine presence 'with unveiled face' (2 Cor. 3:18). But since the word 'freedom' (*eleutheria*) is unqualified in verse 17, one may be permitted to interpret this freedom that is mediated by the Spirit as including release from spiritual bondage of every kind. Finally, there is the intimate association of freedom with the future. Galatians 4:26, in the context of Galatians 4:21–31, makes it clear that the Christian church, as represented by the heavenly Jerusalem, is presently the community of free persons. But it is also true that Christians eagerly wait for the final stage of their adoption as God's children, which Paul defines as 'the redemption of our bodies' (Rom. 8:23). This ultimate emancipation is not release from all embodiment, but freedom from a flesh-dominated body through the receipt of a Spirit-dominated body, the 'spiritual body' (1 Cor. 15:44). Non-human nature, the irrational universe, will also experience a comparable freedom. Instead of being subject to futility (Rom. 8:20) and characterized by 'bondage to decay', as is presently the case (Rom. 8:21a), creation will be set free (*eleutherōthēsetai*) from this inhibiting slavery to transitoriness, decay and death and will thus share the freedom (*eleutheria*) that will accompany the revelation of the glory belonging to God's children (Rom. 8: 21b, 19).

It is the uniform testimony of the New Testament that conversion to God brings freedom on several fronts. Indeed Paul can say that the divine call is 'for freedom' (Gal. 5:13), that is, 'to be free'. We may note the following aspects of this freedom.

1. Freedom from spiritual death. 'I tell you the truth,' Jesus said, 'those who hear my word and believe him who sent me have eternal life and will not be condemned; they have crossed over from death to life' (John 5:24; *cf.* Eph. 2:1, 5; Col. 2:13).

2. Freedom from 'self-pleasing'. 'And he [Christ] died for all, that those who live should no longer live for themselves but for him who died for them and was raised again' (2 Cor. 5:15).

3. Freedom from people-pleasing. 'Am I [Paul] now trying to win human approval or God's approval? Or am I trying to please people? If I were still trying to please people, I would not be a slave of Christ' (Gal. 1:10; *cf.* 1 Cor. 7:23; 9:19).

In none of these cases is it explicitly stated that freedom brings emancipation from a particular form of slavery, but it is implied in each case that there is a force or power that holds sway until release is effected, whether it be spiritual death, self-pleasing or people-pleasing. But in four places conversion is explicitly said to bring release from slavery or captivity. The person who turns to God in repentance and expresses faith in Christ (Acts 20:21) gains:

4. Freedom from slavery to sin. Jesus solemnly declared, 'Everyone who sins is a slave of sin ... If the Son sets you free, you will be indeed free' (John 8:34, 36; *cf.* Rom. 6:14–23).

5. Freedom from bondage to the Mosaic law, especially if observing it is seen as a way of gaining God's approval. 'Now we have been released from the law, in that we have died to what once held us captive' (Rom. 7:6; *cf.* 3:20; Gal. 2:16; 3:10, 13). 'So, my brothers and sisters, through the crucified body of Christ your bondage to the law has been broken' (Rom. 7:4; *cf.* Gal. 5:4, 13).[13] 'For in the case of

---

[13] On Rom. 7:4–6 and Paul's concept of 'bondage to the law', see Moo 1996: 414–423. Dunn (1993: 71–76) argues that for Paul, freedom from the law involved four elements: freedom from the conditions of the law; freedom from the tutelage of the law as a childhood governor; freedom from the 'self-deception which sin uses the law to achieve' (73f.); and freedom to obey the law from the heart empowered by the Spirit.

every believer Christ is the end of the law in its relation to right-eousness' (Rom. 10:4).

6. Freedom from fear of physical death. 'Since the children all share in flesh and blood, he [Christ] too shared in their human nature so that by his death he might destroy him who holds the power of death – that is, the devil – and set free those who all their lives were held in slavery by their fear of death' (Heb. 2:14–15).

7. Freedom from slavery to 'the elemental spiritual forces of the universe'.[14] 'During our minority we were slaves, subject to the elemental spirits of the universe ... Formerly, when you did not know God, you were slaves to gods who are not gods at all. But now that you do acknowledge God – or rather, now that he has acknowledged you – how can you turn back to those feeble and bankrupt elemental spirits? Why do you propose to enter their service all over again?' (Gal. 4:3, 8–9, REB; *cf.* Col. 2:8, 20).

A glance at the verses cited above will show how many of them are Pauline. Word statistics confirm the view that Paul was indeed 'the apostle of freedom'. The noun *eleutheria* ('freedom') occurs eleven times in the New Testament, of which seven are in Paul's letters; the noun *apeleutheros* ('freed person') is found only in Paul (1 Cor. 7:22); the adjective *eleutheros* ('free') twenty-three times, sixteen in Paul; and the verb *eleutheroō* ('set free'), seven times, five in Paul. Many writers have recognized the centrality of the concept of freedom in Paul's thought, particularly in his letter to the Galatians. Two distinguished Pauline scholars, both of whom have written major commentaries on Galatians, will serve to illustrate the point. R. N. Longenecker's doctoral dissertation, completed at the University of Edinburgh, was published under the title *Paul: Apostle of Liberty*, while as the climax of his specialist studies in Paul's writings, F. F. Bruce produced his magisterial work *Paul: Apostle of the 'Free Spirit'* (published in the USA under the title *Paul: Apostle of the Heart Set Free*).

Not without reason has the letter to the Galatians been called 'Paul's charter of freedom'.[15] And nowhere in this epistle is the theme of 'liberty in Christ' (*cf.* Gal. 2:4) more in evidence than in the section 4:21 – 5:1, where Paul interprets the Hagar–Sarah story of Genesis 16:1–16; 21:1–21 in an analogical fashion to illustrate his

---

[14] On the meaning of *ta stoicheia* (*tou kosmou*), 'the elemental spiritual forces (of the universe)', in Pauline usage, see O'Brien 1982: 129–132.

[15] Most recently by L. Morris as the subtitle of his commentary on *Galatians* (1996).

point that believers are emancipated from all spiritual slavery.[16] A sketch of that Genesis narrative will prove helpful at this point.

Because Abraham's wife, Sarah, had borne no children, she suggested to Abraham that he sleep with her Egyptian servant named Hagar. Abraham agreed, and Hagar became pregnant, but then despised Sarah, who proceeded to ill-treat her. Fleeing from her mistress into the desert, Hagar was confronted by the angel of the Lord, who announced that she would bear a son who was to be named Ishmael. Eighteen years later, in fulfilment of a divine promise, Sarah herself gave birth to a son, Isaac. On the day Isaac was weaned, Abraham held a celebration at which Ishmael, now in his late teens, began to mock Isaac. This prompted Sarah to insist to Abraham, 'Get rid of that slave woman and her son, for that slave woman's son will never share in the inheritance with my son Isaac' (Gen. 21:10). Abraham was distressed by this request, but, reassured by God, he sent Hagar and Ishmael off with provisions for their journey.

Paul's treatment of this story in Galatians 4 falls into three parts. In verses 21–23 we have the three basic facts of the story. Then follows, in verses 24–27, the analogical interpretation of the story. Finally, in verses 28–31, Paul applies these interpreted facts to the Galatian and Christian situation. Whether we describe this section of Galatians as 'A tale of two cities: earthly Jerusalem (v. 25) and heavenly Jerusalem (v. 26)',[17] 'A tale of two covenants: law and promise (vv. 24, 28)', 'A tale of two women: Hagar and Sarah', or 'A tale of two sons: Ishmael and Isaac', the paragraph clearly presents a series of antitheses between slavery on the one hand and freedom on the other.

Contrasted with Hagar, the slave women, is Sarah, the free woman, Abraham's free-born wife, although she is not explicitly named. Ishmael too remains unnamed; he is depicted simply as Abraham's 'son by the slave woman' (vv. 23a, 29), someone born 'according to the flesh' (v. 23a), that is, 'in the ordinary way' (NIV), in the course of nature, by natural procreation. Isaac stands opposite Ishmael, as Abraham's 'son by the free woman' (v. 23b), 'born as the result of a promise' (v. 23b) and 'by the power of the Spirit' (v. 29). Then there is the covenant of law that is 'from Mount Sinai and bears children for slavery' (v. 24), which is implicitly contrasted with the covenant

---

[16] For a discussion of the question whether Paul's treatment of the Genesis account is allegorical, typological or analogical, see Fung 1988: 217–220.

[17] The allusion, of course, is to Charles Dickens' classic work, *A Tale of Two Cities*. The use of the term 'tale' in reference to Gal. 4 does not imply that the Hagar–Sarah story in Genesis is unhistorical.

of promise (*cf.* 3:17) that produces children for freedom. Finally, we have 'the present city of Jerusalem' (= Judaism) that 'is in slavery along with her children' (= the Judaizers) (v. 25), which is paired against 'the Jerusalem that is above', that is free and is the mother of the free (v. 26).

The contrasts of the paragraph may be set out in chart form (following Fung 1988: 213, with slight modifications).

Slavery	*Freedom*
Hagar – a slave woman	Sarah – a free woman
Ishmael – born in the course of nature	Isaac – born as the result of a promise and by the power of the Spirit
The covenant of law from Mount Sinai	The covenant of promise (based on faith)
The present city of Jerusalem (= Judaism)	The Jerusalem that is above (= the church)
The children of the present Jerusalem (=legalists)	The children of the Jerusalem above (= Christians)
Righteousness by law	Righteousness by faith

The conclusion Paul draws from all this is stated in 5:1: 'For the enjoyment of this freedom,[18] Christ has set us free. Stand firm, therefore, and do not be tied again to a yoke of slavery.'

It is not difficult to imagine a slave's natural reaction on being emancipated. When people are released from slavery, relief at the sudden change of status and circumstances is naturally expressed in exhilaration.[19] Consider the jubilant Song of Moses and Miriam that

---

[18] Whether the dative *tē eleutheria* is taken as indicating purpose or advantage ('for freedom') or, less probably, the instrument or mode ('with freedom'), it is clear that Christians are intended to benefit from this freedom.

[19] 'The ceremony that effected a move from chattel bondage to legal freedom was a time of celebration in the life of virtually any ancient slave' (Harrill 1995: 193). Just before these Moore Lectures were delivered (in Sydney) in early August 1997, a tragic midnight landslide occurred at the ski resort of Thredbo in New South Wales, which claimed the lives of eighteen people. Some sixty-five hours after the avalanche of earth swept down on the resort, rescuers freed a twenty-seven-year-old ski instructor, Stuart Diver, after digging through two metres of concrete and rubble. Imagine his colossal relief and exquisite exhilaration when freed from his suffocating concrete coffin!

was sung after Israel had been delivered from their bitter bondage in Egypt. 'I will sing to the LORD, for he is highly exalted. The horse and its rider he has hurled into the sea' (Exod. 15:1). Then Miriam, tambourine in hand, led all the women in celebratory dancing and singing (Exod. 15:20–21). Or recall Charles Wesley's famous hymn that begins, 'And can it be, that I should gain / An interest in the Saviour's blood?' The picturesque imagery of the fourth verse was probably prompted by Luke's vivid account of Peter's escape from prison recorded in Acts 12:6–11, and expresses the pure exhilaration felt by sin's captives at the time of their emancipation:

> Long my imprisoned spirit lay
>   Fast bound in sin and nature's night;
> Thine eye diffused a quick'ning ray, –
>   I woke, the dungeon flamed with light;
> My chains fell off, my heart was free,
> I rose, went forth, and followed Thee.

Only the person who has suffered under the rigours of slavery truly appreciates freedom. Indeed, the more intense one's experience of servitude, the greater one's appreciation of emancipation. The joy of freedom is in direct proportion to the pain of slavery. The person who is unaware of being enslaved neither longs for nor appreciates freedom. On the other hand, the person who is painfully aware of grinding slavery will pine after freedom and embrace it with enthusiastic relief if it comes (*cf.* Patterson 1982: viiif., 340f.).

But whenever people feel exhilarated at being set free, they immediately face two new dangers. The first is the danger of converting liberty into licence.[20] Protection against this danger comes when freedom from slavery to sin leads to slavery to righteousness (hence our third topic in this chapter, 'Freedom *for* slavery'). Second, there is the danger of becoming enslaved to liberty. Protection against this danger comes when freedom is expressed in self-imposed slavery for the good of others (hence our fourth and final topic in this chapter, 'Freedom *in* slavery').

---

[20] 2 Pet. 2:19 points to an opposite danger – that of heralding liberty but being enslaved to licentious behaviour. So far from delivering the freedom they promised, the false teachers described in 2 Peter 2 were 'themselves enslaved to corrupt conduct [*autoi douloi hyparchontes tēs phthoras*]'. Because they failed to deliver what was promised, Peter describes them as 'springs without water' (*pēgai anydroi*) (2 Pet. 2:17).

Freedom *for* slavery

For all its emphasis on freedom *from*, the letter to the Galatians indicates that for the Christian a new type of slavery lies on the other side of 'the freedom we have in Christ Jesus' (Gal. 2:4). In 1:10 Paul argues that being a slave of Christ excludes people-pleasing. 'Am I now trying to win human approval, or God's approval? Or am I trying to please people? If I were still trying to please people, I would not be Christ's slave (*doulos*)'. Then there is 5:13: 'Yes, brothers and sisters, freedom became yours when you were called. Only do not use your freedom as an opportunity to gratify your sinful nature; rather, give a slave's service (*douleuete*) to one another in love.'[21] Paul is saying that unbridled freedom can lead to libertinism, whereas bridled freedom expresses itself in mutual enslavement.

If these two themes, freedom *from* slavery and freedom *for* slavery, are found within a single Pauline book (Galatians), they also appear side by side within a single Pauline paragraph, *viz.* Romans 6:15–23, a passage that now warrants our attention.

Verses 15–23 of Romans 6 cohere closely with verses 1–14. There is a clear parallelism between 6:1–2a and 6:15. In each case Paul counters a false inference that could be drawn or had been drawn from a previous statement, by using a rhetorical question followed by an emphatic denial (*mē genoito*, 'By no means!' or 'Perish the thought!'). In 5:20 he had asserted that under the reign of the law an increase in sin had brought an increase in grace. From this truth one could infer that continuance in sin was meritorious, since it afforded a greater opportunity for God's lavish grace to be displayed. So Paul asks, 'Are we to go on sinning, so that grace may increase?' (6:1). Similarly, in 6:14 he had affirmed that the believer is 'not under law but under grace'. This could prompt the inference that living under grace gave grace to sin. 'Are we to sin because we are not under law but under grace?' Paul asks. 'Certainly not!' So it becomes apparent that verses 1 and 15 address basically the same issue, *viz.* whether God's grace accommodates the believer's sin.[22] Although Paul's

---

[21] Alternative renderings of the second part of this verse might be 'act as slaves to one another in the bondage of love', or 'enslave yourselves to one another through active love' (articular *agapēs*).

[22] While it is not impossible that Paul intended to distinguish between continuance in sin (*epimenōmen*, present tense, 6:1) and the act of sinning (*hamartēsōmen*, aorist, 6:15), it is more likely that the aorist here denotes the simple fact of sinning, without

responses to this issue in verses 2b–14 and 16–23 differ, the question answered is essentially identical. His response in verses 2–14 is this: sin has no rightful place in the lives of Christians because in baptism they all shared Christ's experience of death, burial and resurrection and therefore should now exhibit a 'newness of life' (v. 4) – the enjoyment of open and full relations with God ('living to God', vv. 10–11) and the suspension of all relations with sin ('dying to sin', vv. 2, 7, 11). His response in verses 16–23 is that sin should be foreign to believers' experience because at conversion they ceased to be the slaves of sin and became enslaved to God, offering to this new Master an obedient service that results in holiness and eternal life. The main thrust of the whole chapter is unambiguous. Christians, free from sin as a controlling power, are to shun sin. That is, the indicative is the basis for, and leads to, the imperative: 'We are free from the power of sin. Therefore let us not sin.'[23] Freedom *from* sin certainly does not give the freedom *to* sin; rather, it brings the obligation not to sin.

There can be no doubting the centrality of the ideas of freedom and slavery in verses 15–23. We find two uses of the verb 'set free' (*eleutheroō*, vv. 18, 22), one of the adjective 'free' (*eleutheros*, v. 20); four uses of the noun 'slave' (*doulos*, vv. 16 twice, 17, 20), two of the adjective 'enslaved' (*doulos*, v. 19 twice), and two of the verb 'enslave' (*douloō*, vv. 18, 22), as well as the servile terms 'obedience' (*hypakoē*, v. 16 twice) and 'obey' (*hypakouō*, vv. 16, 17).

As was the case with Galatians 4:21–31, so also in Romans 6:15–23, we find a sequence of contrasts. But whereas in Galatians 4 the antithesis was between the states of slavery and freedom, in Romans 6 the crucial contrast is between two types of slavery, slavery to sin and slavery to righteousness, or between two masters, sin and righteousness. Freedom from one means freedom for the other.

Slavery to sin	*Slavery to righteousness*
15: we are not under law	[we are] under grace
16: slaves to sin, which leads to death	[slaves to] obedience, which leads to righteousness

---

specifying the type of action (whether single or repeated or continuous).

[23] *Cf.* the sequence in Col. 3: 'You have died (*apethanete*) [with Christ, to sin, *cf.* 2:20; 3:1]' (v. 3) '... Therefore put to death (*nekrōsate*) your members as used for earthly purposes – immorality ...' (v. 5).

17: you were once slaves to sin	you have become obedient to the pattern of teaching to which you were entrusted
18: you have been set free from sin	you have been enslaved to righteousness
19: you used to offer your bodily members as slaves to impurity and to ever-increasing wickedness	now offer your bodily members as slaves to righteousness which leads to holiness
20: when you were slaves to sin	you were free from (the control of) righteousness
21a: what benefit did you reap … from the things you are now ashamed of?	22b: the benefit you reap leads to holiness
21b: the result of those things is death	22b: the result is eternal life
22a: you have been set free from sin	you have been enslaved to God
23: the wages of sin is death	the gift of God is eternal life

Clearly, then, the overall theme of the passage is the two 'slaveries': the old slavery to sin, from which believers have been set free, and the new slavery to righteousness, to which believers have been committed and now must commit themselves. Verse 18 is thematic: 'You have been set free from sin and have been enslaved to righteousness.' These two masters who vie for human allegiance, Sin (vv. 16, 18, 20, 22, 23) and Righteousness (vv. 18, 19) are given alternative names. Instead of the ruthless despot Sin, we read of 'impurity' and 'wickedness' (v. 19). In the place of the generous sovereign Righteousness, we have 'grace' (v. 15), 'obedience' (v. 16), 'the pattern of teaching' (v. 17) and 'God' (v. 22).

What is stunning about Paul's depiction of the human situation here is that there are only two masters, not three or more, and that allegiance to either is portrayed as slavery. A person is either a slave of sin or a slave of righteousness; neutrality, or an alternative servitude, is impossible. For Paul the natural state of all human beings is one of slavery to sin (Rom. 5:12; 6:6, 17, 22; Eph. 2:1–3). It is not that human existence in itself is slavery ('to be human is to be a slave', Petersen 1985: 245),[24] but the human predicament of natural alienation from God means that all are slaves ('to be a sinful human being is to be a slave'; cf. John 8:34). However, although conversion to God brings release from the thraldom of sin, it marks not the end of all bondage but the beginning of a new bondage. Paul highlights the dramatic substitution of one bondage for another by his characteristic 'then ... now' contrast. 'You used to be slaves to sin ... but you have been set free from sin' (vv. 17–18). 'Just as you used to offer your bodily members in slavery to impurity and to ever-increasing wickedness, so now offer them in slavery to righteousness' (v. 19). 'What benefit did you reap at that time? ... But now you have been set free from sin and have been enslaved to God' (vv. 21–22). This idea of conversion as an exchange of servitude finds classic expression in 1 Thessalonians 1:9. Concerning the Thessalonian Christians it was said, 'You turned (*epestrepsate*) to God from idols to be slaves (*douleuein*)[25] of the living and true God'. At their conversion, slavery to idols[26] was replaced by slavery to God.

To return to Romans 6, it would seem that neither the old nor the new slavery is irreversible. Those who have offered themselves as slaves to the master 'sin' (v. 16) could wholeheartedly obey the pattern of teaching contained in the gospel (v. 17) and thereby become the slaves of a new master, 'obedience' (v. 16). Similarly, those who, by divine intervention, have become enslaved to righteousness (v. 18) or to God (v. 22) are in constant danger of reverting to slavery to sin, albeit temporarily. If this danger were not present, Paul's injunction to the Romans, 'offer your bodily members in slavery to righteousness' (v. 19), would be pointless. Peter's experience at Caesarea Philippi (Matt. 16:13–23) illustrates how the tongue, a bodily member, can at one moment be enslaved to righteousness as an agent of the Father ('You are the Messiah, the Son of the living God', Matt.

[24] *Cf.* Petersen 1985: 246, 249. 'The form of a slave' in Phil. 2:7 does not mean simply 'the human form' as opposed to 'the form of God' seen as 'the divine form', as if Paul were saying that Christ emptied himself merely by assuming humanity. Rather, Christ's self-emptying was by assuming a slave's status (deprivation of rights) and role (humble, obedient service).

[25] *Douleuein* means 'to be a slave' or 'to serve as a slave'. This infinitive may be telic or ecbatic, indicating that slavery to God was the purpose or the result (respectively) of turning to God.

[26] The notion of slavery to idols is implied by the two expressions 'turned ... from' and 'to be slaves'.

16:16), and at the next moment be enslaved to sin as an agent of Satan ('Never, Lord ... This [suffering] shall never happen to you!' Matt. 16:22). 'Conducting oneself under the stimulus of the flesh' (*kata sarka peripatein*, *cf.* Rom. 8:4) is possible even for the believer who normally 'lives by the Spirit' (*pneumati peripatein*, *cf.* Gal. 5:16).

The exquisite attractiveness of the new slavery becomes evident when Paul contrasts the outcome or 'fruit' of the two 'slaveries'. For those on the payroll of sin, the wages are 'death' (v. 23; *cf.* vv. 16, 21), what Paul elsewhere depicts as 'eternal ruin and exclusion from the presence of the Lord' (2 Thess. 1:8). On the other hand, those who are God's slaves will receive as a gracious gift (unrelated to merit) 'eternal life' (v. 23b), that unmediated and beatific participation in the eternal divine life that will exclude both physical and spiritual death.

But it is not only Paul who champions the *for* after the *from*. As seasoned pastors, both Peter and Paul were keenly aware that if slavery to sin was not replaced by slavery to righteousness, liberty could quickly degenerate into licence.[27] We have seen that Paul says to the recently converted Galatians: 'Yes, brothers and sisters, freedom became yours when you were called. Do not use your freedom as an opportunity to indulge the flesh. Rather, enslave yourselves (*douleuete*) to one another in the bondage of love' (Gal. 5:13; *cf.* Matt. 20:27; Mark 10:44). Peter expresses the same sentiment: 'Live as free people, but do not use your freedom as a pretext for evil. Rather, live as God's slaves (*douloi*)' (1 Pet. 2:16). What is remarkable about these two apostolic injunctions is their similarity: first, an unequivocal affirmation of freedom; then a command to express this freedom not in doing wrong but in slavery to God or others. Stated in another way, for people recently emancipated from slavery, the antidote to licence is a new slavery.

Nor is this 'from–for' sequence foreign to the Old Testament, where there is a recurring pattern: release from Egyptian bondage leads to

---

[27] This point is not incompatible with Bruce's (1982: 240) observation that true liberty, the freedom of the Spirit, is itself a protection against licence: 'Many of Paul's friends would have assured him that the tendency to misuse the freedom of the Spirit as an excuse for enthusiastic licence could be checked only by a stiff dose of law. But Paul could not agree: the principle of law was so completely opposed to spiritual freedom that it could never be enlisted in defence of that freedom: nothing was more certainly calculated to kill true freedom. The freedom of the Spirit was the antidote alike to legal bondage and unrestrained licence.' The freedom of the Spirit is expressed in slavery to Christ.

willing servitude to God.[28] Says the LORD God, 'The Israelites belong to me as slaves. They are my slaves, whom I brought out of Egypt' (Lev. 25:55). On the individual plane, the psalmist affirms, 'O LORD, truly I am your slave (LXX, *doulos*); I am your slave (LXX, *doulos*) ... you have freed me from my chains' (Ps. 116:16; LXX 115:7).

Freedom *in* slavery

We have noted that the second danger facing those who are revelling in new-found freedom is so to glorify liberty that it becomes a new god to which they are enslaved. Everything is viewed in terms of freedom, nothing in terms of obligation. 'Freedom! Freedom! Freedom at all costs!' is the watch-cry, and any restriction on that freedom is regarded as an evil to be resisted. But in reality the most convincing evidence of the possession of freedom is the willingness to surrender it to achieve a worthy goal. The supreme example of this, of course, is the incarnation. The divine Logos, who had always been free of the limitations of time and space, chose to surrender that freedom and assume 'the form of a slave (*doulos*)' (Phil. 2:7) in first-century Palestine, so that he might be obedient right up to death (Phil. 2:8) and thus make atonement for the sins of the people (Heb. 2:17). Two instances from Paul's life will illustrate the point still further. Paul was 'free' to derive his support from those to whom he was ministering, but he chose to forgo this freedom so that the gospel he preached might be seen all the more clearly to be free of charge (1 Cor. 9:3–18; 2 Cor. 11:7–12). Or again, Paul could say, 'Though I am free and belong to no-one, I have made myself a slave (*emauton edoulōsa*) to everyone, in order to win as many converts as possible ... I have become all things to all people so that by all possible means I might save some of them' (1 Cor. 9:19, 22b).[29] Freedom expressed

[28] Regarding this pattern, Stek (1978: 148f.) aptly comments: 'The way of salvation in the Old Testament is not out of Egypt into Canaan, but *out of Egypt into the wilderness — and to Sinai!* Out of Egypt into the wilderness to teach Israel that the bread and water of life are gifts from Yahweh (neither man by his ingenuity and toil nor the gods by their alleged powers can assure man's necessary provisions), and that "man does not live by bread alone, but that man lives by everything that proceeds out of the mouth of Yahweh" (Dt. 8:3). Out of Egypt to Sinai that Israel may there become a people under the rule of Yahweh, bound to his service by covenant (of the suzerain–vassal type)'.

[29] 'First Corinthians 9:22 is the testimony of a man who has found security in bondage to Christ, and who is consequently free to relate to all kinds of people and to tolerate all sorts of differences within the context of a common commitment to the gospel' (Chamblin 1993: 138).

85

in self-imposed slavery! F. F. Bruce (1985: 230) has caught the point superbly: 'So completely was he [Paul] emancipated from spiritual bondage that he was not even in bondage to his emancipation.'

According to Stoic thought, external circumstance was irrelevant for the wise person who was in reality spiritually free. For example, someone who bore the marks of slavery should not be assumed to be not free, for the soul could be enjoying true freedom even when the body was in chains. Hence the Stoic paradox, 'a slave, yet free' (*doulos eleutheros*).[30] But in Christian thought, every Christian, whether slave or free, is spiritually free but nevertheless in slavery to Christ: 'free, yet a slave'.

'Freedom in slavery' is an unsettling yet exquisite Christian paradox, comparable to that other quintessential Christian paradox, 'strength in weakness' (*cf.* 2 Cor. 12:9). Just as the Christian's strength comes to its zenith of perfection in the 'weakness' of acknowledged dependence on God, so the Christian's freedom finds its consummation in exclusive and wholehearted devotion to Christ and his people. Yet these two paradoxes are not merely parallel; one is the corollary of the other. The strength of freedom in Christ is displayed in the 'weakness' of slavery to Christ.

So then, in true Christian liberty, freedom *from* is immediately suc-ceeded by freedom *for*. We are set free from slavery to sin precisely in order to be free to choose slavery to Christ, a slavery of perfect freedom. As believers, we have chosen to become slaves of a new Master. Such a transfer of allegiance, such an exchange of masters, saves us from falling prey to the danger of using liberty as an oppor-tunity or pretext for evil and the danger of becoming liberty's slave.

The Christian paradox of 'freedom in slavery' has been captured in a memorable way by two distinguished 'slaves of Christ', one of the sixteenth century, one of the nineteenth. In his *The Freedom of a Christian* (1520), Martin Luther (1943: 5) developed these two complementary propositions: 'A Christian man is a perfectly free lord of all, subject to none. A Christian man is a perfectly dutiful servant of all, subject to all.' That is, a Christian is subject to nobody with respect to liberty, subject to everyone with respect to service. Then in his commentary on Romans, H. C. G. Moule (1896: 11) wrote, 'The liberty of the Gospel is the silver side of the same shield whose side of gold is an unconditional vassalage to the liberating Lord.'

---

[30] This theme, 'a slave in body, yet free in spirit', is common in Greek and Roman literature; *e.g.*, Euripides, *Hel.* 728–731; *Ion* 854–856; Seneca, *Ben.* 3. 20. 1; *Ep.* 47. 17.

Chapter Five

Slavery and lordship

In the last chapter we discovered that in the New Testament the two notions, slavery and freedom, are presented not as mutually exclusive but as potentially complementary ideas. Christians have been freed from their natural slavery to sin so that they might embrace slavery to righteousness, a slavery in which true freedom reaches its zenith.

But these two 'slaveries' do not involve bondage to two abstract principles, sin and righteousness. Slavery to sin is in fact slavery to Satan, who ensnares people (*cf.* 1 Tim. 3:7) and captures them to do his will (2 Tim. 2:26). Slavery to righteousness is in reality slavery to Christ, the Master in heaven (*cf.* Col. 4:1). In the present chapter, I wish to develop this theme of the 'masterhood' or 'lordship' of Jesus.

The earliest Christological confessions

The New Testament records two early and widespread confessions made about Jesus by the first Christians. One focused on his messiahship: 'the Messiah is Jesus' (*ho Christos Iēsous*, Acts 18:5, 28) or 'Jesus is the Messiah' (*cf.* Acts 9:22; 17:3); the other, on his lordship: 'Jesus is Lord' (*Kyrios Iēsous*, Rom. 10:9; 1 Cor. 12:3; *cf.* Phil. 2:11). When a New Testament writer gives Jesus his full name, 'the Lord Jesus Christ' (*e.g.*, 1 Cor. 1:3, 7, 10), these two confessions are being combined, asserting his deity ('Lord'), his humanity ('Jesus') and his messiahship ('Christ'). Such a conflation of confessions is also found in Acts 2:36, where, as the climax of his Pentecost speech, Peter announces: 'So let all the house of Israel know without a shadow of doubt that God has made him both Lord and Messiah – this very Jesus whom you crucified.' Then there is Colossians 2:6, in which Paul reminds his readers that at conversion they had embraced the Christian tradition regarding 'the Messiah, namely Jesus the Lord'.

The term *kyrios*[1]

Originally the term *kyrios* was an adjective, with the sense 'having power', but in the 600-plus New Testament uses of the term it is always a noun, occurring in every New Testament book except Titus and 1, 2 and 3 John. It means 'sir', 'owner', 'master', 'lord' or 'Lord', and is used of a man in his role as an owner of property (Matt. 20:8), a master of slaves (Luke 12:45), a father of children (Matt. 21:30), or a person worthy of respect (John 4:11). It is applied to an angel (Acts 10:4); to Jesus, both during his ministry (Luke 9:54) and after his resurrection (Eph. 6:5–10); and to God (Luke 1:6; Acts 7:33; Jas. 1:7).

In the first-century pagan world, *kyrios* was not a proper name but a title prefixed to a deity's name.[2] So a papyrus records a dinner invitation this way: 'Chaeremon invites you to dine at the table of the lord Serapis in the Temple of Serapis tomorrow' (cited by Barclay 1958: 326). Yet this term became a personal name by which Christians referred to Jesus, as is shown by the Aramaic phrase *Marana tha* ('Our Lord, come!') in 1 Corinthians 16:22. Indeed, Christians are described as 'those who call upon the name of the Lord' (Acts 9:14; 1 Cor. 1:2; *cf.* Joel 3:5, LXX), whether in baptism, prayer, or exorcism. *Kyrios* is the distinctive New Testament title signifying the resurrected and ascended Jesus (2 Cor. 5:6, 8; 1 Thess. 4:15–16), but the concept of his being 'Lord' doubtless arose during his earthly life as a consequence of his authoritative teaching and divine power (see Mark 11:3; 12:35–37, citing Ps. 110:1). That is, the pre-resurrection historical experience of the lordship of Jesus foreshadowed the post-resurrection theological confession of Jesus as Lord.

In a statement that is arresting because it appears to be without exceptions, the apostle Paul insists that no-one can say *Kyrios Iēsous* ('Jesus is Lord') 'except by the Holy Spirit' (1 Cor. 12:3). This Pauline insistence is surprising because it is patently possible for

---

[1] In the following discussion of the meaning and significance of *kyrios*, I make use of sections of my article 'Lord' (Harris 1986: 3. 157f.). Used with permission.

[2] Although in the Hellenistic East the title *kyrios* was regularly applied to rulers in the pre-Christian and Christian eras, in Rome and the West there was a reluctance even during the early Empire to use *kyrios* of the emperor, for Augustus and Tiberius saw themselves as 'First' or the 'Leading Figure' (*princeps*) in a 'principate' rather than as 'Lord' (*dominus*) in a 'dominate'. But by the time of Nero this reluctance had been overcome and Caesar became 'Lord', rather than merely 'First' in the state (see Deissmann 1965: 349–357).

anyone to utter the words 'Jesus is Lord'. What the apostle is saying is that apart from the Holy Spirit's power in enlightening the mind and captivating the will, no person can make this simple confession with understanding and commitment. What, then, did the earliest Christians understand as the implications of this confession? To judge from the New Testament use of *kyrios* in reference to Jesus, whenever worshipping Christians repeat this confession of faith, we are doing several things.

1. We are implying that the Christ of faith is none other than the Jesus of history. Said Peter to his audience on the day of Pentecost, 'This Jesus, whom you crucified, God has made both Lord and Christ' (Acts 2:36).[3]

2. We are acknowledging the deity of Christ. When Thomas addressed Jesus as 'My Lord and my God' (John 20:28), he was applying to the Nazarene an expression used commonly in the Psalms in reference to Yahweh. Moreover, the combination of 'Lord' and 'God' shows that the title 'Lord' connotes divinity.[4]

3. We are affirming the triumph of Christ over death and hostile cosmic powers when God raised him from the dead. The risen Lord addresses John with the words, 'Do not be afraid. I am the First and the Last. I am the Living One; I was dead, but now I am alive for evermore, and I own the keys that unlock death and Hades' (Rev. 1:17–18). Paul speaks of God's 'mighty strength, which he exerted in Christ when he raised him from the dead and seated him at his right hand in the heavenly realms, far above all rule and authority, power and dominion ... And God placed all things under his feet' (Eph. 1:19–22).

4. We are epitomizing the Christian message. 'For we do not preach ourselves,' Paul insists, 'but Jesus Christ as Lord' (2 Cor. 4:5).

5. We are declaring everyone's accountability to the Lord, the righteous judge. 'Judge nothing before the appointed time; wait till the Lord comes. He will bring to light what is hidden in darkness and will expose the motives of people's hearts' (1 Cor. 4:5).

6. We are making a personal and public declaration of faith. 'If you confess with your mouth, "Jesus is Lord", and believe in your heart that God raised him from the dead, you will be saved' (Rom. 10:9).

---

[3] It is of interest that Dunn (1977: 369) identifies the distinctive feature of first-century Christianity and 'the integrating centre for the diverse expressions of Christianity' as 'the unity between the historical Jesus and the exalted Christ' (*cf.* 205–216, 370–372).

[4] On John 20:28, see Harris 1992: 106–129.

7. We are repudiating our former allegiance to pagan 'lords' and reaffirming our loyalty to the one Lord. In 1 Corinthians 8:5–6 Paul declares that 'even if there are so-called gods, whether in heaven or on earth (as indeed there are many "gods" and many "lords"), yet for us there is but one God, the Father, from whom are all things and for whom we exist; and there is but one Lord, Jesus Christ, through whom are all things and through whom we exist.'

The correlativity of lordship and slavery

But there is another connotation of the term *kyrios* that is germane to our discussion. When believers sing or recite the confession 'Jesus is Lord', we are affirming his absolute supremacy,[5] not only over the physical and moral universe (Matt. 28:18; 1 Pet. 3:22), and not only over human history (Rom. 9:5), not only over all human beings (Acts 10:36; Rom. 10:12), whether living or dead (Rom. 14:9), not only over the church (Eph. 1:22), but also over our own lives as his willing slaves. The simple but crucial point is that the two words 'Lord' and 'slave', *kyrios* and *doulos*, are correlatives. That is, they form a matching pair, comparable to 'lightning and thunder'. Not that thunder is the opposite of lightning, or that 'slave' is the opposite of 'lord' – 'slave' and 'free' are opposites – but when you see lightning, you usually hear thunder immediately afterwards; they belong together.[6] So, too, the word 'slave' belongs naturally with the term 'lord'.

This correlativity of lordship and slavery is evident in many New Testament passages. Consider, for example, the following statements where the two terms *kyrios* and *doulos* are used in close proximity.

A student is not above his teacher, nor a slave above his master. It is enough for the student to be like his teacher, and the slave like his master (Matt. 10:24–25).

His master replied, 'Well done, good and faithful slave!' (Matt. 25:21, 23).

[5] In keeping with the original adjectival sense of *kyrios* ('having power'), the cognate verb *kyrieuō* means 'have dominion over', 'exercise lordship over', 'be master' (seven NT uses; all Pauline, except for Luke 22:25). Only the context indicates whether the rule being exercised is regarded as positive (*e.g.*, Rom. 14:9) or negative (*e.g.*, 2 Cor. 1:24, of spiritual imperialism), or neutral (*e.g.*, Rom. 7:1).

[6] Other comparable correlatives are 'parent–child' and 'king–subject'. Where you have a king, there are usually subjects; where subjects, usually a king.

I tell you the truth, no slave is greater than his master, nor is a messenger greater than the one who sent him (John 13:16).

I no longer call you slaves, because a slave does not know his master's business (John 15:15).

We do not proclaim ourselves, but Jesus Christ as Lord, and ourselves as your slaves for Jesus' sake (2 Cor. 4:5).

The Lord's slave must not be quarrelsome (2 Tim. 2:24).

James, a slave of God and of the Lord Jesus Christ (Jas. 1:1).

Now it is true that on occasion there may be a *kyrios* without *douloi* ('slaves'), as when a Roman emperor was given the title *kyrios* as indicating his unquestioned supremacy and authority. Roman citizens were not the slaves of the emperor, although they addressed him as *kyrios*.[7] For example, the Roman procurator of Judea, Porcius Festus, refers to the emperor Nero as 'sovereign lord' (*tō kyriō*) when discussing Paul's fate with Herod Agrippa II (Acts 25:26). But more often than not, when there was a *kyrios*, there were *douloi*.[8] On the other hand, wherever there were *douloi*, there was a *kyrios*.[9] In this case,

---

[7] But see above, n. 2.

[8] Of course, when Sarah is said to have called her husband Abraham her 'master' or 'lord' (*kyrios*, 1 Pet. 3:6, alluding to Gen. 18:12, where the LXX has *ho kyrios mou*, 'my master'), we cannot infer that Sarah was his slave!

[9] It was only in the niceties of Roman legal terminology that the concept of a 'masterless' slave existed. In the standard Roman definition of slavery as 'an institution of the law of nations by which, contrary to nature, a person is subjected to an alien dominion [*dominio alieno*]' (Florentinus, in Justinian's *Digest* 1. 5. 4. 1), it is inappropriate to translate *dominio alieno* as 'to the dominion of another [person]' (as Watson 1987: 7). Buckland (1969: 3) notes: '*Dominus* and *dominium* are different words. The statement that slaves as such are subject to *dominium* does not imply that every slave is always owned. Chattels are the subject of ownership: it is immaterial that a slave or other chattel is at the moment a *res nullius*' ('a chattel belonging to no-one'). A slave who had been abandoned or illegally manumitted, or a free person who had been sold into slavery fraudulently, might technically be ownerless for a temporary period. But as Patterson (1982: 366 n. 13) rightly observes: 'In reality all that being a *servus sine domino* ['a slave without a master'] meant was either that a potential relation of slavery existed, although the person in question – for example, the abandoned slave – was not at the time actually in a slave relationship or in a position to claim free status, or that the person was actually in a relation of slavery but was potentially a free person and could legally claim such a status. Legal technicalities aside, in actual practice all Roman slaves had at least one master.' Even convicted criminals condemned to slavery (*servi poenae*,) and slaves of the Treasury and slaves serving in a temple were effectively responsible to some

'slave' always implied 'lord'. We may summarize the point by saying that 'slave' is the natural concomitant of 'lord', while 'lord' is the necessary corollary of 'slave'.

Now if Jesus Christ was called 'Lord' but there was never a reference to Christians as 'slaves', then it would be *possible* to regard Jesus as 'Lord', a person of exalted status and supreme authority, who nevertheless had no 'slaves'. But even in that case it would normally be expected that he had people whom he called his slaves. But as it is, not only is Jesus regularly called 'Lord' in the New Testament; his followers *are* described or depicted as his slaves, both after and before his resurrection. In Ephesians 6:6 household slaves are called 'the slaves of Christ', while in 1 Corinthians 7:22 the free person is designated as 'Christ's slave'. And even in the gospels there are unambiguous indications that the followers of the earthly Lord were seen as his slaves.[10] Four instances will suffice to establish the point.

Luke 12:35–38 records a parable in which a *kyrios* returns from a marriage celebration to his household of *douloi*. When Peter asks, 'Lord, are you telling this parable specially for us or for everyone?' (v. 41), he receives no direct reply, but Jesus speaks further of a *kyrios* who, on his delayed arrival, metes out reward or punishment to his *douloi*, depending on the nature of their service (vv. 42–48). Clearly, as the coming Son of Man (v. 40), Jesus is the master who will certainly return, and all his disciples, but in particular, leaders must faithfully discharge their duties (vv. 42–43) as his watchful slaves (vv. 35, 37). A similar point is made in the parable of the talents (Matt. 25:14–30; *cf.* Luke 19:11–27). During his absence, Jesus' slaves (*douloi*, six uses) must engage in profitable service, for on his return as 'the master (*kyrios*) of those slaves' (v. 19) he will reward productive, faithful service ('good and trustworthy *doulos*', vv. 21, 23), while unproductive work will incur judgment. In John 13:12–16 Jesus instructs his disciples 'to wash one another's feet' because he, their Teacher and Lord (*kyrios*), had washed their feet (John 13:1–11) and 'a slave (*doulos*) is not greater than his master (*kyrios*)'. Finally, the parallelism in John 15:20 (slave–master//you–I) shows that Jesus is the *kyrios* and his disciples are his *douloi*: 'Remember the word that I spoke to you, "A slave (*doulos*) is not

---

individual who acted in the capacity of a *kyrios*. Moreover, one could argue that such slaves were owned by the state or by a particular temple and so were not 'masterless'.

[10] There are also, of course, passages in the gospels in which God is pictured as the Master and his adherents as slaves (*e.g.*, Matt. 6:24; 18:23–35).

greater than his master (*kyrios*). If they persecuted me, they will persecute you".'

So whether we approach this matter of correlativity from the vantage-point of the word *kyrios* or from that of the word *doulos*, the result is the same: Jesus is 'Lord', and his disciples are his 'slaves'.

Slavery as a yoke

For good reason slavery was often described as a 'yoke' (*zygos*), the piece of shaped wood worn on the necks of draught-animals (Num. 19:2). Figuratively, the yoke was a symbol for humiliating bondage and enforced subjection, any imposed relationship that necessitated obedient service. 'I am the LORD your God, who brought you out of Egypt so that you would no longer be slaves to the Egyptians; I broke the bars of your yoke (Heb. *'ōl*, LXX *zygos*) and enabled you to walk with heads held high' (Lev. 26:13). Early in the reign of Zedekiah, the LORD directed Jeremiah, 'Make a yoke out of straps and crossbars and put it on your neck' (Jer. 27:2), to symbolize the nation's coming subjection to Nebuchadnezzar, king of Babylon. Yet the image of the yoke could also have positive connotations, depicting commendable submission to Yahweh's will – a will that rebellious Israel had repudiated. 'Long ago you broke off your yoke and tore off your bonds; you said, "I will not serve you!"' (Jer. 2:20; *cf.* 5:5).

In the New Testament, too, the yoke is both a negative and a positive symbol. Paul addresses slaves as those who are 'under the yoke of slavery' (*hypo zygon douloi*), directing them to view their masters as worthy of complete respect, 'so that God's name and our teaching may not be slandered' (1 Tim. 6:1). Again, using yoke imagery in a negative sense and figuratively, Paul warns the Galatians who have been liberated by Christ 'for the enjoyment of freedom' (*tē eleutheria*) not to let themselves be burdened again by 'a yoke of slavery' (*zygos douleias*, Gal. 5:1). That is, if the Galatians complied with the Judaizers' insistence that belief in Christ needed to be supplemented by total adherence to the Mosaic law, including the rite of circumcision (*cf.* Acts 15:1, 5), they would once again be submitting to 'a yoke of slavery'. In current Jewish thought, to keep the law of Moses was to place oneself under 'the yoke of the law', which effected the removal of 'the yoke of worldly care' (*Pirke Aboth* 3:5), a saying of Rabbi Neḥunya ben Haqqanah about AD 100. But Rabbi Paul equates subservience to the law, seen as a means of gaining divine approval, with the wearing of a slave's yoke, and he would have wholeheartedly agreed with Peter that 'the yoke of the law' was a burden that the Jews had been unable to bear (Acts 15:10). One aspect of the freedom of the gospel is freedom from the observance of the law regarded as the ground of divine approval.

When we come to the famous invitation and promise of Jesus in Matthew 11:28–30, the image of the yoke is used positively: 'Come to me, all you who are weary and burdened, and I will give you rest. Take my yoke upon you and learn from me, for I am gentle and humble at heart, and you will find rest for your souls. For my yoke is easy and my burden is light.' The background of this saying is probably not the Jewish concept of the law as a pleasant yoke but their view of wisdom as an agreeable yoke. 'Bring your neck under her yoke, and let your soul bear her burden. She is near to those who seek her, and the person who is intent on finding her will do so' (Sir. 51:26). As the embodiment of Wisdom, Jesus is inviting those who are spiritually restless and oppressed to gain peace and serenity by becoming his yoke-bearing slaves. When he says, 'My yoke is easy', he means that 'the yoke I impose on those who come to me fits easily on the neck', because he is a gentle-hearted Master.

Christian conversion may be described as an exchange of yokes. Slavery to sin, to evil powers, to evil desires, is replaced by slavery to Christ. Since life cannot be 'yokeless', conversion must involve an alteration of sovereignty, an exchange of masters, the assumption of a new yoke – that of service to Christ. Whereas the previous yoke was oppressive and chafing, the new yoke is pleasant and emancipating (cf. Matt. 11:30, 'My yoke is easy and my burden is light'). It is true that the New Testament nowhere explicitly depicts the Christian as being under a yoke of slavery to Christ. But inasmuch as Jesus invited the oppressed to take his yoke upon them (Matt. 11:28–29) and the New Testament calls Christians the slaves of Christ (1 Cor. 7:22; Eph. 6:6; Phil. 1:1; Col. 4:12), we may legitimately infer, I suggest, that Christians are 'slaves under a yoke', or those who have submitted to 'a yoke of slavery'. To take on Christ's yoke of slavery is to be under Christ's law, the law of love,[11] which involves carrying one another's burdens (Gal. 6:2; cf. Rom. 13:8–10).

The slave's service

The slave of Christ renders service *to* Christ the Lord. Paul describes

---

[11] Cf. Bengel's dictum: *lex Christi, lex amoris*, 'the law of Christ is the law of love'.

those who live in the newness of life that Christ imparts as living 'no longer for themselves but for him who died and was raised for them' (2 Cor. 5:15; *cf.* Rom. 7:4). To be '*in* Christ' is to live exclusively '*for* Christ', that is, to live at his disposal and for his benefit. The same point is made in Rom. 14:8: 'If we live, we live for the Lord's benefit (*tō kyriō*); and if we die, we die for the Lord's glory (*tō kyriō*)'.[12] What Paul says to actual slaves applies also to all Christ's slaves: 'You are to give a slave's service (*douleuete*) to the Lord (*tō kyriō*) Christ' (Col. 3:24). Notice once again the conjunction of *kyrios* and the *doulos* root.

The essence of slavery is subjection, usually involuntary, to the will of another (*cf.* Vogt 1972: 93f.).[13] Apart from his choice in the matter, a slave is obliged to fulfil an alien will (Xenophon, *Cyr.* 8. 1. 4). Jesus' intimate word to his Father in Gethsemane perfectly sums up the slave's attitude: 'Not my will, but yours be done' (Matt. 26:39). The slave is totally at the disposal of his master,[14] completely subject to his master's will. He lives solely for the benefit of his master, and the service he must render has two elements: obedience to explicit commands, and, where there are no specific directives to follow, action that will please his master.[15] Obeying and pleasing the master – this is the service rendered by a slave. These two aspects of the slave's service must now be considered in greater detail.

The first obligation of the slave has always been to serve by obeying. In Luke's 'Sermon on the Plain', Jesus asks, 'Why do you call me, "Lord, Lord", yet (*kai*) do not do what I tell you?' (Luke 6:46; *cf.* Matt. 7:21). Or again, in the course of requesting Jesus to

[12] *Cf.* the general observation of Watson (1987: 102): 'The main end of slavery is to increase the master's satisfaction, whether he obtains this through pride in the augmentation of social prestige by conspicuous consumption, through the availability of personal services, or through economic betterment.'

[13] Bradley (1987: 18) notes that 'slavery by definition is a means of securing and maintaining an involuntary labour force by a group in society which monopolises political and economic power'.

[14] The story is told of an assistant librarian of German descent who served at Cambridge University Library. Knowing the English idiom, 'to be at someone's disposal', he volunteered his services to the students with the words, 'You may dispose of me however you wish!' The thought was right even if the words were wrong.

[15] The Stoic moralist Seneca distinguishes clearly between 'services' a slave performs for his master as a matter of duty, and 'benefits' he confers on his master out of love (*Ben.* 3. 19. 1–4). He mentions two examples of such 'benefits' that go beyond 'the constraints of necessity' (= duty) – when a slave lays down his life to protect his master from attack (3. 19. 2), or refuses under the pressure of torture to disclose his master's secrets (3. 19. 3).

heal his slave by his powerful spoken word, the centurion at Capernaum commented that even he himself as someone with delegated authority knew the power of the word of command. 'I say to my slave (*tō doulō mou*), "Do this", and he does it' (Luke 7:8). Obedience to commands was not simply required of slaves; it was assumed to be their principal role. In fact, the degree of a slave's faithfulness was determined by the extent of his obedience: a perfectly obedient slave was a completely faithful slave. The verdict on their lives that all Christians hope to hear from their heavenly Lord is just this, 'Well done, good and faithful slave (*doulos*)' (Matt. 25:21, 23). His warm congratulations will be offered to slaves who have been industrious ('good') and obedient ('faithful').[16] The same point emerges from the parable regarding watchfulness in Luke 12:42–48. That steward (*oikonomos*) is pronounced faithful who has complied with the will of the master by careful supervision of the master's household in his absence (Luke 12:42–43). Again, in the parable of the lost son (Luke 15:11–32), the older brother complains to his father: 'All these years I've been slaving for you (*douleuō soi*) and have never disobeyed your orders' (v. 29). Yet again, the slave who is a useful instrument (*skeuos ... euchrēston*) for the master of the house (*despotēs*) is the one who is 'prepared to do any good work' (2 Tim. 2:21). The slave's life revolves around the will of the master. He is a living instrument whose individuality is subsumed in the personality of the master. So, for Paul, slaves were to be obedient to their earthly masters just as they obey Christ (*hōs tō Christō*), and 'as slaves of Christ (*hōs douloi Christou*)' they were to do the will of God from their heart (Eph. 6:5–6). This link between slavery and obedience is perhaps clearest in Romans 6:16: 'Don't you realize that when you give control of yourselves (*paristanete heautous*) to someone to obey him as slaves, you are the slaves of the one you obey – whether you are slaves to sin, which results in death, or to obedience, which results in righteousness?'[17] Notice the phrase, 'when you give control of yourselves to someone to obey him as slaves', or

---

[16] In a context of slavery (vv. 21 and 23 of Matthew 25 both have *kyrios* [2x] and *doulos*), obedience is likely to be the principal ingredient in the faithfulness, especially since in classical Greek *pistos* sometimes had the nuance of 'obedient' and *pisteuein* the nuance 'to obey' (Bultmann 1968: 6. 175, 178).

[17] Gale (1964: 183f.) has rightly pointed out that the surprising antithesis in Rom. 6:16 between 'sin' and 'obedience' (where 'righteousness' [*cf.* v. 19] or 'God' [*cf.* v. 22] might have been expected) indicates the centrality of obedience in Paul's thought in 6:15–23 where he makes extensive use of the analogy of slavery.

'when you present yourselves to someone as obedient slaves'. Obedience to Christ, while an obligation, is voluntary.

But obedience or submission to the Lord Christ may exceptionally be involuntary, being a forced allegiance. This, I believe, is the case at the end of the Christological poem in Philippians 2. It is at the sounding of the name of Jesus (*viz.* 'Lord') in the heavenly court that all sentient, intelligent beings will bow the knee and confess his cosmic dominion as Lord (Phil. 2:10–11). This dominion will be acknowledged, whether voluntarily or involuntarily, by the whole created order – including angels ('those in heaven'; *cf.* Heb. 1:13; 1 Pet. 1:22), human beings ('those on earth'; *cf.* Rom. 14:9; Rev. 1:5), and demons or the dead ('those under the earth'; *cf.* Rom. 14:9). The song of the redeemed, 'Jesus is Lord', will also be the cry of the subjugated.

The other essential ingredient of a slave's service is pleasing his master. If obedience to explicit commands is merely a slave's duty (Luke 17:10), pleasing the master, where there are no particular commands to follow, is a slave's prerogative and goes beyond the performance of duty. A master gives neither wages nor thanks for compliance with his commands (*cf.* Luke 17:9), but ideally he expresses commendation to his slave for using initiative in seeking to please him (*cf.* Matt. 25:14–23). In Titus 2:9 Paul instructs Titus, 'Urge slaves to be submissive to their masters and to please them in every way.'[18] Whereas most slaves served under some degree of compulsion and expected punishment for disobedience, Christ's slaves serve voluntarily, so that what motivates their service is not fear of punishment or even principally the prospect of reward, but the desire to please their Master. In Paul's prayer for the Colossians (Col. 1:9–14), he asks God to give them the spiritual wisdom and discernment that will fill them with the knowledge of God's will and produce behaviour that is worthy of the Lord (Jesus) and that seeks to please him in everything (*eis pasan areskeian*, Col. 1:10), behaviour that aims to give him complete satisfaction. An explicit link between slavery to Christ and divine pleasure is found in Romans 14:18: 'The

---

[18] This assumes that *en pasin* ('in every way') should be contrued with *euarestous einai* (thus 'to please them in every way') (*cf.* Col. 1:10, *eis pasan areskeian*), but it is equally possible to take the phrase with the preceding *hypotassesthai* (thus 'to be submissive in all respects') (*cf.* Eph. 5:24, *hypotassetai ... en panti*; Col. 3:22, *hypakouete kata panta*). In the light of Eph. 6:5–6 (obedience to earthly masters is the will of God), we can infer that slaves would be pleasing to their heavenly Master, Christ (*cf.* 2 Cor. 5:9, *euarestoi autō einai*) when they were pleasing (*euarestous*) to their earthly masters (Titus 2:9).

person who acts as Christ's slave (*ho ... douleuōn tō Christō*) in this way [*viz.* by exhibiting righteousness, peace, and joy in the Holy Spirit, Rom. 14:17] pleases God and wins people's approval.'

But there is another passage that confirms the conclusion that pleasing Christ or God was Paul's preoccupation. In 2 Corinthians 5:1–10 Paul is reviewing the sources of divine comfort afforded the believer who faces the possibility of imminent death: certainty of the future possession of a spiritual body (v. 1); the present possession of the Spirit as the pledge of ultimate transformation (vv. 4–5); and knowledge that death begins a walk 'in the realm of sight' (v. 7) and involves departure to Christ's immediate presence where personal fellowship with him is enjoyed (v. 8). These reassuring truths, and especially the last, form the basis for the ethical consequence drawn in verse 9: 'That is why (*dio kai*) we constantly make it our ambition (*philotimoumetha*) to please him, whether we are at home [in the body] or away [from it].' The movement of thought from verses 1–8 to verse 9 is comparable to Paul's frequent passage from the doctrinal indicative to an ethical imperative ('You are; therefore be!'). After stating profound doctrinal facts, Paul spells out their implications for behaviour. His incessant aim to be pleasing to Christ (v. 9) was the direct outcome of his awareness that death would terminate his relative exile from Christ and inaugurate his walking in the realm of sight in the presence of the Lord (vv. 6–8). To entertain the hope of person-to-person communion with Christ after death (v. 8) naturally prompts the aspiration of gaining acceptance in his eyes before and after death.

Let us consider one further passage. When Paul argues, 'If I were still trying to please people, I would not be a slave of Christ' (Gal. 1:10), the inference is clear. A slave of people is preoccupied with pleasing people; a slave of Christ is passionately committed to pleasing Christ. And it is not that Christians must wait until the second advent to sense Christ's pleasure. Whenever the aim of pleasing Christ is fulfilled, he is pleased. One may recall Eric Liddell's memorable statement in *Chariots of Fire*: 'When I run, I feel his pleasure.'

In both these respects – obeying and pleasing a master – Christ himself is the paradigm. 'He emptied himself by assuming the form of a *slave* (*doulos*) ... and became *obedient* to the point of death' (Phil. 2:7–8).[19] His slavery to God implied his obedience to God. One

[19] The preposition *mechri* in the phrase *mechri thanatou* perhaps expresses both

SLAVERY AND LORDSHIP

crucial aspect of Christ's service as a *doulos* was his exclusive devotion to doing his Father's will.[20] The author of Hebrews indicates that the incarnate Christ addressed his Father using the words of David in Psalm 40:7–8a: '"Here I am – it is written about me in the scroll – I have come to do your will, O God"' (Heb. 10:7). A similar emphasis on Christ's obedience to God throughout his life on earth is a feature of the fourth gospel (*e.g.*, John 6:38; 14:31).

In pleasing a master, Christ is also the model for imitation. 'Christ did not please himself' (Rom. 15:3), but could say without fear of contradiction, 'I always do what is pleasing to him [God]' (John 8:29), and, 'I seek not to please myself but him who sent me' (John 5:30). At the outset of Christ's public ministry, the heavenly voice declared, 'You are my Son, whom I love; with you I am well pleased' (Mark 1:11).

There is another area in which Christ serves as the supreme model which his slaves seek to follow. Just as Christ's servitude to God involved suffering (Phil. 2:7–9), so also the Christian's sharing in Christ's slavery involves suffering. The link between physical slavery and suffering is explicit in 1 Peter 2:18–23. There Peter addresses the plight of Christian slaves who were being treated unjustly by brutish masters even when they served in an exemplary way. He appeals to their awareness that God is the ultimate person whose commendation they must seek (vv. 19–20), and encourages them to submit and show the utmost respect even to surly and overbearing masters (v. 18). Then follows Peter's potent reminder that when they patiently endure undeserved suffering they are following in the footsteps of Christ, who himself did not retaliate when he was reviled and did not make threats when he suffered, but rather entrusted himself and his cause to God who judges justly (vv. 21–23).

---

measure ('to the extremity of death') and time ('right up to [and including] death'). The GNB catches both senses: 'He ... walked the path of obedience all the way to death – his death on the cross.'

[20] It would not have seemed incongruous to Paul's addressees in the Roman province of Philippi for Jesus to be described as both a *doulos* (during his earthly ministry) and a *kyrios* (*par excellence*, at his exaltation) (Phil. 2:7, 11). In fact, a *doulos* could simultaneously be a *kyrios*, for within an urban household a slave could own other slaves and even use their services to accumulate his own private funds. The picture of Christ as a *doulos* who, as the *kyrios*, came to have many *douloi* of his own, prompts a comparison with King Rehoboam. The elders who had served his father, Solomon, advised him to be a slave (LXX, *doulos*) to the people, so that they would always be his slaves (LXX, *douloi*) (1 Kgdms 12:7). Jesus chose to be a *doulos*, and as a consequence he was honoured as a *kyrios* (Phil. 2:7–11) who would always have many *douloi*.

Matthew 10 associates suffering with spiritual slavery to Christ. Verses 16–23 describe the afflictions that will be the lot of the followers of the suffering Son of Man. The next two verses (vv. 24–25) illustrate the inevitability and the necessity of such suffering. If 'disciples are not above their teachers nor slaves above their masters' (v. 24) and 'it is enough for disciples to be like their teachers and for slaves to be like masters' (v. 25), then persecution and rejection should be reckoned as both inevitable and necessary for the disciples and slaves of Jesus. As their teacher and master, he first experienced hostility and suffered persecution (v. 25b). Verse 25a may be paraphrased as follows: 'The slave should be content with sharing the same fate as his master. A better fate cannot be expected, given the principle (v. 24) that "the slave is not superior to his master".' John 15:20 makes explicit this correlation between Master and slave with respect to suffering: 'Slaves are not superior to their masters. If they persecuted me, they will persecute you also.' Indeed, the implication here and in Matthew 10:24 is that if the master is superior to the slave, then the slave should expect more rather than less opposition and suffering. 'If the head of the house has been called Beelzebub, how much more the members of the household!' (Matt. 10:25b).

So then, the slaves of Christ carry out their voluntary service not only to Christ but also in imitation of him.[21] Like his obedience, theirs is to be unquestioning and complete. Like Christ's pleasing of his Master, theirs is to be enthusiastic and creative. And just as he patiently endured suffering, they too should do the same.

Slavery to other people

Thus far we have seen that when believers confess 'Jesus is Lord', they are also affirming, by implication, that 'we are his slaves'. But how does this confession affect horizontal relationships between fellow-confessors, and between believers and non-believers? Are there limits to the Christian's slavery?

Paul's injunction, 'Do not become slaves of people' (1 Cor. 7:23), follows the simple statement, 'You were bought at a price', without a connective. This stark juxtaposition points to the relation of the two statements. It is because Christians were bought at a price – the price of blood – that they can belong to no-one other than their Purchaser.

---

[21] 'Christ is pre-eminently the Servant of God, and Christians are servants of the Servant of God' (Richardson 1958: 305). *Cf.* also Russell 1968: 41, 67, 88–89.

Slavery to people's whims and fancies, to their requests and demands, compromises the prior and exclusive claim of Christ to the Christian's total devotion. Any slavery to people amounts to a repudiation of slavery to Christ. 'Precisely because the slave is both free and slave in Christ, and the free person is both slave and free in Christ [v. 22], they must not let themselves come under the bondage of mere humans' (Fee 1987: 320).[22] It is unlikely that Paul is addressing the issue of self-sale into slavery, but it is entirely possible that this aphorism, 'Do not become slaves of people', castigates the Corinthian tendency to champion particular leaders, whether Paul, Apollos, Cephas or Christ (cf. 1 Cor. 1:12), or any of the 'countless guides' at Corinth (cf. 1 Cor. 4:15).

Another indication of Paul's rejection of bondage to others is found in 1 Corinthians 10:23–33, where he is discussing motivation for Christian living and the limitations of Christian freedom. 'If some unbeliever invites you to a meal and you are disposed to go, eat whatever is set in front of you without raising any question based on conscientious scruples' (1 Cor. 10:27). Then follows a parenthetical exception (vv. 28–29a; so, rightly, RSV). 'For why should my freedom be judged by another's conscience?' (1 Cor. 10:29b). That is to say, 'Why should the expression of my Christian liberty be determined by another person's unexpressed scruples?' Just as there are limits to freedom, so too there are limits to the Christian slave's accommodation to others.

But alongside his repudiation of one type of bondage, Paul embraces another type of slavery. 1 Corinthians 9 is both a defence of Paul's freedom and rights and a statement of his self-imposed restriction of those apostolic rights (see especially v. 15, 'I have made no use of any of these rights'). In a tantalizing paradox, he enunciates his *modus operandi* in verse 19: 'Though I am free from all, I have enslaved (*edoulōsa*) myself to all people [cf. Mark 10:44], so that I might win the largest number of converts possible.'[23] Paul was 'free from all', not only in the sense that he was financially independent of

[22] According to Martin (1990: 64–68), however, 1 Cor. 7:22–23 relates not to the abolition of status distinctions but to their reversal, to 'status improvement', so that the expression 'slave of Christ' is 'a *lower* status indicator' than 'freedperson of Christ' (67). On this, see chapter 7.

[23] In 1 Corinthians 9 Paul draws on 'two traditionally opposed concepts of status, that of the free man and of the slave. One of honour the other of shame. He is a free man who has the right and power to act as he chooses (vv. 1–14). He is a slave who has no rights and is bound to carry out his obligations (vv. 15–18)' (P. Marshall 1987: 304).

his converts (vv. 12b–18), but also in the sense that he was in bondage to no human being (*cf.* 1 Cor. 7:23) and to no circumstance (*cf.* Phil. 4:11–12) and had been emancipated from sin and the law. Yet, in Christlike fashion (*cf.* Phil. 2:7), he had assumed the role of a slave, surrending his liberties and devoting himself to the cause of evangelism, whether that entailed accommodation to the Jews or to the Gentiles or to the weak (vv. 20–22). This self-imposed slavery aimed at extending the borders of the kingdom, at enabling as many people as possible to share in the blessings of the gospel (v. 23).

But the horizontal implications of slavery to God or Christ stretch still further. Not only are Christian believers, like Paul, the slaves of unbelievers for the gospel's sake; they are irrevocably committed to give to one another a slave's service. Matthew 20:20–28 records the request of the mother of the sons of Zebedee for positions of pre-eminent honour for her two sons in Jesus' coming kingdom. When the other ten disciples became indignant at the forwardness and selfishness of these two brothers (their mother was their initial spokesperson), Jesus addressed all of his disciples. 'You know that the rulers of the Gentiles rule over them like lords (*katakyrieuousin autōn*) and their high officials exercise authority over them. It is not to be so among you. Instead, whoever wants to be great among you must be your servant (*hymōn diakonos*), and whoever wants to be first among you must be your slave (*hymōn doulos*) – just as the Son of Man did not come to be served (*diakonēthēnai*) but to serve (*diakonēsai*) and to give his life as a ransom for many' (vv. 25–28). In verses 26–27 the words 'great' and 'first' reflect the woman's request for the 'right-hand' and 'left-hand' positions for her sons (v. 21), and are starkly contrasted with the terms 'servant' and 'slave', their virtual opposites in the estimation of the twelve disciples.[24] Jesus was teaching that greatness in the community of his followers is marked by humble, self-effacing servanthood or slavery, modelled on his own selfless devotion to the highest good of others.[25] Then there is John 13:16, that applies the dictum 'The slave (*doulos*) is not greater

---

[24] The emphatic position of *diakonos* and *doulos* at the end of their respective clauses focuses attention on this 'great reversal' in Jesus' teaching.

[25] In the Markan account of this episode (Mark 10:35–45) the *diakonos–doulos* parallelism is also found, but instead of 'your slave' (*hymōn doulos*, Matt. 20:27) we find 'slave of all' (*pantōn doulos*, Mark 10:44). Yet it is unlikely that Mark is emphasizing that the obligation of servitude is universal (true though that be), for like Matthew (20:26) he earlier has the words, 'It is not to be so *among you* [my disciples]' (Mark 10:43); in the context, '(slave) of all' refers to all Jesus' disciples, *viz.* the Twelve and others.

than his master' to the obligation that falls on those who call Jesus 'Teacher' and 'Lord' (*kyrios*) (v. 13) to do as their Master had done (vv. 4–5) and 'wash one another's feet' by self-sacrificial service (vv. 14–15).

In the epistles, too, the obligations of Christians to one another are expressed by the metaphor of slavery. In 2 Corinthians 4:1–6 Paul describes the Christian gospel as God's agent for the dispelling of the spiritual darkness created by Satan, the god of the present age. The gospel light consists of the glory of Christ, who is the outward and perfect representation (*eikōn*) of God (v. 4). This being so, it comes as no surprise that the apostle then affirms, 'It is not ourselves that we proclaim, but Jesus Christ as Lord (*kyrios*)' (v. 5a). The lordship of Jesus the Messiah is at the heart of the good news. But the same Greek sentence continues, 'and ourselves as your slaves (*doulous hymōn*) for Jesus' sake' (v. 5b). It is tempting (and certainly grammatically possible) to regard the conjunction *de* here as meaning 'and therefore', and not simply 'and':[26] 'It is not ourselves that we present, but Jesus Christ as Lord, *and therefore* ourselves as your slaves.' However that be, there is clearly a precise parallelism between 'Jesus Christ as Lord' and 'ourselves as your slaves'. This parallelism and the natural sequence of thought from lordship to slavery (*kyrion ... doulous*) suggests that acknowledgment of the lordship of Jesus leads naturally and inevitably to lowly, unquestioning service to one's fellow-believers. To confess 'Jesus is Lord' is to say to other followers of Jesus, 'I am your slave.' Slavery to Christ is exhibited in slavery to Christians. Because of their willing servitude to Christ, and as part of it, Christians are unconditionally obligated to serve Christ's people. Following Paul's example, they are to view their relationship to Christ *and* their relationship to fellow-Christians as one of slavery, as a relationship in which they render unquestioning service for the benefit of others. There were, however, two important differences between these two relationships of which Paul speaks. First, the Corinthians were not Paul's lord any more than he was their lord (*cf.* 2 Cor. 1:24). His service to them was 'for Jesus' sake' – only Jesus was 'Lord'. Second, Paul not obliged always and everywhere to obey and please the Corinthians as he was his heavenly Lord.

---

[26] There is certainly no contrast between v. 5a and v. 5b, as though Paul were saying, 'We do not proclaim ourselves (as Lord) but as your slaves'. In v. 5b the implied *kēryssomen* will bear a general sense such as 'we present', or we may supply *logizometha* ('we consider'), or this may be a case of zeugma.

John 13:16 and 2 Corinthians 4:5 stand alone in the New Testament in directly associating slave-like service to fellow-believers with the recognition of the lordship of Christ, and suggesting that one follows naturally from the other. But without the slavery imagery, 2 Corinthians 8:5 creates a comparable parallelism. As Paul describes the nature of the Macedonians' 'rich generosity' (2 Cor. 8:2) in contributing to the collection 'for the poor among the saints in Jerusalem' (Rom. 15:26), he notes that they gave far more generously than their slender means and adverse circumstances really permitted them (2 Cor. 8:2); that, acting on their own initiative, they urgently pleaded with Paul for the privilege of fellowship in the collection (2 Cor. 8:3c, 4); and that they outstripped Paul's expectations by not restricting their contribution to financial aid. 'On the contrary', says Paul, 'they gave themselves [in glad service] first to the Lord (*kyrios*) and then [as a consequence] to us, in keeping with God's will' (2 Cor. 8:5). Clearly they recognized that dedication to Christ involves dedication to his servants, and that dedication to them was in reality service for Christ. All was part of God's will. Finally, Galatians 5:13 makes the horizontal obligation explicit, using the figure of slavery but with no reference to Christ's lorship. 'You were called, my brothers and sisters, to be free. But do not use that freedom as an opportunity for fleshly indulgence. Rather, with acts of love (*dia tēs agapēs*),[27] render a slave's service (*douleuete*) to one another.' Slavery and love are perfectly compatible in the divine economy!

There is a beautiful example of this dual slavery, upwards and outwards, in the last chapter of Colossians. Epaphras was a trusted colleague of Paul who had been involved in the evangelization of the Lycus Valley (*cf.* Col. 1:7–8). He is described as 'a slave (*doulos*) of Christ Jesus', and then a twofold outworking of this slavery is given. He was always wrestling in prayer for the Colossians, that with maturity and conviction they would stand firm in doing all the will of God. Also, he toiled hard for the three churches of the Lycus Valley (Col. 4:12–13). Slavery to Christ was expressed in earnest prayer and strenuous toil for his people.

The term *doulos* expresses both a vertical and a horizontal relationship of the Christian, who is both the willing vassal of the heavenly Master and the submissive servant of fellow-believers. The term epitomizes the Christian's dual obligation: unquestioning devotion to

---

[27] This articular use of *agapē* points to specific, concrete expressions of love (see Zerwick 1963: 57 §176).

Christ and to his people.[28] But the vertical relationship is prior and the horizontal secondary. Christians are devoted to one another as a direct result of being devoted to Christ. When they serve each other, they are demonstrating and expressing their slavery to the Lord Christ.

[28] This twofold obligation mirrors the two primary senses of Paul's ubiquitous 'in Christ' formula (a correlation suggested by G. A. Okesson in his 1993 MA thesis at Wheaton College, Illinois, entitled 'Pauline Usage of *doulos* as a Paradigm for Living in Christ'): 'in [personal union with the risen] Christ', which is the individual dimension of the phrase; and 'in [the body of] Christ', the church, which is the corporate aspect of the formula.

Chapter Six

Slavery and ownership

Thus far I have generally illustrated my points from New Testament verses in which some form of the *doulos* root appears. In this chapter I shall often move beyond the technical terms related to slavery, to a group of broader concepts associated with slavery. Ownership is one such concept, and this will afford a convenient focal point for discussion of several crucial aspects of the slavery metaphor.

The fact of ownership

In a fundamental sense slavery involves the absence of rights, especially the right to determine the course of one's life and the use of one's energies. What is denied the slave is freedom of action and freedom of movement; he cannot do what he wishes or go where he wishes. The faculty of free choice and the power of refusal are denied to him. The slave is basically 'a possession, something owned, which itself cannot own' (Westermann 1974: 18).[1] To be a slave was to be the property of another person, who could use or dispose of that 'property' as if it were some inanimate chattel. In fact, the creation of the Roman legal category of a 'corporeal thing', as opposed to an 'incorporeal thing', was prompted by the phenomenon of slavery (see Patterson 1982: 31f.). The slave was the only human 'thing' (*res*)[2] and

---

[1] Westermann is summarizing A. Zimmern's view of the 'chattel slave'. The 1926 Convention of the League of National defined (chattel) slavery as 'the status or condition of a person over whom any or all of the powers attaching to the right of ownership are exercised' (cited by Fisher 1993: 5).

[2] But when Aristotle says that 'a slave is a living tool [or, instrument]; a tool [or, instrument] is a lifeless slave' (*Nic. Eth.* 8. 11), 'he is not telling us how he and his contemporaries saw, let alone treated, their own slaves, but conceptualizing the relationship between the man who give orders and the man who carries them out: a (free) ship's crew is equally the 'instrument' of the ship's captain' (Wiedemann 1981: 13). On the Aristotelian view, see above, chapter 2, n. 16. But Patterson (1982: 7) is using the word 'tool' in a derogatory sense when he asserts that 'the slave was the ultimate human tool, as imprintable and as disposable as the master wished'.

'the one human being who could be owned' (Buckland 1969: 3, 10).

Slavery, then, is a social institution in which one person owns another, and uses that person, forcibly if necessary, to perform his or her will.[3] Both the person and the labour are 'owned'. It is artificial to distinguish between the two, as if the labour could be forced yet the person not owned. In ancient slavery, it was the slave himself, and not simply his labour, that was the commodity for sale. What the master owned was not merely the slave's potential as a worker or his actual production, but his very person. Finley (1980: 74f.) expresses the point memorably: 'The slave, by being a slave, suffered not only "total loss of control over his labour" [O. Patterson] but total loss of control over his person and his personality: the uniqueness of slavery ... lay in the fact that the labourer himself was a commodity, not merely his labour or labour-power. His loss of control, furthermore, extended to the infinity of time, to his children and his children's children unless ... the owner by a unilateral act broke the chain through unconditional manumission'.[4]

Not without reason was a master of slaves called a slave-*owner*. This ownership was reflected in the identification of a slave as 'of' (= 'belonging to') a particular master or place. So, for example, a personal slave such as Onesimus (Philem. 10) would be known as 'Onesimus, [slave] of Philemon'; an imperial slave would be referred to as '*X* of our Caesar' (*Caesaris nostri*); and a public slave as '*X* of the settlement of Placentia' (*coloniae Placentinae*). When Paul speaks of *hoi Chloēs*, literally, 'those of Chloe' (1 Cor. 1:11), he is probably referring to 'slaves belonging to [the household of] Chloe'.

In a similar way, when Christian slaves are called 'slaves of Christ' (Eph. 6:6) and the Christian free person is designated 'the slave of Christ' (1 Cor. 7:22), the Greek word *Christou*, 'of Christ', is a genitive of possession, signifying 'belonging to Christ'. However, the Christian's slavery to Christ is never depicted by the simple genitive case without the term *doulos*; this word is always required to make the reference to slavery explicit. So, whereas *hoi Chloēs* (1 Cor. 1:11)

[3] When we say in English that a person is 'a slave to duty' or 'a slave to fashion', we are suggesting that the person is a helpless and hapless victim to an overpowering influence that in effect 'owns' the person. As Peter expresses it, 'That by which someone is overcome, by this he is enslaved', or 'People are slaves of anything that masters them' (2 Pet. 2:19).

[4] Finley (1974: 145) himself defines slavery as 'roughly the status in which a man is, in the eyes of the law and of public opinion and with respect to all other parties, a possession, a chattel, of another man'.

may mean 'Chloe's slaves', the parallel expression *hoi tou Christou* (1 Cor. 15:23; *cf.* Gal. 5:24) means simply 'those who belong to Christ', 'Christ's people', not 'Christ's slaves'. Or again, when Paul wishes to introduce himself as 'a slave of Christ Jesus', he writes *doulos Christou Iēsou* (Rom. 1:1), not simply *Christou Iēsou*, 'of Christ Jesus'.

'Belonging to Christ' (*Christou einai*, 2 Cor. 10:7) is the essence of the Christian faith.[5] To the Corinthian Christians Paul can say simply, 'You belong to Christ' (*hymeis [de] Christou*, 1 Cor. 3:23; *cf.* Gal. 3:29).[6] When he affirms that 'anyone who does not have the Spirit of Christ does not belong to him' (Rom. 8:9), the implication is clear: possession of Christ's Spirit is evidence of belonging to Christ. Later in Romans (14:8) Paul insists that in both life and death believers 'belong to the Lord'. Whereas Roman emancipation from slavery brought release 'not merely from ownership, but from the capacity of being owned' (Buckland 1969: 715), Christian emancipation from slavery to sin leads to new ownership. 'So, my brothers and sisters, through the crucified body of Christ you too died to the law, so that you may belong to another husband [= Christ], who was raised from the dead, in order that we might bear fruit for God' (Rom. 7:4).

We may profitably view baptism as a rite that marks a transfer of ownership – from being 'in subjection to the ruler of the realm of the air' (Eph. 2:2), 'the god of the present age' (2 Cor. 4:4), to being part of 'a people claimed by God for his own' (*laos eis peripoiēsin*, 1 Pet. 2:9, NEB). Baptism is sometimes described as being '*in* the name of Jesus Christ' (Acts 10:48), where the preposition *en* is used; sometimes, as being '*upon* [the confession of] the name of Jesus Christ' (Acts 2:38), where the preposition *epi* is used. But twice in Acts the distinctive phrase '*into/in* the name of the Lord Jesus' is found (Acts 8:16; 19:5), with the preposition *eis* being employed, as also in the Great Commission, 'Go and make disciples of all nations, baptizing them *into/in* the name of the Father and of the Son and of the Holy Spirit' (Matt. 28:19). Now while the prepositions *eis* and *en* are sometimes interchangeable or confused in Luke-Acts and Mark,

---

[5] In 2 Cor. 10:7, D* F G it[a] vg[mss] Ambrosiaster read *Christou doulos einai*, a reading that may reflect a claim of Paul's opponents to be the *douloi* of Christ as well as the *diakonoi* of Christ (2 Cor. 11:23; *cf.* 11:13).

[6] Although Paul dramatically reversed three of the Corinthian slogans – 'I belong to Paul', 'I belong to Apollos', and 'I belong to Cephas' (1 Cor. 1:12) – to read 'All things belong to you, whether Paul or Apollos or Cephas; all belong to you' (1 Cor. 3:21–22), he could not say, 'Christ belongs to you' to correspond to 'I belong to Christ' (1 Cor. 1:12), but only 'and you belong to Christ' (1 Cor. 3:23).

Matthew is not prone to this confusion (*cf.* Zerwick 1963: 35 §106), so that *at least* in the baptismal logion in Matthew we must reckon with the distinctive expression, baptism '*into* the name' (*eis to onoma*). In commercial usage this Greek phrase *eis to onoma* denoted a transference of ownership, as when money is paid 'into or to the account' of a certain individual, or is credited 'to the name of' someone (thus Heitmüller 1903: 127). On this understanding, the person being baptized passes into the possession of the Triune God (Matt. 28:19) or the Lord Jesus (Acts 8:16; 19:5), and comes under new control and protection. Support for this view comes from 1 Corinthians 1, where Paul equates being baptized into his name (*eis to onoma*) with belonging to him: 'One of you says, "I belong to Paul" … Were you baptized into the name of Paul? I am thankful that I did not baptize any of you except Crispus and Gaius, so that no-one can say that you were baptized into my name' (1 Cor. 1:12–15). So then, just as in commercial usage payment 'into' someone's name indicated a transfer of money into someone's account, so in baptism there is signified a transference of believers into the permanent possession and safe keeping of the omnipotent Trinity. In baptism God says to the believer, 'You belong to me. You are my adopted son, my adopted daughter, for ever.' And in response the believer says to God, 'I belong to you. I will be your willing slave for ever.' Believers are Christ's *indentured* slaves in the sense that, through baptism, they have become eternally bound to him by mutual agreement. Like the Hebrew slave whose ear lobe was pierced with an awl to signify that he loved his master and wished to be his slave for life (Exod. 21:5–6; Deut. 15:16–17), the disciples of Jesus submit to baptism as an indication that they love their new Master and pledge to serve him wholeheartedly as long as they live.

In Roman law a master's ownership of his slaves was absolute. The slave stood under the *dominica potestas*, 'the master's total sway'. Even under the Empire the absolute right of the 'head of the household' (the *paterfamilias*) to punish a slave with death – the so-called 'right of life and death' (*ius vitae necisque*) – remained intact, although that right was circumscribed, for a court's approval of such an execution was needed. K. R. Bradley (1994: 24) maintains that 'from a legal point of view the Latin words for power (*potestas*) and slaveownership (*dominium*) could be regarded as synonymous, which means that, above all, slaveowning was an expression of power'.[7]

---

[7] On *dominium* as absolute ownership and power, see Patterson 1982: 29–32.

So, being the subject of another person's right, the slave had no legal status as a person. 'The tension between the slave's total rightlessness in law and the fact that he was a human being meant that there had to be limits to the brutality which society would tolerate in practice – but these rules had to be phrased in such a way as not to challenge the absoluteness of the owner's theoretical rights' (Wiedemann 1981: 9)[8]

Not only the slave himself, but also the fruit of his toil, was 'owned' by the master. As Hopkins (1978: 117, cf. 126) notes: 'By buying a slave in the first place, a master had acquired the right of all the slave's labour and produce for the rest of his life, without further payment.' As a result, the services rendered by a slave did not place the owner under any obligation to the slave. Neither wages nor thanks became a slave's right after he had done his duty. Obedience did not merit reward; it was merely a fulfilment of duty. This is the background to Jesus' instruction to his followers who are his slaves. 'So you also, when you have obeyed all the orders given you, must say, "We are unworthy slaves (*douloi*): we have only done our duty"' (Luke 17:10). As slaves, we are unworthy of reward; but as slaves of a generous heavenly Master, we are the recipients of reward (Matt. 25:21, 23; cf. 1 Cor. 4:5).

Two Greek terms highlight the absoluteness of a master's ownership. The word *sōma* ('body') ranges in meaning in Greek literature from 'corpse' to 'person', with an emphasis on physicality. But as early as the third century BC, this word, without any qualifying adjective, was used to describe a slave (see LSJ, 1749), who was seen as basically a 'body', possessed by his master for his use. Aristotle

---

According to Patterson (*passim*), at the core of slavery is domination, which is exhibited in three ways: the coercion exercised by the slave-owner who possesses absolute power; the alienation of the slave from community life and rights; and the constant dishonouring of the slave. Patterson's 'preliminary definition of slavery on the level of personal relations' is as follows: 'slavery is the permanent, violent domination of natally alienated and generally dishonored persons' (13).

[8] Dealing with this 'rightlessness' of Roman slaves, Wiedemann (1981: 10) comments that 'whipping served to symbolize the absoluteness of the owner's power', and later (11) he notes that the Emperor 'Claudius' legislation in favour of sick slaves [is no] evidence for the theory that Roman emperors systematically attempted to improve the treatment slaves received, under the influence either of powerful *liberti* or of Stoic humanitarianism. The advice on how to make the most of slaves in earlier Greek philosophical handbooks discussing practical ethics may strike us as cynical, but there are no grounds for believing that in the Roman world humanitarian ideals of Jewish or Stoic provenance led to restrictions upon an owner's rights in law.'

(*Pol.* 125. 4a. 16) went one stage further: 'The slave is part of the master, in the sense of being a living but separate part of his body.' The plural *sōmata* is used once in the New Testament in reference to slaves, in an itemized list of cargo, but it is immediately qualified by the explanatory phrase, 'that is, human beings' (Rev. 18:13).[9]

The other term is *despotēs* ('master', 'lord') which originally referred to an 'owner' or 'possessor' of persons or things within a household – a sense made explicit by the compound word *oikodespotēs*, 'the master of the house'.[10] When this term is applied to God[11] or to Jesus,[12] it emphasizes absoluteness of ownership, of authority, and of power. Clearly *despotēs* and *kyrios* largely overlap in meaning; both may be rendered 'lord' or 'master'. If we are to distinguish the two terms with regard to emphasis, *kyrios* signifies 'sovereign Lord', and *despotēs* 'absolute Lord'.

Nowhere in the New Testament is the absoluteness of the Lord's ownership of his *douloi* depicted more clearly than in Romans 14:7–8: 'None of us [Christians] lives for his own benefit alone, and none dies in relation to himself alone. If we live, it is for the Lord's benefit; and if we die, it is to the Lord's glory. So then, whether we live or die, we belong to the Lord.' Notable is the threefold repetition of *kyrios* in verse 8: the Master is the focal point of the slave's life; everything is evaluated in terms of the Master's pleasure and profit. The absoluteness is depicted in temporal terms – the Master's good reigns supreme, whether in continuation of his slave's life or with the advent of his slave's death. Believers are divine property, invested at the discretionary will of the Master for his own profit.

Another characteristic of slave ownership in the ancient world was exclusivity. The slave was not only at his master's disposal (= absoluteness), but also at *only* his master's disposal, unavailable for service to another. This is reflected in Paul's response to his own rhetorical question. 'Who are you', he asks the 'strong' and the 'weak' in Rome, 'to judge someone else's slaves? To their *own* master (*tō idiō kyriō*) they stand or fall' (Rom. 14:4). Now exceptionally, one and the same slave could in fact belong to more than one master. An inscription that dates from about AD 100 refers to a slave

[9] On this verse see further Appendix 2, n. 10.

[10] As with *kyrios*, the terms *despotēs* and *oikodespotēs* are naturally associated with *doulos* (*e.g.*, Titus 2:9 and Matt. 13:27 respectively).

[11] Luke 2:29; Acts 4:24; 2 Tim. 2:21; Rev. 6:10.

[12] Only at 2 Pet. 2:1 and Jude 4 (which has 'our only Master and Lord, Jesus Christ', *ton monon despotēn kai kyrion hēmōn Iēsoun Christon*).

who belongs in common to three brothers.[13] Sometimes even a share in a slave could be bought and sold. But, from a psychological standpoint, the aphorism of Jesus is certainly true: 'No-one can be a slave (*douleuein*) to two masters' (Matt. 6:24; Luke 16:13).[14] C. Spicq (1994: 1. 381 n. 4) notes that Euboulos had already stated this axiom memorably: 'a slave with two masters is a nobody from nowhere.'[15] No person can simultaneously please two masters who have different desires. No-one can serve two masters wholeheartedly since no-one can simultaneously belong exclusively to two masters.

The *Shema* is the Jewish confession of faith in the oneness and uniqueness of God: 'Hear, O Israel: the LORD our God, the LORD is one' (Deut. 6:4).[16] 1 Corinthians 8:6 is a Christianized *Shema*: 'For us there is one God, the Father, from whom are all things and for whom we exist, and one Lord, Jesus Christ, through whom are all things and through whom we exist.' When believers confess their allegiance to the 'one Lord, Jesus Christ', they are not only repudiating any adherence to other 'lords' (1 Cor. 8:5) but also acknowledging the exclusive rights that the Lord Jesus has over every domain of their lives. Corresponding to Christ's absolute and exclusive ownership of believers in him is their total and sole devotion to him. Isaiah 44:5 indicates that after the exile some faithful Jews would unashamedly say, 'I belong to Yahweh', while others would actually write 'Yahweh's' on their hands, to indicate whose slaves they were.[17] Most Christians do not bear any 'brand-marks of Jesus' (Gal. 6:17) as Paul did, but they may rightly say, 'I belong to Christ' (*cf.* 1 Cor. 1:12), and may, figuratively speaking, write 'Christ's' on their hands, to indicate whose slaves they are.

---

[13] For details, see Spicq 1994: 1. 381 n. 4. For Jewish examples, see Rengstorf 1964: 2. 270 n. 66.

[14] 'Jesus is not attacking the actual position of a *doulos* under two masters. He is attacking the man who suffers from the illusion that he could do what is implied by *douleuein* without concentrating all of his powers on rendering *douleia* ['a slave's service'] in the sense of an exclusive commitment and obligation' (Rengstorf 1964: 2. 270f.).

[15] *Amphidoulos = oudamothen oudeis.*

[16] This credal declaration is called the *Shema* because the first (Hebrew) word of Deut. 6:4 is *šᵉma'* ('hear').

[17] A fifth-century BC Aramaic papyrus from Elephantine refers to a Jewish female slave who had the name of her master ('Of Meshullam') inscribed on her right hand (Pritchard, ed., 1969: 548).

The means of ownership

We move on now to consider the ways in which literal slavery was entered and metaphorical slavery is entered. I do not mean to suggest that there is any correspondence between the two, as though some New Testament writers, knowing the ways in which people became slaves, used that knowledge in describing slavery to Christ. Nevertheless, to treat literal and figurative slavery together, with regard to means of entry, may shed light on some New Testament imagery.

In the ancient world a person became a slave, the disposable property of another, in one of four basic ways:[18] (a) by birth into a family of slaves; (b) by self-sale; (c) by capture; and (d) by purchase. Each of these may now be considered in more detail. But let me stress again that nowhere does the New Testament explicitly link any one of these ways of becoming a literal slave with a person's becoming a slave of Christ. Indeed, *slavery by birth* is unlikely to be so linked, since the New Testament clearly indicates that by nature, that is, by literal birth, we become, figuratively speaking, 'slaves of sin' (Rom. 6:17; *cf.* Eph. 2:3; Titus 3:3). That is, what is already associated with 'birth' is slavery to sin, not slavery to righteousness.

Although the Stoics viewed voluntary slavery as despicable (Seneca, *Ep.* 47. 17), self-sale was not an uncommon practice in the first century AD (see Bartchy 1973: 46–49, 109 nn. 416f.).[19] There were three main motives behind *self-sale into slavery*, whether it was temporary enslavement or became permanent: to relieve economic pressure or actually prevent financial disaster; to gain special posts that might prove lucrative; and even (on occasion) to climb the social ladder and so gain prestige and ultimately wealth.[20] Paul may allude

---

[18] There were, of course, other ways in which people became slaves, such as the sale of children by their parents, either because of abject poverty or because of famine; conviction of serious crime (such convicts [*servi poenae*, 'penal slaves'] often worked in the mines or quarries); piracy and brigandage, which was a very profitable enterprise when slaves were scarce; and exposure of infants, which led to their slavery if they were rescued. See further Harrill 1995: 30–42.

[19] Among Ancient Near Eastern law codes, only OT legislation mentions voluntary slavery (Mendelsohn 1962: 4. 384).

[20] On the latter point, persons sometimes sold themselves into slavery so that as slaves with responsibility within the household of a Roman citizen they might soon become freed persons enjoying not merely a better financial situation than before the self-sale but also the rights of citizenry and the possibility of becoming the parent of free-born children. See further, chapter 7.

to this practice when, in Romans 6:16, he writes: 'Don't you know that when you offer yourselves as someone's slaves to obey him, you are the slaves of the one you obey?' On the other hand (*pace* Bartchy 1973: 48, 181), it is improbable that Paul is addressing this issue when he says to the Corinthians, 'Do not become the slaves of people' (1 Cor. 7:23), which is more probably an injunction against submission to legalists of any type. But we do know from 1 Clement 55:2 (written about AD 96) that some Christians in Rome were selling themselves into slavery – no doubt temporary slavery or indentured servitude – in order to provide money for the manumission of others or for food for the needy: 'We know that many among us have given themselves over to bondage in order to ransom others. Many have given themselves over to slavery and provided food for others with the sale-price they received for themselves.'

Is slavery to Christ in any sense self-imposed? From one perspective, people become Christ's slaves by his purchase of them: 'You do not belong to yourselves, for you were bought [by Christ] at a price' (1 Cor. 6:19–20). Yet from another perspective, 'conversion' may be seen as a human act. 'You turned to God from idols, in order to serve (*douleuein*) the living and true God' (1 Thess. 1:9). Note the active sense, 'you turned' (*epestrepsate*), and the purpose, expressed by a verb of the *doulos* family. Both these aspects of the issue – the divine and the human – are represented in Romans 6:15–23, which also refers to ongoing slavery (v. 19): 'You were enslaved to righteousness … you were enslaved to God' (vv. 18, 22), where the passive voice implies divine agency and a state of slavery is assumed. On the other side, we have several references to human action. 'When you offer yourselves to someone' (v. 16); 'you wholeheartedly obeyed the pattern of teaching to which you were entrusted' (v. 17); 'now offer them [the parts of your body] in slavery to righteousness' (v. 19). The two truths are complementary, not antithetical. Entering into slavery and continuance in slavery are the result of both divine and human action – provided we never forget the prevenience of God's grace with respect to all human virtue.

Christian slavery, then, is *unlike* self-sale into slavery in that Christ bought his slaves (Rev. 5:9) and they did not sell themselves; but it is *like* self-sale into slavery in that they voluntarily embraced slavery to Christ and were not forced into slavery against their will. Only in a limited sense, then, can we say that the practice of self-sale formed the cultural background to the New Testament call to Christians, whether freeborn or slave, to regard themselves as 'the slaves of Christ'.

We turn now to *slavery through capture*. We could surmise that the practice of slavery began when prisoners of war were not slain (as had been the practice *ex hypothesi*), but were spared and retained as a free labour force for the victors. Whatever the origin of slavery, Roman military success meant that many thousands of captives were regularly brought to the slave markets of Italy for sale.

We have seen (pp. 53f.) that Paul excoriates kidnapping or dealing in slaves (1 Tim. 1:10). Consequently he is unlikely to portray conversion as an act of divine brigandage or as spiritual kidnapping! Nevertheless, there are several places where he appears to depend on the notion of 'capture' in describing conversion or the Christian life.

1. The first is Philippians 3:12, where, referring to his own conversion, Paul says that Christ 'laid hold of him' or had 'made him his own'. This graphic verb, *katalambanō*, means 'seize with a firm grip', as when a person is apprehended as a wrongdoer. It was as though Paul had been overtaken and arrested in his flight from God. To use Petrine terminology, Christ had 'mastered' Paul, so that Paul became Christ's possession or slave, on the principle that 'a person is a slave to whatever has mastered him' (2 Pet. 2:19).

2. Another colourful verb expressing capture occurs twice in the Pauline corpus. *Thriambeuō* means 'lead in triumphal procession', the picture being that of a Roman 'triumph' (*triumphus*). When a Roman general had conducted a successful military operation abroad, it was the prerogative of the senate, or later the emperor, to appoint a day on which the populace could join in a public expression of gratitude to the general and his soldiers – and to the gods – for their success in warfare. The whole proceedings were called a 'triumph'. At the head of the procession were the senators, dressed in white, followed by musicians and dancers, then samples of the trophies of war such as golden objects and art, and finally the wretched prisoners of war driven in chains in front of the general's chariot and the jubilant soldiers. In Colossians 2:15 we read that 'after disarming the powers and authorities, he [God] boldly displayed them in public by leading them in triumphal procession in the person of Christ'. Clearly, in this use of the imagery, the 'powers and authorities' are the enemy captives of Christ, the triumphant general. In 2 Corinthians 2:14, however, it is the apostles or Christians in general who are led in triumphal procession, as Paul pictures the irresistible advance of the

gospel, in spite of temporary frustration: 'But thanks be to God, who always leads us in Christ's triumphal procession, and through us spreads everywhere the fragrance of the knowledge of him.' Now it could be that Christians are here seen as exultant soldiers who share in the benefits of Christ's victory (*cf.* Rom. 8:37), but it is more likely, since the object of the verb *thriambeuō* is usually the war captives, that Christians are being viewed as Christ's willing captives who count it a privilege to be caught up in Christ's magnificent 'triumph'.

3. On three occasions Paul calls a colleague his *synaichmalōtos*, which means literally, 'fellow-prisoner of war': Andronicus and Iunia(s) in Romans 16:7, Aristarchus in Colossians 4:10 and Epaphras in Philemon 23. Now it is possible that these four colleagues had earlier actually been imprisoned with Paul or that (in the case of Aristarchus and Epaphras) they were voluntarily sharing Paul's imprisonment at the time of writing.[21] But since Paul was not technically an *aichmalōtos*, a 'prisoner *of war*', and he does not use one of the three Greek terms for a literal 'fellow-prisoner',[22] it seems more likely that this term is figurative, not literal, in meaning,[23] and describes these four fellow-workers as the voluntary bondslaves of Christ, along with Paul (*cf. syn-*, literally 'with' or 'fellow-').[24] Accordingly, the NEB renders the term 'Christ's captive like myself' in Colossians 4:10 and Philemon 23, and 'comrades in captivity' in Romans 16:7.

4. In several places we encounter the phrase, 'the prisoner of Christ Jesus' (*desmios Christou Iēsou*, Eph. 3:1; Philem. 1, 9) or its equivalent, 'his prisoner' (*ton desmion autou*, 2 Tim. 1:8). In the case of these three letters – Ephesians, Philemon and 2 Timothy – it is clear that Paul is incarcerated (see Eph. 6:20; Philem. 10, 13, 22; 2 Tim. 1:16), so that this self-description may simply refer to the literal imprisonment that he is currently experiencing.[25] Indeed, the presence

[21] In each of the three verses, the GNB has 'who were/is in prison with me'.

[22] *Viz., syndesmios, syndedemenos,* or *syndesmōtēs.*

[23] In defence of the figurative sense, see Kittel 1964a: 1. 196f.; 1964b: 2. 43 (in *synaichmalōtos* there is an 'application of the image of the apostle's subjection to bondage to Christ'). The verb *aichmalōtizō* bears a figurative sense in Rom. 7:23; 2 Cor. 10:5; 2 Tim. 3:6.

[24] It is also significant that Epaphras, whom Paul calls 'a fellow-prisoner [of Christ]' (Philem. 23), is during the same period described by Paul as 'a fellow-slave [of Christ]' (*syndoulos*, Col. 1:7) and 'a slave (*doulos*) of Christ Jesus' (Col. 4:12).

[25] Rapske proposes that while Paul saw himself as a slave of Christ at all times, he 'only calls himself Christ's prisoner as it is temporally and circumstantially appropriate;

of the phrase 'and now also' (*nyni de kai*) in Philemon 9 would dictate that there physical incarceration must be principally in Paul's mind: 'Paul, an ambassador, *and now also* a prisoner of Christ Jesus ...' There are, indeed, some commentators and translators who settle for the literal sense of 'prisoner' (*desmios*), taking the genitive 'of Christ Jesus' as one of purpose, 'a prisoner *for the sake of* Christ Jesus'.[26] But there is no reason not to regard this particular genitive as pointing to a multifaceted relationship:[27] 'for the sake of Christ Jesus' (purpose), 'because of [my service for] Christ Jesus' (cause); and also 'belonging to Christ Jesus' (possession), 'captured by Christ Jesus' (agency).[28] On this view the word 'prisoner' is both literal and figurative in meaning.[29] I suggest that Paul saw himself not merely as someone who was in prison because of his witness for Christ and for Christ's sake but also as someone whom Christ himself had captured and imprisoned and now possessed as his slave.

Now it must be admitted that capture need not lead to slavery, but since in the ancient world prisoners of war were generally reduced to slavery, the movement of thought from 'prisoner' to 'slave', in either a literal or a metaphorical sense, is minimal. The ideas of capture and enslavement are so closely related that they may be said to belong to the same semantic domain.

The fourth way in which a person became enslaved was *by purchase*, usually at a slave market. By the first century AD there was a decline in the number of war captives, so that the demand for slaves elevated their price. We saw in chapter 2 that an unskilled male adult slave cost between 500 and 600 denarii, with a skilled slave, who might be used as a tutor, craftsman or a vinedresser, fetching as much as 2,000 denarii. When one remembers that Roman soldiers received

---

i.e., when he is *actually* a prisoner' (1991: 194 n. 45).

[26] *E.g.*, with reference to Philem. 1, O'Brien 1982: 271; GNB. It is of interest that while the RSV has 'a prisoner for Christ Jesus' in Philem. 1, 9, the NRSV has the more open-ended 'a prisoner of Christ Jesus'.

[27] Regarding the similarly rich genitive *tou Christou* ('of Christ') in 2 Cor. 5:14 and Mark 1:1, Zerwick (1963: 13 §36) writes: 'In interpreting the sacred text ... we must beware lest we sacrifice to clarity of meaning part of the fulness of the meaning.' For a different analysis of the phrase *desmios Christou Iēsou*, see Wansink 1996: 147–156, 173f.

[28] Winer (1872: 189) remarks that '*desmios Christou a prisoner of Christ* means one whom Christ (the cause of Christ) has made and keeps a prisoner'.

[29] See also M. Barth 1974: 360f. Caird (1976: 218) comments: 'Not only is Paul in a Roman prison for Christ's sake, he is also Christ's prisoner, and the metaphorical imprisonment is the cause of the literal.'

a salary of only 225 denarii per year, one can see that an unskilled slave cost two to three times the annual keep of a Roman soldier, and a skilled slave almost ten times as much.

The main New Testament verb denoting purchase is *agorazō*, meaning 'buy in the market-place', and more generally, 'buy', 'acquire as property'. Most of its twenty-five New Testament uses are in the gospels, with purely commercial overtones; but on several occasions it depicts the 'purchase' of Christians. Twice the purchaser is indicated, *viz.* Christ (2 Pet. 2:1; Rev. 5:9); once, the purchase price, *viz.* the blood of Christ (Rev. 5:9); once, the ultimate possessor, *viz.* God (Rev. 5:9); and once, the thing from which the purchase separates, *viz.* the earth (Rev. 14:3 of the 144,000).

The two uses of *agorazō* in 1 Corinthians (*viz.* 6:20; 7:23) are of special relevance to our theme, since in one of these verses (7:23) the term *douloi* occurs. In the second half of 1 Corinthians 6 (vv. 12–20) Paul is countering the libertines at Corinth who apparently believed, on the basis of the premiss that matter was inherently evil, that actions involving the physical body were morally indifferent. So their watch-cries were, 'Everything is permissible for me' (v. 12), 'Food is meant for the stomach, and the stomach for food' (v. 13), and 'The body is intended for immorality' (*cf.* v. 13), as they sought to justify their actions in visiting prostitutes. Paul enumerates a succession of reasons why sexual immorality must be repudiated. The body is meant to honour the Lord (v. 13); resurrection involves the body (v. 14); the body is a member of Christ (v. 15); physical unity with a prostitute compromises spiritual unity with the Lord (vv. 16–17); sexual immorality is a sin against one's own body (v. 18); the body is the temple of the Holy Spirit (v. 19); as purchased property, Christians do not belong to themselves (vv. 19–20). In establishing this latter point, Paul introduces a slogan of his own, 'You were bought at a price.' Neither the purchaser nor the price is mentioned, which suggests that this was a stock phrase of Pauline theology. There can be no doubt about the identity of the purchaser, for Christ is the subject of the compound verb *exagorazō* ('buy out', 'redeem') in Galatians 3:13 and 4:5. As for the price paid, it is clearly the blood of Christ, given the close parallels in Revelation 5:9 ('with your blood you purchased (*ēgorasas*) people for God') and 1 Peter 1:18–19 ('you were redeemed … with the precious blood of Christ').[30] The

---

[30] Peter can be said to hint at an association between purchase and slavery. Redeemed from futility by means of 'the precious blood of Christ' (1 Pet. 1:18–19), believers have

movement of Paul's thought seems to be: 'You do not belong to yourselves, but are the exclusive property of Christ, for (*gar*) he purchased you at the price of his own blood'.[31] That is to say, purchase gives the right to possession; ownership is the corollary of purchase. The same point is made in 2 Peter 2:1: 'There will be false teachers among you who will secretly introduce destructive heresies, even denying the Master (*despotēn*) who bought (*agorasanta*) them.' The effrontery of these false teachers was seen in their rejection of divine ownership after divine purchase.

The second place where Paul uses his streamlined theological slogan is 1 Corinthians 7:23: 'You were bought at a price; do not become slaves (*douloi*) of people.' As at 1 Corinthians 6:20, the imagery is that of transfer of ownership, of becoming someone's slave through purchase. But what is perhaps implicit in 6:20 become explicit in the immediate context of 7:23: the aphorism applies both to the situation of the free person who becomes enslaved and to the situation of the slave who becomes free. By one and the same purchase of Christ, the free person becomes Christ's slave (*cf.* 7:22b) and the slave becomes the Lord's freed person (*cf.* 7:22a).[32] For the one, the purchase leads to slavery; for the other, the purchase leads to freedom. But either way, the result was the same – they were not to let themselves become enslaved to mere human beings (v. 23b). Slave or free, they were now the exclusive property of Christ; they were his slaves.[33]

---

collectively become 'a people that is God's own property' (1 Pet. 2:9) and individually people who are 'God's slaves (*douloi*)' (1 Pet. 2:16).

[31] The next verse (1 Cor. 6:20) may be paraphrased, 'So, then, honour your new owner, God, with your whole personality.' While, in NT thought, the purchaser and the price paid are uniform (*viz.* Christ and his blood), the new owner as the result of the purchase is seen as either Christ (Rom. 14:8; 1 Cor. 3:23; 7:22–23; 15:23; Gal. 3:29; 5:24; Titus 2:14) or God (Acts 20:28; 1 Cor. 6:19–20; Rev. 5:9).

[32] Whereas Seneca argues that a slave *may* be a free person, and a free person *may* be a slave, Paul asserts that in Christ a free person *is* a slave, and a slave *is* free (Sevenster 1961: 191).

[33] 'The man who belongs to the slave class is actually, like all Christians, a freedman while the freedman in society is actually, like all Christians, a slave of the Lord. All, regardless of their social class, have been freed and all have, as a result, been reduced to servitude' (Russell 1968: 49–50). We should note that in 1 Cor. 7:22 Paul distinguishes between the person born free (*eleutheros*, Lat. *liber*) and the freed slave (*apeleutheros*; Lat. *libertus* or *libertinus*). A freed person was called *libertinus* in reference to his status in society, but *libertus* with respect to his former master, his manumitter. Metaphorically, in reference to sin, the believer is a freed slave (*apeleutheros*), freed by Christ from slavery to sin. In relation to Christ, the believer is an enslaved freed person, enslaved to

G. A. Deissmann (1965: 322–330) found the background to these two Corinthian passages in the process of 'sacral manumission' by which a god fictitiously purchased a slave 'for freedom' (*ep' eleutheriai*) from his earthly master.[34] Let Deissmann himself explain the process: 'The owner comes with the slave to the temple, sells him there to the god, and receives the purchase money from the temple treasury, the slave having previously paid it in there out of his savings. The slave is now the property of the god; not, however, a slave of the temple, but a protégé of the god. Against all the world, especially his former master, he is a completely free man; at the outset a few pious obligations to his old master are imposed upon him' (322). A sample inscription from Delphi, dating from 200/199 BC, records the transaction:

> Apollo the Pythian bought from Sosibius of Amphissa, for freedom, a female slave, whose name is Nicaea, by race a Roman, with a price of three minae of silver and a half-mina. Former seller according to the law: Eumnastus of Amphissa. The price he has received. The purchase price, however, Nicaea has committed to Apollo, for freedom (323).[35]

From this it becomes clear that the purchase by Apollo is merely fictitious, as is his ownership of the slave. Nicaea purchased her own freedom, no doubt using her *peculium*, with the temple priest simply acting as an intermediary between owner and slave. The main point of the god's involvement was to guarantee the contract and protect the ex-slave from any further enslavement.

There are, indeed, certain striking similarities between this form of manumission and Christian redemption, *viz.* a price paid for the permanent release of a slave; a divine figure and sacrifice were involved in the transaction; the manumission was 'for freedom' (*ep' eleutheriai*; *cf.* Gal. 5:1, 13). But the differences are also significant: (a) in the New Testament concept of redemption, it is the divine figure, Christ, who pays the price for release, not the slave who is to

---

Christ after being freed from sin. Ignatius, however, regarded his becoming Christ's freedman (*apeleutheros*) to be a future experience after suffering and through resurrection (*Rom.* 4:3).

[34] For a critique of Deissmann's view, see Bömer 1960: 2. 133–141; and, more briefly, Büchsel 1964: 1. 124–126; Bartchy 1973: 121–125.

[35] More than 1,000 Delphic manumission contracts have been found, dating from 200 BC to about AD 75.

be freed; (b) there is no indication of the former master nor of the one to whom the price is paid; (c) while Christians are permanently free, they are also enslaved to a new Master; (d) Christ's ownership of his new slaves is real, not fictitious; (e) the Christian has no obligation of any sort to his former master; and (f) the verb denoting purchase is *agorazein*, not *priasthai* (as in the Delphi contracts), a word never found in the New Testament.

Given these significant differences, we would be wiser to locate the background to 1 Corinthians 6:20 and 7:23 in the Old Testament concept of God's 'redemption-acquisition' of the people of Israel after their Egyptian bondage (*e.g.*, Exod. 6:6; Ps. 74:2) to become his treasured possession (Exod. 19:5–6; Deut. 26:18; Mal. 3:17) (thus Cruz 1990: 118) and in the contemporary practice of manumission seen as effecting a 'change of ownership as a result of payment of a price' (I. H. Marshall 1974: 159).[36]

The theme of 'purchase leading to ownership' may also be present in Acts 20:28, but more probably we find there the broader motif of 'ownership through acquisition'. In his farewell speech at Miletus, Paul exhorts the Ephesian elders 'to shepherd the church of God which he obtained (*periepoiēsato*) with the blood of his own Son'. Although this verb *peripoieomai* may mean 'preserve for oneself' (something already possessed), here it means 'acquire for oneself' (something not yet possessed). The phrase that follows, 'with the blood' (*dia tou haimatos*), specifies the means by which the acquisition was made, not the price of a purchase (which would be *en tō haimati* or simply *tou haimatos*). Just as God had originally acquired a people to be his treasured possession through a covenant ratified by blood (Exod. 19:5–6; 24:3–8; Is. 43:21, *periepoiēsamen*), so now he has secured for himself the church to be his distinctive people, 'a people belonging to God' (*laos eis peripoiēsin*, 1 Pet. 2:9), by means of the shed blood of his own Son. In this verse the church is said to be 'the church *of God*', because he acquired it 'for himself' or 'as his own' (the sense of the middle voice here).

We conclude that whether believers are seen as belonging to Christ as his slaves because of their own choice of this slavery, or as a result

---

[36] I. H. Marshall (1974: 159) recognizes this same dual background. He also refers to the background proposed by Elert 1947: 265–270: prisoners of war were sometimes 'released and returned to their native land on payment of a ransom by a fellow-citizen. The freedman stood under certain obligations to the person who had redeemed him, as a *libertus* to his *patronus*, until he had paid back the cost of his ransom' (I. H. Marshall 1974: 158).

of his capture of them, or as a consequence of his purchase of them, the fundamental truth is that they are 'a people of his very own' (*laos periousios*, Titus 2:14).

The mark of ownership

It is a universal custom to indicate ownership of an item by some distinctive mark. Personal ownership may be indicated, for example, by initials on a bag, by a label on clothing or by a formal certificate of ownership. In a similar way, manufacturing ownership may be shown, for example, by a trademark on a tool, by an emblem on a vehicle or by a tune in an advertisement. Is there, correspondingly, some specific mark that points to God's ownership and possession of those purchased by Christ's death?[37]

We have seen that recaptured runaway slaves were sometimes branded on the forehead with the letter F or the three letters FVG, standing for the word FVGITIVVS, 'runaway (slave)'. But it was not uncommon for any temple or domestic slave to be branded, as certifying his or her ownership by a particular master. This, I believe, is the cultural background to Paul's comment at the end of Galatians, 'In future let no one make trouble for me, for I bear the marks (*ta stigmata*) of Jesus branded on my body' (Gal. 6:17, NEB), not the 'ear-marking' of voluntary slaves mentioned in Exodus 21:6 and Deuteronomy 15:17; or religious tatooing, such as with the initial X (chi) of *Christos* (*cf.* Lev. 19:28). Though in themselves such 'brand-marks' were symbols of dishonour (*cf.* Pseudo-Phocylides, *Sent.* 225), for Paul they became a badge of honour because they marked him out as a slave belonging to his Lord, Jesus. Evidently Paul interpreted the scars and wounds on his body (*cf.* Acts 14:19; 2 Cor. 11:23–27), received as a result of persecution, as the visual evidence of his being Christ's slave (so also Burton 1921: 360f.; Bruce 1982: 275f.). He was Christ's 'marked man', possessed and protected by him.[38]

But not all believers have suffered as Paul did! So we cannot regard these 'brand-marks of Jesus' (NASB) as the uniform sign that believers belong to God. For this we must turn, I believe, to the notion of the

---

[37] I shall not be dealing here with 'the image of God' as his mark of 'manufacturing ownership' placed on humans.

[38] In Gal. 6:17 Paul is issuing a warning 'that he should not be troubled further since he is Christ's "marked man", with those markings suggesting, positively, that he is under Christ's ownership and protection, as well as, negatively, that those who try to harass him will come under Christ's judgment and retribution' (Longenecker 1990: 300).

divine sealing as it is expounded in the first chapter of 2 Corinthians.

In 2 Corinthians 1:17–22 Paul is defending himself against the charge of fickleness (1:17) levelled against him by his Corinthian opponents. In verses 21–22, he appeals to the constant activity of God in producing stability in himself and the Corinthians – stability, not fickleness! This one Greek sentence contains four participles, each of which has God as its subject. The first, in the present tense, refers to God's ongoing activity of strengthening believers in their faith in Christ and enriching their knowledge of Christ (*ho bebaiōn*, v. 21a). The other three participles are in the aorist tense, here indicating what took place at the time of conversion and baptism. The phrase 'he anointed (*chrisas*) us' follows immediately after a reference to Christ (*Christos*, 'the Anointed One') and speaks of God's commissioning believers for his service and imparting the gifts necessary for that service (v. 21b). The next two Greek participles ('he sealed', *ho sphragisamenos* … 'he gave', *dous*, v. 22) are associated by a single article (*ho*) and an explicative 'and' (*kai*), indicating that 'sealing' is God's giving of the Spirit as a downpayment and pledge (*arrabōn*). So we may render verse 22, '[God] set his seal on us in that he put his Spirit in our hearts as a deposit, guaranteeing what is to come.'

The verb *sphragizō* means 'I mark as my own, by sealing'. Associated with sealing are three ideas: (a) ownership: believers are 'branded' as God's property; (b) authentication: the reality of their faith is attested; and (c) security: safety in transit is guaranteed 'until the day of redemption' (Eph. 4:30).

In three Pauline passages (2 Cor. 1:22; 5:5; Eph. 1:14) the Spirit is called the *arrabōn* that God has given to believers.[39] This technical term had two basic meanings in Greek commercial usage. It was a first instalment of a purchase, a downpayment or deposit, that required further payments but gave a legal claim to the goods in question. Sometimes this partial payment was a sizeable portion of the total, but on other occasions it was merely a token deposit. In its other sense, *arrabōn* denoted a pledge or guarantee that differed in kind from the actual payment but rendered it obligatory. Some modern translations prefer to retain both senses (*e.g.*, Moffatt, 'pledge and instalment', NIV; 'a deposit, guaranteeing what is to come'). 2 Corinthians 5:1–4 indicates that 'what is to come' is the acquisition of an immortal body through the transformation of the mortal body. Confirmation of this comes from Ephesians 1:13–14, where the

---

[39] I am here drawing on material from Harris 1983: 143f.

promised Holy Spirit is described as 'a deposit guaranteeing our inheritance until the redemption of those who are God's possession' (NIV). God's gift of the Spirit is therefore not only the fulfilment of promise (Gal. 3:14; Eph. 1:13) but also the promise of fulfilment (2 Cor. 5:5; Eph. 1:14).

So then, the mark of God's ownership, his seal, which is set on all believers, is his giving of his Spirit as a downpayment and pledge of the acquisition of a resurrection transformation that will issue in immortality.

What are the main points to emerge from this consideration of slavery and ownership? There is a sense in which all people are Christ's possession because he created them and now sustains them; he is the one 'through whom all things were made and through whom we live' (1 Cor. 8:6). But in every sense believers are his special possession, a people of his very own, because he purchased them as his slaves (1 Cor. 6:19–20; 7:22–23) along with their freedom from all iniquity (Titus 2:14). As a result of that purchase they belong to him totally, and only to him, a comprehensive ownership that his slaves voluntarily embrace. He is their absolute and exclusive Master. His rights over what he purchased are unlimited and he tolerates no rivals to his lordship, for no slave can adequately serve two different masters. 'Proof of purchase', or the mark of this ownership, is the presence and activity of his Spirit in the believer's life. And that same Spirit is the guarantee that this divine 'property' will reach its destination intact.

Chapter Seven

Slavery and privilege

Paul's letter to the Romans begins, surprisingly, not with the words 'Paul, an apostle of Christ Jesus', as we might be led to expect by the salutations in seven of his other letters,[1] but with the expression, 'Paul, a slave (*doulos*) of Christ Jesus, called to be an apostle'. But it is not only in this letter that Paul describes himself as 'a slave of Christ'. In Philippians 1:1 he introduces himself and Timothy as 'slaves of Christ Jesus', while in Galatians 1:10 he argues that if he were still trying to please people, he would not be 'a slave of Christ'. What did Paul intend to signify by this phrase in these three places?

Two representative and influential answers to this question deserve detailed consideration. Both scholars agree that Paul here sees himself in a privileged leadership role as an agent representing Christ, but whereas G. Sass (1941) finds the background of Paul's usage in the Old Testament, D. B. Martin (1990: 51–60 and *passim*) discovers it in contemporary Greco-Roman society.

The view of G. Sass

As he examines the Old Testament use of the Hebrew word *'ebed* (usually rendered by *doulos* in LXX), Sass argues for (a) the loss of the etymological sense of 'slave', 'bondsman' or 'servant' in the latest stages of development, and (b) the emergence of a new theological meaning, that of instrumentality (rather than servitude), of being Yahweh's chosen instrument (as in the case of Moses, Joshua or David) or tool (as in the case or Nebuchadnezzar or Cyrus) for the

---

[1] 1 Cor. 1:1; 2 Cor. 1:1; Gal. 1:1; Eph. 1:1; 1 Tim. 1:1; 2 Tim. 1:1; *cf.* also Titus 1:1. If we ask why Paul does not introduce himself as an apostle of Christ in his other letters (*viz.* Philippians, 1 and 2 Thessalonians, and Philemon), the answer is probably that his apostleship had not been called into question in the province of Macedonia, where Philippi and Thessalonica were situated. In the case of the letter to Philemon, he chooses to forgo his right as an apostle to issue a command, preferring rather to appeal to Philemon as an ambassador and prisoner of Christ Jesus (Philem. 8–9).

achievement of his purposes among humankind. He denies that *doulos* in Romans 1:1 (and, by implication, in Gal. 1:10 and Phil. 1:1) expresses the idea of 'unconditional subjection and bondage' (1941: 31), and affirms that *doulos* is an official title of honour that stresses instrumentality and is reserved for a few men who are 'entrusted by God with special tasks in and for the church' (32).

We must be grateful to Sass for highlighting the significance of *doulos* as a 'title of honour' (*Ehrentitel*).[2] Usage of the term *doulos* in the Greek Old Testament certainly shows that when it is qualified by a divine name (*kyriou*, 'of the Lord'; or *theou*, 'of God'), it indicates that the bearer of such a title is highly privileged, being a worshipper of God or in some way a representative or agent of God.[3] But we may legitimately question whether such a sense of *doulos* is restricted to certain church leaders. While it may be technically true to say that Paul nowhere explicitly refers to Christians in general as 'slaves of Christ' (29),[4] such an inference may be fairly drawn from Romans 6:16, 22 and 1 Corinthians 7:22–23 within the Pauline corpus.[5] And would not this putative late and specialized theological sense of *doulos* emanating from Septuagintal usage have been lost on Paul's readers in Rome, Galatia and Philippi, for whom the term *doulos* would first and foremost have the sociological connotation of unconditional obedience to and service for a master? In any case, this idea of 'instrumentality without servility' (as we might express Sass's view of the significance of *doulos* in these three Pauline passages) would be more naturally expressed in Greek by other more neutral terms such as *skeuos* ('vessel', 'instrument'; *cf.* Acts 9:15), or *hypēretēs* ('servant', 'assistant'; *cf.* Acts 26:16; 1 Cor. 4:1) or *diakonos* ('servant', 'helper'; *cf.* Col. 1:23; 1 Tim: 4:6).

The view of D. B. Martin

Martin (1990: 51f., 56–60) contends that in our three passages the phrase 'slave of Christ' is a title of leadership, denoting those who, as

---

[2] Sass is followed by Ollrog 1979: 75, 76 n. 73, 184 n. 108.

[3] See Appendix 1.

[4] Nor does Paul call believers 'the slaves of God', although Rom. 6 implies as much. The slavery to righteousness mentioned in v. 18 becomes slavery to God in v. 22: 'Now that you have been set free from sin and have become enslaved to God (*doulōthentes ... tō theō*), the benefit you reap leads to holiness, and the result is eternal life.' Those enslaved to God may be called 'slaves of God' (*cf.* RSV).

[5] See the discussion of the whole NT data below.

agents of the founder of their communities, are representatives of his authority. But Martin's principal focus is on 1 Corinthians 9:16–18, where, he argues, Paul presents himself as an *oikonomos*, a middle-level, managerial slave who has both authority and high standing in the household of Christ (68–85, 117–149).

This scholar has performed the necessary and useful service of demonstrating that in first-century Greco-Roman society slaves could be seen not only negatively, as those who gave 'unconditional obedience to a merciless master', but also positively, as 'indisputable, authoritative representatives' of a powerful owner (60). Nevertheless, several pressing questions remain concerning Martin's work.

1. It is true that Paul says, 'I have been entrusted with a commission' (*oikonomian pepisteumai*, 1 Cor. 9:17), but that fact in itself scarcely validates the inference that Paul views himself as a high-status managerial slave (*oikonomos*) in Christ's household, especially since Paul has already used that actual term *oikonomos* twice in the same letter in reference to stewards who are commissioned to expound 'the mysteries of God' (1 Cor. 4:1–2), 'managers' authorized to divulge God's hidden truths (= the gospel), a role that in fact makes Paul 'the scum of the earth' (1 Cor. 4:13). Nor does the expression 'slave of Christ' appear in 1 Corinthians 9:16–18 (but see 1 Cor. 7:22).

2. One may readily grant that for some people in the Greco-Roman world *becoming* a slave provided a means of social advancement *if* they were then 'upwardly mobile' within patron–client relationships, although the evidence that Martin adduces for this is meagre.[6] On the other hand, *being* a slave of a high-ranking, powerful owner could lead to or enhance education, wealth, authority and prestige. But such 'middle-level, managerial slaves'[7] formed such a small minority[8] that

---

[6] After noting 'both actual cases and fictional accounts of upwardly mobile slaves in the Roman Empire', Martin (1990: 41f.) adduces 'a few texts' as evidence of 'actual voluntary enslavement for social advancement': the freedman at Trimalchio's banquet in Petronius, *Sat.* 57; rural children whose parents sell them into urban slavery (Cassiodorus, *Complex.* 8. 33 [sixth century AD!]; and Cyrus, in the history of Nicolaus of Damascus (text in Jacoby 1926; 2A. 361–370, frag. 66).

[7] 'By middle-level slaves I mean these who ran a business or worked as an agent or manager, those who occupied positions somewhere between top imperial slave bureaucrats and the slaves involved in common, manual labor and services' (xxi; *cf.* 15–22, 30, 49).

[8] Martin himself speaks of a 'small but significant minority of slaves' (1990: xiii), 'a select few' (32), or a highly visible minority (48). And he admits (42) that 'in spite of the ambiguous social position and the upward social mobility of some slaves, few people in the Roman Empire actually experienced real social mobility'.

we may question whether that particular connotation of slavery would have ousted the dominant notion of slavery as humble subjection to a master in the minds of Paul's converts. Would not Paul's Corinthian readers or any typical Greco-Roman urbanites have interpreted the term *doulos* in light of their own experience or observation of slavery? And would that understanding of slavery not correspond precisely to the contextual indicators of 1 Corinthians 9, where the slave is someone who has no rights (vv. 12, 15, 18) and is under obligation to serve another person (vv. 16–17)? What is more, with regard to Paul's intent, these two characteristics – absence of rights and the obligation to serve – are associated with slavery in other Pauline texts (Rom. 6:16; Gal. 5:13; Phil. 2:6–8).

3. Martin's association of slavery to Christ with 'status-improvement' is suspect (1990: 63, 65, *cf.* 137). Any suggestion of Paul's personal concern about 'status' – whether upward social mobility in the case of the phrase 'slave of Christ', or deliberate self-lowering in the case of 'slave of all' – seems foreign to an evangelist-pastor who earlier in 1 Corinthians has depicted himself and the other apostles as doomed gladiators entering the arena of human scorn at the end of the procession (1 Cor. 4:9–10), and who aligned himself with menial slavery by pursuing the servile, manual trade of tent-making (Acts 18:3). Was Paul really the patron of the patronless, lower-status members of the Corinthian church, seeking to improve their chances of eventually overcoming 'the oppressions of hierarchy to reach high positions in the household of Christ' (149)? Rather, Paul's use of the metaphor of slavery in 1 Corinthians 9 (especially vv. 19–23) would lead his converts to recognize their own obligation to adopt a slave's role of obedient service in relation to Christ and others.

4. The title of Martin's book – *Slavery as Salvation* – raises the issue of what he means by 'salvation' and the precise relation between slavery and this salvation. Although he once speaks of 'Christian salvation as slavery to Christ' (on 1 Cor. 7:22) (65), else-where salvation is defined in purely sociological and temporal terms. 'To raise one's status by becoming a slave of a good and powerful master was to be saved from a harsher and less honourable fate' (63). 'Salvation is here [*viz.* in 1 Cor. 7:22–23] depicted as upward mobility within slavery' (63; similarly 65, 68, 132). To be the slave of Christ is to gain power and authority from 'status-by-association', to be assured that there is no need to be 'trapped forever in the slavery of obscurity' (149). On the relation between slavery and

salvation, Martin proposes that the image of slavery 'symbolized' (xvii, 62), 'represents' (xix, xxii, 129, 132, 180 n. 12), 'expresses' (xix), or 'depict(s)' (61) salvation; or that slavery to Christ 'mean(s)' (63) or brings (xxii, 129, 132) salvation. Would it not be simpler – and truer to Pauline usage – to reverse the two crucial terms and say that salvation in Christ involves slavery to Christ? Stated more fully, those who have been delivered from the domain of sin and transformed into the kingdom of Christ (cf. Col. 1:13) enter into two-dimensional slavery – slavery to Christ (the individual and vertical dimension) and slavery to other people (the corporate and horizontal aspect).

The approaches of Sass and Martin are complementary, not antithetical. When we are investigating the background to the titular use of *doulos* in Paul and the New Testament in general, we are not, I believe, obliged to choose between Old Testament or Greco-Roman settings. Both are relevant,[9] but greater precision is possible in describing the Old Testament background since all New Testament writers were immersed in the terminology and usage of the Septuagint.

In spite of the difficulties that persist about the overall theses of these two scholars, one point emerges clearly from both studies. For Paul, the title *doulos* could, on occasion, denote representative agency and privileged leadership: *doulos* was sometimes the designation or self-designation of a Christian leader who was a privileged agent chosen to represent an absent Master. But now, in a more systematic way than has been possible before, we must address the question that naturally arises. Do Paul and other New Testament authors see slavery to Christ or God as a privilege reserved for certain leaders in the church, or as the prerogative of all Christians without distinction?

---

[9] Westermann (1948: 55–64), for example, finds a dual source for Paul's concept of believers as slaves of God or Christ. The 'methods' of this idea come from the continuing indentured services of the Greek *paramonē* contract, and the 'spirit' from the Semitic notion of lifelong service to the deity, the idea of free persons who became slave-devotees of a deity (*e.g.*, 1 Sam. 1:11–28). In a similar way, Willink (1928: 46f.) proposes that in calling himself 'a slave of Jesus Christ', Paul (a) claimed a place in the succession of OT figures who occupied pivotal postitions at turning-points in God's dealings with the world; and (b) possibly saw himself as having a special administrative role in the church comparable to the slaves of the emperor to whom, as 'secretaries of state', were entrusted great fiscal responsibilities.

Slavery to Christ — for the few?

Two lines of evidence — one indirect, one direct — lead us to conclude that slavery to God or Christ is indeed a privilege conferred on every believer. The indirect evidence comes from the Septuagint's usage of the term *doulos*, the direct evidence from the New Testament application of the titles 'slave of God' or 'slave of Christ'. The basic data in these two areas have been set out elsewhere in this book,[10] so all that is necessary here is to review parts of that material and draw the relevant conclusions.

In the Greek Old Testament most uses of *doulos* refer to literal slaves and occur in the historical books. As for the figurative use of *doulos*, the combination 'slave of God' (*doulos theou*) is rare,[11] but the expression 'slave of the Lord' (*doulos kyriou*, rendering *'ebed YHWH*) is common. On occasion Israel as a nation is depicted as Yahweh's slave and Israelites as a whole as his slaves. When *doulos* is applied to individuals, the reference may be to the individual patriarchs, Abraham, Isaac and Jacob; or to national leaders such as Moses, Saul, David or Solomon; or to particular prophets such as Elijah or Jonah, or prophets as a whole. What all these individual applications have in common is the idea of national or religious leadership as chosen representatives of Yahweh. But this title is used not only of the nation of Israel, of Israelites considered corporately, and of leaders within the nation.[12] It is also applied to individuals who are worshippers of Yahweh, desire to reverence his name or are his humble suppliants. Such usage is particularly prominent in the Psalms, the prayer-book of individual Israelites. In the Greek version of Psalm 119 (Psalm 118, LXX), for example, the psalmist refers to himself as 'your slave' (*[ho] doulos sou*) no fewer than thirteen times.[13] Further evidence that individuals could relate to God as *douloi* comes from the cognate verb *douleuō* ('be a slave', 'give a slave's service'), the general word in the Septuagint for the service of God. It can describe both corporate allegiance to God (*e.g.*, Judg. 2:7) and individual devotion to him (*e.g.*, Pss. 2:11; 99:2; Is. 56:6).

---

[10] The use of *doulos* in the LXX is set out in Appendix 1. The NT use of the expressions 'slave(s) of God' and 'slave(s) of Christ' is analysed at the end of chapter 1 (pp. 20–24).

[11] The phrase 'slave of God' (in the form *'ebed 'ēl* or *'ebed 'elōhîm*) has thus far not been found at Qumran.

[12] See Appendix 1, Observation 4 (pp. 174f.).

[13] *Viz*. Ps. 118:17, 23, 38, 49, 65, 76, 84, 122, 124–125, 135, 140, 176, LXX.

We turn now to the New Testament data. If we analyse the use of the expressions 'slave(s) of God' and 'slave(s) of Christ', not according to the number (whether singular or plural) as in the Introduction, but in terms of the referent, the following results emerge.[14]

1. 'Slave of God' is found nine times, twice of an angel (Rev. 19:10; 22:9), once of Moses (Rev. 15:3), twice of apostles (Titus 1:1, Paul; Rev. 1:1b, John), once of a Christian leader (Jas. 1:1, James), and *three times of individual believers* (Luke 1:38; 48, Mary; Luke 2:29, Simeon).

2. 'Slaves of God' occurs thirteen times, once of Christian martyrs (Rev. 19:2), three times of Christian leaders (Acts 16:17; Rev. 10:7; 11:18), and *nine times of any or all Christians* (Acts 2:18; 4:29; 1 Pet. 2:16; Rev. 1:1a; 6:11; 7:3; 19:5; 22:3, 6).[15]

3. "Slave of Christ' appears ten times, three times in reference to apostles (Rom. 1:1 and Gal. 1:10, Paul; 2 Pet. 1:1, Peter), six times of Christian leaders (Col. 1:7 and 4:12, Epaphras; Col. 4:7, Tychicus; 2 Tim. 2:24, of any Christian leader; Jas. 1:1, James; Jude 1, Jude), and *once of any Christian free person* (1 Cor. 7:22).

4. 'Slaves of Christ' is found three times, once in reference to Paul and Timothy (Phil. 1:1), *once of any slaves who are Christians* (Eph. 6:6), *and once of Christians in general* (Rev. 2:20).

So then, if Septuagintal usage made it antecedently probable that in the New Testament the figurative and titular use of *doulos* would not be restricted to leaders of God's people, the actual texts confirm this and indicate that being a slave of God or of Christ is a privileged role open to all believers.[16]

'Slave of Christ': its relation to 'slave of God'

If Christians are called both 'slaves of God' and 'slaves of Christ', how should we describe the relation between the two expressions? Do Christians have two masters, each vying for their total allegiance?

We should observe, first of all, that there is no reason to believe that the content of the slavery to Christ differs in any regard from what is

---

[14] I have included in the following statistics the uses of *syndoulos* (see pp. 22–24).

[15] Rengstorf (1964: 2. 273) notes the OT flavour of many of the NT uses of *doulos/douloi theou*.

[16] Never is the church, considered corporately, spoken of as the slave of God or Christ, although in the LXX Israel as a nation is depicted as Yahweh's *doulos* (Ps. 79:5, Heb. *'am*) or *douloi* (Deut. 32:36; Neh. 1:6). In the *Shepherd* of Hermas (?c. AD 150), *doulos theou* is a synonym for 'Christian' (*e.g.*, 38:6; 46:1; 48:2, 4).

implied by being God's slave. Since in each case the willing service is given to divine beings who have not merely a personal affinity to each other but an identity of nature and purpose (John 10:30), it will involve the same reverent submission and obedient servitude. Indeed, we may go one step further and confidently assume that to be Christ's slave is to be God's slave and *vice versa*.[17] The New Testament gives no hint that the Christian is in the service of two competing masters. Rather, the slaves of Christ do the will of God, as Ephesians 6:6 expresses it, so that competitive servitude is excluded. Consequently, one and the same person can be said to be, simultaneously, 'a slave of God and of the Lord Jesus Christ' (Jas. 1:1). Just as to see Christ is to see God the Father (John 14:9), just as to believe in Christ is to believe in God (John 12:44), just as to know Christ is to know the Father (John 14:7), just as to be inseparable from Christ's love is to be inseparable from God's love (Rom. 8:35, 39), just as the Spirit of Christ is none other than the Spirit of God (Rom. 8:9), so also, to give a slave's service to Christ is indistinguishable from giving such service to God. James is the only New Testament author explicitly to associate slavery to Christ with slavery to God (Jas. 1:1). His purpose in doing so may well be to show that service to the Messiah is in reality service to the God of Israel.

The very existence of the phrase 'slave of Christ' alongside 'slave of God' in New Testament usage testifies to the early Christian belief in Christ's deity. Knowing the expression 'slave of the Lord' from the Septuagint, several New Testament writers – John, Peter, Paul, James and Jude – quietly substitute 'Christ' for 'the Lord', a substitution that would be been unthinkable for a Jew unless Christ was seen as having parity of status with Yahweh. Commenting on Paul's use of the phrase 'slave of Christ Jesus' in reference to himself and Timothy in Philippians 1:1, F. W. Beare (1959: 50) astutely observes that 'this passionate defender of freedom would not own himself a slave except of one to whom he accords divine prerogatives'.

Connotations of *doulos*

In the first century, *doulos* (or the Latin equivalent, *servus*) was a standard and effective term of abuse.[18] And for slaves themselves it

---

[17] Compare the similar pair 'servants of God' (*theou diakonoi*, 2 Cor. 6:4) and 'servant of Christ Jesus' (*diakonos Christou Iēsou*, 1 Tim. 4:6).

[18] See Dio Chrysostom, *De Lib*. 2. 1. Among the Rabbis, too, the word 'slave' constituted 'one of the worst insults one man could hurl at another' (Rengstorf 1964: 2. 271,

was generally true that to be addressed as 'slave', or to be referred to as a slave, was a reminder of their inferior and dishonourable status. 'There is only one thing that brings shame to slaves – the name itself' (Euripides, *Ion* 854). When an 'upwardly mobile' slave gained some honour and status through his association with a prestigious and powerful master, this was simply the exception that proved the rule. In any case, as J. A. Harrill observes, 'from a historical perspective any "honour" conferred even on high-ranking servile persons was always fragile, as the imperial freedman Thallus discovered when Augustus broke his legs'.[19] So it comes as no surprise to learn that in Greco-Roman society it was not customary for devotees of a deity to describe themselves as 'slaves' (*douloi* or *servi*) of that deity.[20]

How, then, could ordinary first-century Christians who held no positions of leadership in the church have found pleasure in being called the 'slaves of Christ', especially since Christ himself had taught that to be a 'slave' was the opposite of being 'first', of having a position of dignity and honour (Matt. 20:26–27)? Why did that title seem sweet, not sour, and dignified, not demeaning? The answer, I suggest, lies in the nature of the Master they were serving and in the example of slavery to God that he himself afforded.

The nature of any slavery is determined by the nature of the master. Who and what the master is, determines the status of the slave, the attitude of the slave, and the significance of the slave's work.[21] For example, to be in the employ of the emperor, as a member of 'the household of Caesar' (some 20,000 in number), gave the slave a significant status and certain prestige, which was usually reflected in a positive 'work attitude' (as we would call it), and a sense of contributing in some way, however insignificant, to the smooth running of that massive machine called the Roman Empire.[22] At the

---

citing the proverb, 'A dog is more honourable than a slave', *Mekilta* on Exod. 22:30).

[19] In a review of Martin's book in *JR* 72 (1992) 427, citing Suetonius, *Aug.* 67.

[20] Martin (1990: xiv–xvi) cites several examples that show conclusively 'that metaphorical slavery to a god was not a completely unlikely construction in Greco-Roman society' (xvi).

[21] The thought that conversion was merely an exchange of one form of slavery for another would have seemed utterly repugnant to the ancient pagan mind. Why would anyone who had gained freedom choose to be enslaved? If to be a slave was to lack human dignity, why would a freedman opt for a return to slavery? The answer, of course, is determined by the nature of the master and of the work he requires.

[22] 'For the slave almost everything depended on the character of the master ... Within slavery were possible virtue, happiness, culture, wealth; but whether the slave enjoyed any of these depended on his master' (Barrow 1968: 52).

other end of the spectrum, a slave who found himself in the household of an unreasonable and cruel master,[23] would, more often than
not, become bitter and resentful or oppressed and cringing, and his
reluctant service would be minimal, motivated by anger or fear.

When we recognize this correlation between kind master and
compliant slave, and cruel master and reluctant slave, we can begin to
understand why the early Christians found their slavery sweetly
attractive. To be the slave of a Master who is himself 'gentle and
humble-hearted', and whose yoke is so easy to wear that his load is
light (Matt. 11:29–30), is to be a highly privileged and readily
obedient slave. When the Master is the omnipotent Lord of the
universe, the slavery is a consummate privilege and a passionate
delight, as well as being infinitely worthwhile. The eloquent words of
Philo (*Cher.* 107) regarding slavery to God are equally applicable to
slavery to Christ:

> The purified mind rejoices in nothing more than in confessing
> that it has for its master the One who is Lord of all. For to be
> the slave of God (*to ... douleuein theō*) is the greatest human
> boast, and is a more precious treasure not only than freedom
> but even than wealth or dominion or anything that mortals
> cherish.

In his drama *Amphitryo*, the Roman playwright Plautus places on
the lips of one of his characters the words: 'It's no fun being a slave.
And it's not just the work, but knowing that you're a slave, and that
nothing can change it.'[24] The slave of Christ, on the other hand, says:
'It's a delight being Christ's slave. And it's not just the work, but
knowing that you're his slave, and that nothing can separate you from
his love.'

The other reason why being a 'slave of Christ' would have been
attractive and not repulsive to the first Christians was that in some
circles, if not in all, the condition of Jesus himself during his
incarnation was described as that of a slave. The pre-incarnate Son of
God 'emptied himself by assuming the form of a *doulos*' (Phil. 2:7).
While there may be here an indirect allusion to Jesus as the Servant
of Yahweh (LXX, *pais kyriou*), given certain linguistic echoes of

---

[23] A slave was clearly subject to his master's capricious outbursts of anger, as is shown
by Seneca's diatribes on the need to curb anger against slaves in particular (*De Ira* 3. 24.
2; 3. 32. 1).

[24] Cited, without reference (perhaps lines 173f.), by Hopkins 1978: 99.

Isaiah 52:13 – 53:12 highlighted by J. Jeremias,[25] it seems preferable to see Christ's own slavery as involving the deprivation, or better the surrender, of his inherent rights and his giving humble, obedient service. As a slave without rights, the incarnate Son was obedient to God until death (Phil. 2:8). And Jesus had dramatized this self-emptying and provided an example of a slave's self-effacing service when he laid aside his outer clothes and, girded with a towel, washed and dried his disciples' feet (John 13:2–5). If, then, Jesus had himself been a humble, obedient slave, those who followed his example were indeed privileged imitators.[26] 'The slave is not greater than his master' (Matt. 10:24; John 13:16; 15:20), but Christians become great as the slaves of Christ because of their Master's greater greatness as the slave of God. It is Christ's voluntary role as God's *doulos* that prevents the Christian's slavery from being a distasteful experience and makes it a privilege and honour.

How highly the early Christians prized the honour of being 'slaves of Christ' is forcefully shown by the way four New Testament authors begin their epistles. It must be significant that Paul begins his letter to the Romans (1:1), 'Paul, a slave of Christ Jesus, called to be an apostle', not 'an apostle of Christ Jesus [*cf.* 1 Cor. 1:1] and his slave'. So also Peter, as he begins his second letter (2 Pet. 1:1): 'Simeon Peter, a slave and apostle of Jesus Christ', not 'an apostle and slave of Jesus Christ', as we might have expected. May we not infer that both these principal figures in the early church believed it was a higher privilege to be a slave of Christ than to be an apostle of Christ?[27] Then we have the testimony of James and Jude, two of the brothers of Jesus. James begins (1:1), 'James, a slave of God and of the Lord Jesus Christ', while Jude starts (v. 1) with 'Jude, a slave of Jesus Christ and a brother of James'. Neither writer begins, '... a brother of Jesus and also his slave', yet *Paul* can call James 'the Lord's brother' (Gal. 1:19).[28] May we not infer that both James and Jude regarded it

---

[25] See the discussion of these linguistic echoes in O'Brien 1991: 194, 220, 268–271.

[26] Russell (1968: 31 n. 19, 38, 41) argues that both in his active ministry of proclaiming salvation and in his passive suffering, Paul was following in the footsteps of Christ, who had fulfilled the prophecies of Isaiah 40 – 55. 'It was perhaps Paul's conviction that he was continuing the work of Christ the *Ebed* which motivated him to call himself and those associated with him in his apostolic work "slaves"' (26).

[27] The very association of *doulos* with *apostolos* in Rom. 1:1 and 2 Pet. 1:1 shows clearly the high honour of slavery to Christ. Russell (1968: 28, *cf.* 50) maintains that when *doulos* is linked with *apostolos* in Rom. 1:1, it points to Paul's role as an evangelist and 'his total availability for this work no matter what it cost him'.

[28] See the discussion of this point in Bauckham 1983: 23f.

as a more exalted privilege to be a slave of Jesus than even a brother of Jesus?

From all of these considerations two major conclusions emerge.

First, to be a slave of Christ is not a right reserved for the favoured few in the church but is the privilege of all believers, unrelated to their giftedness or their particular role in the church. Septuagintal use of the related phrase, 'slave of the Lord', shows that although it was often an honorific title applied to prominent leaders of the nation, it could also denote the relationship to God of any member of the covenant community. So, too, in the New Testament, the term *doulos* in the metaphorical sense of slavery to the deity is applied not only to the apostles and their colleagues and to church leaders in general, but to all Christians. It has become, in a Christian context, a title of exquisite honour describing accredited representatives of the risen Christ.

Second, while for Christian leaders *doulos* was already a title of honour, it gained its positive connotations in the ears of all Christians because the divine Master they were serving was kind and generous and himself had blazed an exemplary trail of lowly service. What all the *douloi* of this *Kyrios* gained through being associated with him was not so much authority and power as unparalleled honour and the assurance that their service, whatever its nature, was of supreme value, simply because it was done for *him*.

Chapter Eight

'Slave of Christ': its significance in the New Testament

Slave imagery and its origin

Slave imagery cannot be eradicated from the New Testament, and owes its origin to two sources: Greco-Roman society and Ancient Near Eastern custom, especially as seen in the Old Testament.

However much we moderns, living on the other side of the abolition of slavery, may be scandalized by the New Testament use of the image of slavery to depict one aspect of our ideal relationship to the Deity, we cannot eradicate such imagery from the New Testament without compromising its message. Not only is there slavery to sin or lust, which is condemned, but slavery to God or Christ, which is encouraged. In fact, terminology that is drawn from the sphere of slavery and is used in a figurative sense abounds in the New Testament (see Appendix 2). Moreover, God and his exalted Messiah are both given the titles *kyrios* ('Sovereign Lord') and *despotēs* ('Absolute Lord'), terms which themselves imply absolute sovereignty over slaves.[1] Nor should we overlook the fact that the final picture the New Testament gives of the eternal state is one where 'slaves' (*douloi*) are completely devoted to the worship and service (*latreusousin*) of the Lord God and the Lamb (Rev. 22:3). The redeemed remain 'slaves', although their service is that of priests (*cf.* Rev. 1:6; 5:10; 20:6).[2] According to the New Testament, spiritual slavery to Christ is an integral part of Christian discipleship, since the slave's Master is also his Teacher (John 13:13–14).

We have seen that one of the leading authorities on slavery in the ancient world, Professor Moses I. Finley (1976: 819), argued that

---

[1] *Kyrios*, of God (*e.g.*, Rev. 11:15, 17), of Christ (*e.g.*, 1 Cor. 8:6); *despotēs*, of God (Luke 2:29; Acts 4:24; Rev. 6:10), of Christ (2 Pet. 2:1; Jude 4).

[2] If the name that is inscribed on the foreheads of these slaves (Rev. 22:4) is 'holy to Yahweh' (*cf.* Exod. 28:36–38), the emphasis is on the entire consecration ('holy') of glorified believers to the worship and service of God.

among ancient cultures slavery as an institution essential to the production and lifestyle of a society was found only in classical Greece and classical Rome.[3] These societies were based on slavery. Since slavery still flourished in first-century AD Greco-Roman society, it is *a priori* likely that the New Testament motif of spiritual slavery should have one of its roots in the contemporary practice and language of physical slavery. This *a priori* assumption proves to be factual, for we discovered numerous places where the New Testament description of spiritual servitude to God or Christ corresponds to the practice of slavery in Greco-Roman society.

But another sturdy root of New Testament usage is to be found in the Ancient Near East. E. Yamauchi (1966: 31) has convincingly demonstrated that 'one has great difficulty in finding a culture in the Near East that does *not* have the "slave of God" motif'.[4] He reviews the evidence for the use of 'slave of God' names under ten categories – Egyptian, Babylonian, Ugaritic, Mycenaean Greek, Phoenician, Old Testament, Aramaic, Hellenistic, Late Northwest Semitic, and Arabic – and concludes that 'the practice of designating oneself as the Slave of one's God has been maintained for at least 4000 years to this day' (35). In particular, all Israelites were regarded, or regarded themselves, as the 'slaves' of God the King on the analogy of the subjects of an earthly sovereign, who were regarded as the sovereign's slaves whether or not they were in physical servitude. So it is, for example, that J. Vogt (1972: 94) contends that in his parables Jesus drew on the Old Testament concept of the 'slave of God' – *viz.* complete subjection to another's will – for the paradigm of the ideal God–human being relationship.

The negative connotations of slave terminology

In the first century AD, the *doulos* word group would have generally evoked feelings of repugnance in the hearts of free persons and the vast majority of slaves, although for a small minority of slaves the emotional connotations of slave terminology may have been positive. That is, for most people, whether slave or free, the very term *doulos* or *servus* (the Latin equivalent) would have aroused negative feelings – feelings of dehumanized and unwilling servitude.

What C. E. B. Cranfield (1975: 1. 50) says regarding the Greek

---

[3] See above, p. 44.

[4] He notes here that 'the reasons for the designation were not always the same'.

mindset applied equally, *mutatis mutandis*, to the Roman outlook: 'For the Greek in the classical tradition it was well-nigh impossible to use a word of the *doulos* group without some feeling of abhorrence. That the subjects of an oriental monarch could willingly describe themselves as his *douloi* was to him revolting, and to use such language with reference to men's relations to the gods never came naturally to him.' To be made a slave was to be disgraced and undergo social death. To call a person a slave was to insult him. Crucifixion, the most execrable form of capital punishment, was described as 'suitable for slaves' (*servile*; e.g., Tacitus, *Hist.* 4. 11) because they were regarded as forming the lowest and most contemptible stratum of society.

Now it is true that for a few slaves — especially some of those in the service of the emperor — slavery was a means of upward social mobility. Twice Martin makes the claim that in Greco-Roman society 'it mattered less that one was a slave than whose slave one was' (1990: 85, 132). But this assertion would be hard to demonstrate — and is not established even by the massive inscriptional evidence he appeals to — 'in the face of a tradition that so often claimed to see the power and promotion of slaves as a grotesque inversion of nature'.[5] The most one can say with assurance is that 'it mattered' whose slave one was, in the sense that a certain dignity, at least in the eyes of other slaves, attached to those slaves whose owners were wealthy and influential. But whether slave-owners and other free persons appreciated those distinctions among slaves must remain highly improbable. For them, a slave was a slave, whatever his role and whoever his master was. Only when a slave had become a freedman, had attained Roman citizenship, and had entered a client–patron relationship with his former master would the status of an ex-slave become significant in the eyes of free persons. And even then a freedman's background was not forgotten.

We have seen that for Jews and Christians steeped in the Old Testament, especially in its Greek form, the term 'slave' could be a title of honour, describing someone who was an accredited representative of God among his people, either as a leader or as a prophet. But such a 'pure' sense of *doulos* was well-nigh impossible in the first century. With K. C. Russell (1968: 16, *cf.* 88) we may ask, 'Was it really possible in a society where slaves were encountered as

---

[5] I. A. H. Combes, in a review of Martin's book, *JTS* n. s. 43 (1992), 202. But note Martin's comments on this matter (1990: 43–44; 180 n. 16).

part of daily life to use the word "slave" as a title of honour empty of
its note of essential subservience and dependence?'

Slavery to Christ as a wholly positive image

In its description of figurative slavery to Christ, the New Testament
has eradicated those negative features that attached to the notion of
slavery, so that the metaphor has become a wholly positive image
depicting the believer's exclusive devotion to the Lord Christ. As
used of all Christian believers, the term *doulos* is not partially sweet
and partially sour, but totally sweet.

It should occasion no surprise that the New Testament uses slave
imagery both negatively and positively. On the one hand, we read of
those who are enslaved to sin, to depravity, to passion, to drink, to
spiritual powers, to false gods, or to other people.[6] On the other hand,
positively, Christians are described as being or are urged to be
enslaved to God, to Christ, to righteousness, to obedience, or to
fellow-believers.[7] 'The social reality of slavery was so multifaceted
and ambiguous that one could appropriate its terminology for
different metaphorical uses without self-conscious reflection' (Martin
1990: 60, *cf.* xviii). Whether used positively or negatively, servile
imagery may have a variety of applications.

The Paul who called himself 'a slave of Christ Jesus' (Rom. 1:1)
and spoke of all Christians, whether slave or free, as the slaves of
Christ (1 Cor. 7:22; Eph. 6:6) affirms that believers have not received
'the spirit of slavery' (*pneuma douleias*) or 'the spirit of a slave' that
would prompt a return to fear (Rom. 8:15).[8] Such a spirit is an attitude
of cringing servility, fear of displeasing the master and particularly
fear of the punishment that may follow. Abject submission to a
master, born of fear, has no place in the Christian's slavery to Christ.
Not only is this Master gentle (Matt. 11:29) and gracious (2 Cor.
13:14); he himself gave humble, obedient service as God's slave
(Phil. 2:7–8).

If slavish fear is explicitly excluded in the case of Christ's slaves,

---

[6] (Respectively) Rom. 6:17; 2 Pet. 2:19; Titus 3:3; 2:3; Gal. 4:3, 8; 1 Cor. 7:23.
Compare the indictment of Seneca: 'Show me someone who is not a slave: some are
slaves to lust, others to greed, some to social prestige, and all are slaves to fear' (*Ep.* 47.
17; *cf. Ben.* 3. 28. 4).

[7] (Respectively) Rom. 6:22; 1 Cor. 7:22; Rom. 6:18, 16; Gal. 5:13.

[8] It is also possible to interpret this verse to mean 'You did not receive a Spirit who
enslaves you again and makes you afraid' (*cf.* LN 475 §37. 26).

what are the distinctive marks of his slaves? What is implied by *doulos* and its cognates when these terms refer to the followers of Jesus?

Here we may appeal to our initial definition of a slave (whether a slave literally or figuratively): 'A slave is someone whose person and service belong wholly to another.' As Christ's purchased possession, the Christian is wholly devoted to the person of the Master (Rom. 14:8).[9] As Christ's 'movable property', the Christian is totally available for the Master's use (2 Tim. 2:21). This complete devotion to Christ includes three elements:

1. Humble submission to the person of Christ. This involves an acknowledgment that, as supreme Lord, he has absolute and exclusive rights to the will and affections and energy, now and for ever. It is a case of the devotion of the whole person for the whole of life.[10]

2. Unquestioning obedience to the Master's will.[11] Slavery, we say, involves subjection to another's will, whether voluntarily or involuntarily. The faithful slave is basically the obedient slave, just as the first requirement for commendable military service is compliance with commands.

3. An exclusive preoccupation with pleasing Christ. Believers give satisfaction to their Master not only by obeying him, but also by devising innovative ways of pleasing him. 'We make it our ambition', says Paul, 'to be constantly pleasing to him' (2 Cor. 5:9). This was Paul's magnificent obsession, an obsession that had the effect of expelling inferior – albeit legitimate – pursuits.

---

[9] There is a delightful example of the total devotion of a *doulos* to his *kyrios* in 2 Sam. 15. Forced to flee from Jerusalem because of the success of Absalom's conspiracy, David remonstrates with Ittai the Gittite, encouraging him to return to Jerusalem with his foreign mercenaries. 'But Ittai replied to the king, "As surely as the Lord lives, and as my lord (*ho kyrios mou*) the king lives, wherever my lord (*ho kyrios mou*) may be, whether it means life or death, there will your servant (*ho doulos sou*) be"' (2 Kgdms 15:21).

[10] With this compare the incisive comments of Finley 1976: 819: 'What distinguishes the chattel slave from all other forms of involuntary or compulsory labour is ... not this or that obligation, the lack of this or that right – for which parallels can easily be shown – but the totality of his rightlessness, his powerlessness, in two respects, which must be taken together. One is the totality of the duration, not only for the whole of his life but also for the whole of the lives of his descendants. The other is the totality of the subjection, over the whole of his personality, so to speak.'

[11] Bristol (1958: 79) suggests that in using the word *doulos* of himself (Rom. 1:1), Paul 'considered himself to be wholly in the *possession* of Jesus Christ ... recognized Christ's *direction* of his life ... [and] saw the need for his own *obedience* to the divine purposes'.

John 15:15, Galatians 4:7, and the limitations of the metaphor

The two passages that at first sight seem to disqualify the idea of slavery from being in any way applicable to the relation between Christ or God and the Christian – John 15:15 and Galatians 4:7 – in fact simply point to the limitations of that imagery.

John 15:15

We have noted that in several places in the gospels Jesus portrays himself as a master with slaves.[12] What, then, did Jesus mean when he spoke of his disciples as 'friends', not 'slaves'?

> You are my friends if you do what I command you. No longer do I call you 'slaves', because a slave does not understand what his master is doing. Rather, I have given you the name of 'friends', because I have made known to you everything that I heard from my Father (John 15:14–15).

We should observe, to begin with, that Jesus is not making a blanket affirmation that all his disciples are his friends. 'You are my friends *if ...*' Obedience to Jesus does not create his friendship but it is a mark and proof of that friendship. Nor is Jesus implying that whereas his obedient disciples are his friends, disobedient disciples are his slaves. Rather, his point is that a slave obeys his master's orders without understanding his master's motives and plans; he has no intimate knowledge of his master's purposes. So then, because Jesus *has* disclosed to his disciples a full knowledge of his Father's secret counsels (*cf.* John 8:38), they cannot any longer be called 'slaves'.[13] The only designation appropriate for them in this regard is 'friends', for a friend does have the privilege of intimate knowledge that is denied to a slave.

But by calling his obedient disciples his friends and 'no longer' slaves,[14] Jesus cannot be affirming that the notion of slavery is

---

[12] See p. 92.

[13] 'Everything' (John 15:15) is not contradicted by John 16:12, 'I still have much to say to you, but you cannot bear it now.' This latter passage refers to the coming work of the Paraclete in giving the disciples a deeper understanding of what Jesus had revealed (John 16:13–14).

[14] The expression 'no longer' (*ouketi*) could point back to John 13:13, 16 where the

inapplicable to his disciples' relationship to him. There are several reasons for this:

1. In the immediate context Jesus still sees himself as a Master who gives commands that must be obeyed (John 15:14). This implies that his disciples are his slaves.

2. In John 13:13 Jesus commended his disciples for calling him 'Lord' (*kyrios*), which indicates their slavery to him.

3. Jesus actually directed his disciples to say, 'We are unprofitable slaves' (*douloi*, Luke 17:10).

4. When Jesus stood before Pilate, he spoke of his kingship, and, by implication, of his 'servants' or 'slaves' (*hypēretai*, John 18:36).[15]

It should be observed that although Jesus the Lord calls his obedient disciples *his* friends, they are not thereby authorized to call him *their* friend. In the Old Testament, Abraham (2 Chr. 20:7; Is. 41:8) is called God's friend.[16] But this leads James to say, not that 'God was called the friend of Abraham', but that 'he [Abraham] was called the friend of God' (Jas. 2:23). Not, of course, that God or Jesus is *un*friendly, but each remains a Lord to be obeyed, not a colleague to be befriended.

This assurance of the Master's friendship is all the more remarkable when compared with the common Latin proverb, *quot servi, tot hostes*, which means (literally) 'as many slaves, so many enemies', that is, 'all slaves are enemies'.[17] The idea of 'friendship within slavery' would not have been altogether foreign to first-century ears,[18]

---

use of *kyrios* (= Jesus) implies that his disciples were *douloi*; but more probably it alludes to the radical newness of the era introduced by Jesus' disclosure of the Father. Special knowledge of God's purposes and ways had not been given to his covenant people at large, only to select persons he called his friends (Gen. 18:17; Exod. 33:11; 2 Chr. 20:7; Ps. 103:7). Now, however, intimate knowledge of the Father's character and plan of salvation had been brought by Jesus to all his disciples (John 1:18; 17:26).

15 John 18:36 reads: 'Jesus said, "My kingship does not belong to this world. If my kingship did belong to this world, my servants (*hypēretai*), would be fighting, so as to prevent my being handed over to the Jews. But, as it is, my kingship does not belong here."' This verse implies, but does not explicitly state, that Jesus was a king (but see John 18:37) and that his kingdom did have 'servants', perhaps here 'subjects'. But in the ancient world the king–subject relation was in effect simply the master–slave relation on a grand scale.

16 Moses, too, is called the friend of God (Exod. 33:11; by implication).

17 This proverb appeared in various forms. See, *e.g.*, Macrobius, *Sat.* 1. 11. 13. Seneca insisted that slaves were not enemies when they were acquired; rather, slave-owners made them enemies by maltreating them, as if they were mere beasts of burden (*Ep.* 47. 5).

18 See, for example, Pliny the Younger, *Ep.* 5. 19.

but, generally speaking, friendship and slavery were thought to be incompatible, so that a master's friendship with a slave was regarded as bizarre. So, whereas a Roman would say, 'as many slaves, so many enemies', Jesus says, in effect, 'as many slaves, so many friends'.

As those privileged to gain an intimate knowledge of God, believers are the friends of Jesus, not slaves. But as those privileged to serve the Lord Christ (Col. 3:24), believers are the slaves of Jesus, not friends.

Galatians 4:7

As we have shown, in many places in the Pauline corpus use is made of slave imagery, sometimes in a negative sense, sometimes in a positive. According to Paul, both Christian slaves and Christian free persons are slaves of Christ (1 Cor. 7:22; Eph. 6:6). Indeed, the characteristic Christian confession, 'Jesus is Lord (*kyrios*)' (Rom. 10:9; 1 Cor. 12:3), points unmistakably to his being (figuratively) a Lord or Master (*kyrios*) with slaves – so much so that Paul could twice introduce himself to his readers as 'a slave of Christ Jesus' (Rom. 1:1; Phil. 1:1). How, then, could Paul say to the Galatian Christians, apparently unequivocally, 'You are no longer a slave but a son' (Gal. 4:7)?

Galatians 4:7 states the conclusion that may be drawn from 3:26 – 4:6, but in particular from 4:1–6, which is linked with 3:26–29 by the term 'heir' (3:29 and 4:1). It will be useful to trace the course of Paul's argument in verses 1–6 so that the climactic nature of verse 7 becomes clear.

During his legal minority as a child (*nēpios*), the heir is under the supervision and direction of guardians and trustees. It is only at the time set by his father for him to take over the inheritance that he becomes free of that supervision. So with regard to legal status, there is no practical difference between an under-age heir and a slave, in spite of the fact that the minor by right owns the whole estate: both are under supervision, neither one is his own master (vv. 1–2).[19] So too with believers, whether Jew or Gentile. During their spiritual infancy or minority (that is, until the time appointed by the Father for their receipt of adoption), believers were in perpetual slavery (*ēmetha dedoulōmenoi*) to the elemental powers of the universe, including the

---

[19] Alternatively, the similarity may be that neither one has had the experience of claiming an inheritance. Dunn (1993b: 222) suggests that where the son differed from the slave was 'in potential for inheritance'.

law (v. 3). But with the arrival of the time for believers to receive instatement as sons (*huiothesia*), God sent his Son, born of a woman, born under law (v. 4), in order to free from slavery to the elemental forces those who were under law and so grant them the status and rights of full-grown sons of God (v. 5). Proof of that new status may be seen in God's gift to believers of his Son's Spirit, the Spirit who prompts them to utter the filial cry 'Abba' – that is, 'Father' (v. 6). The consequence of all this? Slavery has been replaced by sonship and heirship: the believer is no longer (*ouketi*) a slave, but a son of God, and consequently an heir of his kingdom, all as a result of God's gracious act of adoption (v. 7).[20]

We could encapsulate the topic of the paragraph with the words, 'From childhood to adulthood', 'From spiritual minority to spiritual majority', 'From restriction to freedom', or 'From slavery to sonship'.[21] The basic contrasts are clear: the child who is an under-age heir (vv. 1–2) *versus* the full-grown son who is the heir come of age (vv. 5–6); and the slave (v. 1) *versus* the adopted son (vv. 6–7).

As in John 15:15, so here, the word *ouketi*, 'no longer', appears. But whereas there it pointed generally to the progress of salvation history and the distinctiveness of the new era brought by Jesus, with no implication of previous slavery,[22] here it points to an actual previous bondage to 'the elemental forces of the universe' (v. 3), including the law (*cf.* v. 5),[23] which was terminated with the coming of Christ and faith in him (Gal. 3:24–25). So if John 15:15 says that followers of Jesus are 'no longer' like slaves denied an intimate knowledge of

[20] The change from the plural, 'you are sons' (*este huioi*, v. 6), to the singular, 'you are ... a son' (*ei ... huios*, v. 7) has the effect of individualizing the sonship; each believer is a son or daughter of God.

[21] A similar contrast between servitude and sonship is found in three other places. (a) As Jesus seeks to show that the Jews, as slaves to sin, had forfeited their status as true descendants of Abraham, and that he, as God's Son, was able to set them free, he cites an axiomatic truth: 'A slave (*doulos*) has no permanent place in the household, but a son (*huios*) belongs to it permanently' (John 8:35). Jesus is probably alluding to the fact that a Jewish slave had to be released in the seventh year (Exod. 21:2–4; Deut. 15:12), or to the possibility that any slave could be sold or set free at any time. (b) In Rom. 8:15–16 slavery is associated with fear, and sonship with intimacy and confidence. (c) In the course of demonstrating the superiority of Jesus over Moses, the author of Hebrews contrasts Moses, who was a faithful servant (*therapōn*) within (*en*) God's household, with Jesus, who was a faithful Son (*huios*) over (*epi*) that household (Heb. 3:5–6).

[22] See above, n. 14. In John 15:15 the reference to 'slaves' is virtually a foil for the subsequent reference to 'friends'.

[23] I take *ta stoicheia tou kosmou* (Gal. 4:3; *cf.* 4:9) to be 'the elemental powers/forces/spirits of the universe', everything that usurps the place of God and then becomes the object of human trust.

their master, Galatians 4:7 affirms that they are 'no longer' actual slaves to 'the elemental powers of the universe', and suggests that they are 'no longer' like slaves, who lack the status and rights of sons.

As in John, so in Paul, the reference to the disciples of Jesus being 'no longer slaves' does not invalidate the other references to his disciples as his slaves. As those who are no longer in bondage to 'the elemental powers of the universe' but have been adopted into God's family and are destined to receive an inheritance, believers are God's sons and daughters, not slaves. But as those who render service to God (Rom. 6:22; 1 Thess. 1:9; 1 Pet. 2:16), believers are his slaves, not sons and daughters.

Limitations of the metaphor

No metaphor that is used to picture the believer's relationship to Christ or God can or should be applied at every point of the comparison. Indeed, to do so would lead to serious distortions of the truth. For instance, to deduce from the image of the potter and the clay (Rom. 9:20–24) that God views humans as impersonal objects, or to infer from the picture of the church as 'betrothed' to Christ (2 Cor. 11:2–3) that he never actually becomes the bridegroom, is to pervert the truth. Each figure that depicts the divine–human relationship illustrates some aspect or aspects of the truth, but none illustrates every aspect. So we may speak with justification of the complementarity of New Testament metaphors that describe the Christ–Christian relationship. Together, they present a balanced, accurate picture; considered alone and pressed at every point, they give a distorted and erroneous picture.[24]

So too with the metaphor of slavery. It affords an extraordinarily vivid and permanently relevant picture of the believer's relationship to Christ, but, as with all pictures, its limitations are clear and therefore its usefulness is limited.[25]

---

[24] A splendid discussion of these issues, with copious and detailed illustrations, may be found in Gale 1964: passim.

[25] No passage in the NT makes a more sustained use of the imagery of slavery than Rom. 6:15–23 (see pp. 80–84). It is possible that in the parenthesis of v. 19a Paul is hinting at the inadequacies of the metaphor: 'I am using this human analogy because of your fleshy limitations.' But it seems more likely that he is explaining why he was continuing to develop the imagery. It was because of the limitations of understanding imposed by their fleshly outlook (dia tēn astheneian tēs sarkos hymōn), because of the need to drive home to their dulled understanding his point about submission and obedience to the new Master. But one may not infer that a spiritual understanding of truth would dispense with any need for the image of slavery. After all, Paul began

In the two places where we are told that Christians are 'no longer' slaves (John 15:15; Gal. 4:7), we may deduce from the context the aspects of slavery that do not apply in Christian experience:

1. A slave did not know his master in the sense of having an intimate acquaintance with his master's thoughts and plans; a master did not count his slaves as his friends (*cf.* John 15:14–15).

2. A slave did not expect to be adopted into his master's family or to receive an inheritance (*cf.* Gal. 4:1–7).

Now there may have been isolated execeptions to these two general rules, but as generalizations these rules are undeniably true and may therefore form the backdrop to the statement that Christians are 'no longer slaves'. As matters now stand, the followers of Jesus, unlike the slave, have gained an intimate knowledge of the Master, have been adopted into the Master's family, and will receive the Master's inheritance.

If, then, we understand that these two aspects of slavery, among others, are not applicable to the divine–human relationship, we can comfortably accommodate the two apparently conflicting truths, 'no longer slaves' and 'slaves of Christ'. Christianity is replete with similar paradoxes.

The ideal conditions of slavery to Christ

As a result of the New Testament's transformation of the metaphor of slavery, the conditions under which slavery to Christ is experienced may be described as ideal.

An ideal Master

The Master who is served is not only peerless in status (Matt. 28:18; Phil. 2:9) and meek and gentle in character (Matt. 11:29; 2 Cor. 10:1; see above, ch. 7). He provides for his slaves generously, protects them jealously, and rewards them handsomely.

A slave was a costly investment in the ancient world, for the corollary of the ownership of the master was the dependence of the slave. The slave-owner was obliged to provide the food, clothing, and accommodation which the slave could not provide for himself and his family.[26] The slaves of Christ, for their part, relax in humble

---

this very letter with the words, 'Paul, a slave of Christ Jesus' (Rom. 1:1).

[26] If the word 'advantage' is in any sense applicable to the state of physical slavery, this was the advantage of being a slave.

dependence on the limitless resources of their Owner. 'His divine power', says Peter, 'has granted us everything necessary for a godly life' (2 Pet. 1:3). Their attitude is summed up in the psalmist's words: 'As the eyes of slaves (*doulōn*) look to the hand of their master (*kyriōn*), as the eyes of a female slave (*paidiskēs*) look to the hand of her mistress (*kyrias*), so our eyes look to the Lord our God, till he shows us mercy' (Ps. 122:2, LXX). Such an attitude is diametrically opposed to the Cynic and Stoic ideal of *autarkeia*, that self-sufficiency that made a person independent of external aid or support. It was only through the power of Christ that strengthened him that Paul was able to 'do all things', *viz.* face plenty and hunger, affluence and poverty (Phil. 4:12–13).

One consequence of the expense of slave ownership was the master's jealous protection of his property. The more expensive the slave, the more vigorous the protection. Anyone who harmed the slave attacked the owner's rights to his property.[27] If the essence of Christianity is belonging to Christ (Rom. 14:8; 1 Cor. 3:23), and the purchase price was blood (Rev. 5:9), there can be no doubt that Christ, as the Purchaser, has a vested interest in protecting his property (*cf.* Acts 9:4–5). For instance, in the high-priestly prayer of John 17, Jesus affirms that during his ministry he had protected and guarded (*ephylaxa*) his followers by mediating the revelation of the Father ('in the name you gave me', v. 12; *cf.* 1:18; 14:9), and prays that after his return to heaven his Father may keep them fully true to the revelation he had brought them (v. 11) and protect them from the evil one (v. 15; *cf.* Matt. 6:13). Paul refers to this protective role of a *kyrios* when he reassures the Thessalonians that 'the Lord (*kyrios*) is to be relied on, and he will give you strength and protect (*phylaxei*) you from the evil one' (2 Thess. 3:3, Goodspeed).[28] But in addition to caring for and guarding his slaves, Jesus the Lord rewards them. It was Jesus himself who reminded his disciples in the parable of the obedient slave (Luke 17:7–10) that a slave's performance of duty never places his master under an obligation to thank or reward him for that service. Yet in the case of Jesus, it is precisely in his role as

---

[27] In Roman law the master was identified with his slave to the extent that crimes against the slave were regarded as offences against his master, and the master – not the slave – could sue for damages.

[28] Christ's care and protection of his own are given in his capacity as *dominus* ('Lord') rather than as *patronus* ('patron'). Believers were not enslaved to Christ before their 'manumission' by him, whereas the 'patron' was the former slave-owner. But for a different view, see Lyall 1984: 43–45.

kyrios that he both commends his slaves warmly and rewards them handsomely. '"Well done, good and trustworthy slave," said his master (*kyrios*). "You have been trustworthy with a few things; I will put you in charge of many things. Come on in and share your master's happiness!"' (Matt. 25:21, 23). 'You know that each of you will be rewarded by the Master (*para kyriou*) for any honest work done, whether you are slave or free' (Eph. 6:8; *cf.* 2 Cor. 5:10; Col. 3:24).

Before we leave this discussion of the ideal nature of Christ's lordship, we must briefly address the question, 'Can Christ's relation to the believer be properly described as "domination", and the believer's relation to Christ as "submission"?'

D. Cupitt (1972: 106) has contended that 'the language of the great monotheistic religions – Judaism, Christianity and Islam – is shot through with imagery of domination and submission. God is described as King, Lord, Judge, and Father, and the believer appears before him as subject, servant, defendant and obedient child.' In his call for a radical moral purging of the Christian tradition, Cupitt argues that Master–servant imagery in particular must be discarded, since 'nowadays a man feels he ought, so far as possible, to be his own master' (120).[29] He himself despairs of an alteration of imagery, rightly recognizing that a change of basic images amounts to the creation of a new religion (120f.).

We have already seen that the New Testament is indeed 'shot through' with the imagery of slavery. But in the Christian transformation of the metaphor, while the notion of voluntary submission to the divine will remains intact, the idea of domination finds no place – if by 'domination' we mean not simply a sway or a state of being ruled, but the imposition of one person's will on another who is either unwilling or reluctant to accept that imposition.

It is the central thesis of Patterson in his magisterial study of slavery in ancient and modern times (*Slavery and Social Death*, 1982) that slavery is basically a relation of human 'parasitism', in which domination characterized the master and social death was the lot of the slave. 'Because the slave had no socially recognized existence outside his master, he became a social nonperson' (5).[30] In the language of

---

[29] 'Master–servant imagery suggests that we still live in a universe in which petition is the ordinary fellow's best recourse. And this is not true, either in the political or in the natural realms' (1972: 120).

[30] 'We may summarize the two modes of representing the social death that was slavery by saying that in the intrusive mode the slave was conceived of as someone who did not

social biologists, parasitism is a form of symbiosis in which one partner – the parasite – benefits while the other partner suffers, although parasitism may range from minor to major dependence on the 'host'.[31] Says Patterson, 'Interpreting slavery as a relation of domination rather than as a category of legal thought has been an important departure' (334). He tries to interpret the social process of slavery from the viewpoint of the persons dominated, in an effort partially to redress the balance in a historiography which has often interpreted slavery from the perspective of the dominator or exploiter (335). Thus the master is the parasite, the slave the host. In the process of dominating another person, the dominator himself becomes dependent or parasitical.[32]

In ancient and modern 'slavery to Christ', the relation is certainly not that of 'parasitism' – in either direction. That is, it cannot be said that, as a result of the symbiosis of Christ and the believer, Christ benefits and the believer suffers, or that Christ suffers while the believer benefits. Nor can the relation be described as 'mutualism', where both partners benefit,[33] for while believers benefit from their relation to Christ, he gains no benefit – although he does gain pleasure – from our relationship to him. He is complete and perfect in himself. Perhaps the most we should say is simply that we are in a symbiotic relationship with Christ,[34] in which we are privileged to participate in his life, to be wholly dependent on him for our spiritual

---

belong because he was an outsider, while in the extrusive mode the slave became an outsider because he did not (or no longer) belonged. In the former the slave was an external exile, an intruder; in the latter he was an internal exile, one who had been deprived of all claims of community' (1982: 44, *cf.* 38–45).

[31] The other major types of symbiosis are 'commensalism' in which one party benefits and the other neither benefits nor suffers; and 'mutualism', in which both partners benefit (E. O. Wilson, *The Insect Societies* [Cambridge, MA: Harvard University Press, 1971], 389, as cited by Patterson 1982: 453 n. 1).

[32] 'The master remains a moral parasite, however well he treats his slave; the slave remains a parasitized victim, however much he or she enjoys thralldom' (Patterson 1982: 445 n. 3). In this 'ideological inversion of reality' or 'ideological self-deception', the slave-holder camouflaged his own parasitism paradoxically by defining the slave as dependent (337–339). 'It is precisely those societies in which slave-holders sought to maximize leisure ... that we find the relation [between master and slave] moving closer to, though never of course reaching, cooperation and mutualism between holder/parasite and slave/host' (337).

[33] See n. 31 above.

[34] *Cf.* Fitzmyer 1989: 90: 'The most common use of *en Christō* ['in Christ'] is to express the close union of Christ and the Christian, an inclusion that connotes a symbiosis of the two.'

sustenance and well-being, and to be submissive to his will.

Said the Stoic philosopher, Seneca: 'All of life is slavery', in the sense that everyone is fettered to the capricious dictates of Fortune. 'For some, the chain is made of gold and is loose; for others, it is tight and made of baser metal – but what difference does it make?' (*Tranq.* 10. 3). For the Christian, on the other hand, all of life is slavery under the beneficent lordship of Christ, whose yoke is easy and whose burden is light (Matt. 11:30).

Willing service

Christians form a community of emancipated people who have become 'fellow-slaves' in the service of Christ. They serve him voluntarily and enthusiastically, motivated by love and sensing their high privilege in belonging to and representing him and yet also their ultimate accountability to him.

One of the classic Christian paradoxes is that freedom leads to slavery and slavery leads to freedom. As soon as people are set free through Christ from slavery to sin, they enter a new, permanent slavery to Christ. Indeed, the one slavery is terminated precisely in order to allow the other slavery to begin. While that emancipation happens individually, the persons who are freed are not simply isolated 'slaves of Christ'. They form a worldwide community of 'fellow-slaves', all belonging to the one Master who purchased their freedom and all committed to obeying and pleasing him. In this individual and corporate servitude to Christ, believers discover true freedom,[35] or as *The Book of Common Prayer* puts it, his (God's) 'service is perfect freedom'.[36] This true freedom means release from self-centredness and self-seeking, the power to do what one ought, and the full realization of personal potential. The sentiment is captured in George Matheson's celebrated hymn (1890):

> Make me a captive, Lord,
> And then I shall be free;
> Force me to render up my sword,
> And I shall conqu'ror be.

---

[35] Dunn (1993a: 103f., *cf.* 20–24, 78–102) has shown that whereas for John Stuart Mill 'liberty meant essentially liberty *from* society', for Paul 'liberty is liberty *in* society, as part of society, a liberty which functions not simply as freedom of the individual, but in and as responsibility towards society'.

[36] In 'The Second Collect, for Peace' in 'The Order for Morning Prayer'.

That is, freedom from slavery is followed by freedom in slavery.

Among New Testament authors it is Paul in particular who uses slave imagery to depict the believer's relation to God or Christ. For him the Christian may be simply and aptly described as someone who serves the Lord as a slave or someone who is the Lord's slave. Twice he issues the command: 'Give a slave's service to the Lord [Christ]' (Rom. 12:11; Col. 3:24), where the verb *douleuō* is used.[37] The Christian life is nothing other than slavery to Christ.[38] In his speech to the Ephesian elders at Miletus (Acts 20:18–35), Paul claims that his conduct during his three years of ministry in Ephesus had been that of a slave of the Lord (Jesus, see Acts 20:21): 'You yourselves know the kind of life I lived the entire time I was with you: I served the Lord as his slave (*douleuōn tō kyriō*) with great humility and with tears' (Acts 20:18–19).

Christ's slaves render their services voluntarily, not under external compulsion. They may confess, to be sure, that Christ Jesus has 'laid hold' of them (*cf.* Phil. 3:12), but they serve him by their own choice, grateful that he has set them free. They have committed themselves to him totally and unconditionally – all of life for the whole of life.[39] Slavery to Christ is not an irksome necessity imposed from without; it is a pleasurable commitment motivated from within.[40]

Half-heartedness has no place among Christ's slaves;[41] they serve with an enthusiasm generated by Christ's Spirit. In Romans 12:11 it is significant that immediately after saying, 'Be aglow with the Spirit',

[37] In Rom. 12:11 the participle *douleuontes* is imperatival in force, and in Col. 3:24 the form *douleuete* is more probably an imperative than an indicative (see Harris 1991: 185f.). Compare Rom. 7:6; 16:18; Eph. 6:7; Phil. 2:22, where the same verb is used in reference to serving God or Christ.

[38] Bultmann (1955: 2. 214) suggests that in its 'technical sense' the expression 'slave of God' (or 'of Christ', or 'of the Lord') is 'approximately equivalent to "Christian"'.

[39] In discussing the unity and variety of NT teaching, C. F. D. Moule (1962: 9, *cf.* 211) proposes that 'the common factor holding all together is devotion to the person of Jesus Christ – the historical Jesus acknowledged as Messiah and Lord'.

[40] As he defends the retention of the figure of slavery to denote Christian obligation, Cranfield (1975: 1. 326) comments that 'it is doubtful whether there is any other [figure] which can so clearly express the total belongingness, the total obligation, the total commitment and the total accountability, which characterize the life under grace'. 'The question may well be asked whether the expurgation of our exposition of the Christian life by the removal of the slavery figure is not more likely to prove a serious impoverishment and distortion than a genuine purification' (326 n. 2).

[41] Rengstorf, the author of the important article on *doulos* in *TDNT*, makes the brutally honest observation that 'when it is taken seriously this formula [slave of God] presupposes a self-dedication which not all Christians are either prepared or able to accept' (1964: 2. 274).

Paul adds, 'Serve the Lord as his slave (*tō kyriō douleuontes*)', as if to suggest that 'the real proof of the presence of this fire of the Spirit would be not effervescent religious excitement but renewed energy and determination in the humble and obedient service of the Lord Jesus' (Cranfield 1979: 2. 635).

Motivation for devoted service comes not only from gratitude for emancipation but also from love. The story of Simon Peter's encounter with Jesus by the Sea of Tiberias after the resurrection (John 21:1–19) illustrates the priority of love over service. 'Do you love me? ... Feed my sheep' (v. 17). The service of slavery to Christ must be prompted by love for him. Matching the paradox of 'slavery in freedom' is the paradox of 'love in slavery'. Within Christian freedom there is slavery; within Christian slavery there is love. This prevents freedom from becoming unbridled licence and prevents slavery from becoming cringing bondage.

There can be no higher and more ennobling privilege than to have the Lord of the universe as one's Owner and Master and to be his accredited representative on earth. Yet that is the privilege of those who address him as 'My Lord and my God' (John 20:28). To be his slave is to be more privileged than to be his apostle (*cf.* Rom. 1:1; 2 Pet. 1:1) or his brother (*cf.* Jas. 1:1; Jude 1).

By definition a *kyrios* holds his *douloi* accountable for their stewardship (1 Cor. 4:1–2, 4–5). When all Christ's slaves appear before his tribunal, there will be an assessment of their works (2 Cor. 5:10), to determine not their destiny but their reward (Eph. 6:8; *cf.* Col. 3:24). Such a prospect instils into Christ's slaves a healthy reverential awe (*phobos*) before their heavenly Lord (2 Cor. 5:10–11).

The book of Romans is the flagship of the Pauline fleet. Flying proudly at the top of the mast of this ship is a flag bearing the words, 'Paul, a slave of Christ Jesus' (*Paulos, doulos Christou Iēsou*, Rom. 1:1). This flag is two-toned, its white indicating complete freedom yet total surrender, and its purple symbolizing royal ownership and therefore incomparable privilege. The slave of Christ is the emancipated dependant of Christ as well as the willing bondservant of Christ, the exclusive property of Christ as well as the honoured representative of Christ.

It is one thing for us to follow a grand custom and stand during the singing of the Hallelujah Chorus at the unforgettable climax of Part II of Handel's *Messiah* and so celebrate the ultimate victory of Christ. It is quite another thing for us to bow the knee before the crucified and exalted Lord of the universe and receive the metaphorical piercing of the ear as a sign and pledge of our joyful and willing slavery to him as long as we live.[42] If we do this, then when we do stand in his presence at the conclusion of our lives, and ourselves sing the song of the Lamb, we shall hear those unforgettable words from our Master's lips, 'Congratulations, good and faithful slave!'

---

[42] *Cf.* Exod. 21:5–6: 'If the slave [the Hebrew slave who has served his master for six years] declares, "I love my master and my wife and children; I do not want to be freed", then his master must bring him before the judges. He shall take him to the door or the doorpost and pierce his ear with an awl. Then the slave will be his for life.'

Chapter Nine

'Slave of Christ': four New Testament examples

What would the life of a twenty-first-century 'slave of Christ' look like? With regard to character, such a person will be marked by the humility of spirit and preoccupation with the interests of others that characterized the model slave, Jesus Christ (Phil. 2:3–8). But as far as action is concerned, how might we expect Christ's slaves to behave as they seek to display his character? Let me try to answer that pressing – and needful – question by focusing attention on four case studies of first-century Christians, two of them less well known (Dorcas and Onesiphorus), and the other two better known (Priscilla and Aquila). Neither the noun *doulos* nor the verb *douleuein* is used in connection with these early disciples, but, as we shall see, there can be little doubt that they deserve inclusion in the gallery of the heroes of Christian slavery.[1]

Dorcas

The gospels record at least three but probably four instances of dead persons being restored to life before Jesus himself rose from the dead (*viz.* Mark 5:21–24, 34–43; Luke 7:11–17; John 11:1–44; and probably Matt. 27:52–53). But the New Testament also recounts two such cases after Jesus rose, *viz.* Peter's raising of Tabitha at Joppa (Acts 9:36–42), and Paul's raising of Eutychus at Troas (Acts 20:7–12).

Luke tells us that Tabitha was a disciple (*mathētria*) who lived at Joppa (modern Jaffa) and that her name, when translated, means Dorcas.[2] He continues: 'Her life was full of helpful deeds [*ergōn agathōn*] and acts of charity [*eleēmosynōn*] which she constantly did'

---

[1] I have already pointed to Paul's colleague, Epaphras, as a sterling example of the upward and outward aspects of Christian slavery (chapter 5, p. 104).

[2] *Tabitha* is the Gk. transliteration of the Aramaic word *taby^eta* meaning 'gazelle'. The Gk. equivalent of Tabitha is *Dorkas*, 'an animal of the deer species', in Syria and Africa signifying 'gazelle' (LSJ, 445).

(Acts 9:36).[3] Both of these Greek expressions refer to actions directed towards others, so it is unlikely that the former phrase includes activities such as prayer and fasting. What these 'helpful deeds' and 'acts of charity' involved is indicated in verse 39 — the making and giving away of cloaks (*himatia*) and tunics (*chitōnas*). But following an illness Dorcas died. She was washed in accordance with the Jewish rite of Purification of the Dead and placed in an upstairs room (v. 37), perhaps where the local Christian congregation met (*cf.* Acts 1:13; 20:8). The fact that she was not anointed (as was customary after the washing) and buried suggests that Dorcas's friends hoped she would be miraculously restored to life. At any rate, when it became known that Peter was at Lydda, some ten miles away, Dorcas's friends despatched two men to Lydda with the urgent request, 'Please come over to us without delay!' (v. 38). Quite clearly, Peter was not being summoned to conduct a funeral service! He agreed to go, and on arriving in Joppa he was taken upstairs to where Dorcas lay and many widows had gathered.[4] As they stood beside Peter, they pointed with pride to all the (*hosa*) garments they were wearing,[5] clothes made by Dorcas,[6] as evidence of her generosity and the reason for their weeping (v. 39).[7] Whether or not Dorcas was an expert seamstress, she had apparently specialized in making coats and undergarments, for which the recipients were profoundly grateful.

Peter sent all the mourners out of the room, knelt and prayed, and then addressed the corpse with the words, 'Tabitha, get up!' She opened her eyes, and on seeing Peter she sat up (v. 40). He helped her to her feet and presented her alive to the local believers whom he had gathered together (v. 41). When Luke observes that Peter called in the believers 'and (*kai*) the widows', we need not infer that all the widows were unbelievers; nevertheless, the phrase 'the believers (*tous*

[3] Note the similar expressions in Rom. 15:14 ('full of goodness', of the Roman believers) and Jas. 3:17 ('full of mercy and good fruit', in reference to 'the wisdom that comes from heaven'). The imperfect *epoiei* is iterative, signifying repeated action: it was Dorcas's pattern of life to engage in such activities.

[4] 'As in 6:1, widows are mentioned not as members of an organization or ecclesiastical order (*cf.* 1 Tim. 5:3–16) but as natural recipients of charity' (Bruce 1990: 249).

[5] The middle voice of *epideiknymenai* has the sense 'displaying on themselves'. See BAGD 291 *s. v.*, citing Socrates, *Ep.* 23. 3, *toiauta epideiknymenoi*, 'show such things on oneself'.

[6] *Met' autōn* ('with them') should be construed with *ousa*, 'while she was with them', not with *epoiei*, as though Dorcas and the widows shared a workshop, for this would leave *ousa* unattached.

[7] 'There lay a certain self-consciousness, yea, a grateful ostentation, in their being able to show the pledges of her beneficence' (Meyer 1889: 195 n. 3).

hagious) and the widows' shows that at least some of Tabitha's acts of charity were directed towards unbelievers.

1 Corinthians 12 contains two lists of the 'spiritual gifts': verses 8–10 and verse 28.[8] Unlike the former list, which focuses exclusively on the persons who are gifted by the Spirit ('to one ... to another'), the latter list of eight items contains three genres of persons ('apostles ... prophets ... teachers'), followed by two gifts ('miracles ... gifts of healing'; *cf.* vv. 9–10), then two deeds of service ('helps ... administrations'), and finally the gift of glossolalia ('diversities of tongues').[9] The sixth item is *antilēmpseis*, literally 'helps', which may refer to 'forms of assistance' (NRSV) or 'helpful acts' (NJB). Expressed in personal terms, it denotes 'those who give assistance to others'. This gift is probably equivalent to two items in Romans 12:8: sharing one's resources with others (*ho metadidous*, 'the one who shares'), and caring for those in need or distress (*ho eleōn*, 'the one who shows mercy'),[10] be they aliens, orphans and widows (a common Old Testament trilogy)[11] or the poor, the sick, the aged, and the disabled. And, more generally, those who exercise the gift of 'helps' are involved in 'helping the weak' (Acts 20:35, where the cognate verbal form *antilambanesthai*, 'help', is used).

So, then, it is clear that as an expression of her total commitment to Christ, her slavery to Christ, Dorcas was constantly devoted to meeting some of the material needs of the widows in Joppa. As she did so, she was exercising her God-given gift of 'giving assistance' (1 Cor. 12:28).

Onesiphorus

This associate of Paul is mentioned only twice in the New Testament, and at that within one Pauline letter (2 Tim. 1:16–18; 4:19). A key theme in the paragraph 2 Timothy 1:8–14 is the idea of shame (the verb is *epaiskynomai*, 'I am ashamed'). Paul encourages Timothy not to be ashamed to testify about the Lord (= Christ), nor to be ashamed of Paul, Christ's prisoner (v. 8). Paul himself is not ashamed of

[8] For the other listings in the Pauline corpus, see Rom. 12:6–8 and Eph. 4:11.

[9] Some translations convert this mixture of categories (personal and impersonal) into purely personal functions. For example, the RSV (but not the NRSV) has 'apostles ... prophets ... teachers ... workers of miracles ... healers, helpers, administrators, speakers in various kinds of tongues'.

[10] Cassirer renders *antilēmpseis* in 1 Cor. 12:28 by 'works of mercy'.

[11] Deut. 24:19–21; 26:12–13; 27:19; Jer. 22:3.

suffering for the gospel (v. 12). To confirm this admonition to Timothy, the apostle appeals to the negative example of the many throughout Asia,[12] including Phygelus and Hermogenes, who had deserted Paul by abandoning his gospel (v. 15), and the positive example of Onesiphorus, who, says Paul, 'was not ashamed of my chains' (= my being imprisoned,[13] v. 16). This loyalty to Paul, as an outcome of his slavery to Christ, had been expressed in three ways.

1. On his arrival in Rome, he mounted an operation to locate Paul, and his persistence was finally rewarded: 'When he got to Rome, he took great pains to seek me out (*spoudaiōs ezētēsen me*) and he found me' (v. 17).[14] With 'stubborn perseverance' (Spicq 1969: 2. 734) Onesiphorus followed all the leads, some useful, some useless, that might bring him to Paul.[15] He probably felt a novice in moving about the imperial capital; perhaps the Christians in Rome themselves were unaware of the place where Paul was detained. The memory of this self-effacing determination shown by Onesiphorus prompts Paul to interject (see RSV) a 'prayer-wish': 'May the Lord [Jesus] grant that he will find mercy from the Lord [God the Father] on that day!' (v. 18).[16]

2. He had many a time 'refreshed' (*anepsyxen*) Paul (v. 16).[17] That

---

[12] Paul's expression 'everyone (*pantes*) in the province of Asia' is undoubtedly hyperbolic, to express general and widespread desertion: 'almost all' or 'people everywhere'.

[13] The term *tēn halysin* ('chain', singular) could refer to the actual chain by which Paul was bound, since the noun *halysis* commonly denotes a literal chain (*e.g.*, Mark 5:3; Acts 12:6–7) or handcuffs (Acts 28:20), but more probably it is a case of 'the concrete for the abstract' or of metonymy, 'chain' signifying imprisonment (as in Eph. 6:20), with the singular being generic.

[14] Verse 17 begins with the conjunction *alla*, 'on the contrary', which indicates that far from being ashamed of Paul's status and shunning him as a prisoner who was likely to be condemned to death (v. 16), Onesiphorus actually sought Paul out.

[15] Onesiphorus's uncertainty about Paul's whereabouts suggests a situation different from that of Paul's first Roman imprisonment, when his friends all knew of the location of his *libera custodia* (see Acts 28:30).

[16] In Paul the articular *ho kyrios* ('Lord') normally refers to the Lord Jesus (as in v. 16) and the anarthrous *kyrios* ('Lord') to Yahweh or God the Father. It seems probable that Onesiphorus was no longer alive at the time Paul wrote. (a) In v. 16 he refers abruptly to 'the household of Onesiphorus', not to 'Onesiphorus and his household'. (b) The timeless wish that the Lord Jesus should show mercy to the household of Onesiphorus (v. 16) suggests that they were in special need of divine aid and grace because of Onesiphorus's permanent (not temporary) absence. (c) The 'prayer-wish' in v. 18 regarding Onesiphorus himself relates to 'that [last] Day' only, not to the present also. Paul did not write *kai nyn kai en ekeinē tē hēmera*, 'both now and on that Day' (*cf.* Jude 25), or omit any reference to time, as in the similar prayer-wish in v. 16.

[17] This verb, a New Testament *hapax legomenon*, means 'make cool (*psychō*) again

---

is, he had often invigorated Paul like a breath of fresh air, reviving Paul's flagging spirits during his frequent visits, and probably also meeting his physical needs such as for adequate food and clothing. Onesiphorus was living up to his name, 'the help-bringer', and was exercising the gift of encouragement (Rom. 12:8; *cf.* Acts 4:36; 11:22–23). To such as Onesiphorus the Son of Man will say on the last Day (*cf.* v. 18), 'I was in prison and you came to visit me' (Matt. 25:36; *cf.* Heb. 10:34; 13:3).

3. In addition (*kai*) to this recent service to Paul in Rome, numerous were the times when earlier he had rendered service to Paul and others in Ephesus (v. 18).[18] Of this Timothy personally was fully aware (*beltion su ginōskeis*).

In the life of Onesiphorus, then, we see one of Christ's slaves in action, as he showed energetic persistence on Paul's behalf, gave invigorating encouragement to Paul and performed many services for the Ephesian believers.

Priscilla and Aquila

We come now to a pair of Christians over whose lives may be inscribed the words, 'Total Devotion'.[19] Before we examine their lives as 'slaves of Christ', it will be helpful to set out the New Testament data about them in chart form. References and material in brackets represent inferential or conjectural information. No suggested date can be regarded as firm, but some are closely related to the chronology of Paul's life and letters.

	Year (AD)	Place	Reference	Events
1	Birth ?40	Pontus	Acts 18:2	Aquila, a Jew, born and raised in Pontus on Black Sea

---

(*ana-*)', that is, 'refresh'. The cognate noun *anapsyxis* ('respite', 'refreshing') occurs only in Acts 3:20 (EVV, 3:19). In 1 Cor. 16:18 Paul credits Stephanas, Fortunatus and Achaicus with having refreshed (*anepausan*) his spirit (*cf.* Rom. 15:32).

18 *Hosa ... diēkonēsen* (v. 18), 'how many services he rendered', need not be restricted to help given to Paul – there is no *moi* '(to) me' – but may include all the loyal Christian service of Onesiphorus rendered to the church in Ephesus.

19 Treatments of the life and role of Priscilla and Aquila may be found in Bruce 1985: 44–50; Hiebert 1973: 33–45; LaSor 1965: 138–146; Lees 1918: 47–67; Moody 1995: 95–101; Murphy-O'Connor 1992: 40–51; Ollrog 1979: 24–27; and Robertson 1922: 52–70.

			(Acts 2:9)	Converted, perhaps by Pontian Christians who had been at Pentecost
2	?40–49	Rome	(Acts 18:3)	Practised his trade as tentmaker
			(Acts 18:2)	Met and married Prisca (= Priscilla), a high-born Roman lady
			(Rom. 16:3)	(Became stalwart members of the church in Rome)
			Acts 18:2	Expelled from Rome by the edict of Claudius against Jews
3	49–52	Corinth	Acts 18:3 (2 Cor. 11:9)	Showed Paul hospitality, and plied their trade with his help
4	52–?55	Ephesus	Acts 18:18–19	Sailed with Paul from Corinth to Ephesus
			Acts 18:19–21	(Carried on Paul's ministry when Paul left for Syria)
			(Acts 18:26)	Worshipped regularly in the synagogue
			1 Cor. 16:19	Part of the Ephesian church met in their home
			Acts 18:26	Instructed Apollos in Christian doctrine
			Acts 18:27	Encouraged Apollos to visit Corinth (*cf.* 1 Cor. 1:12; 3:4–6, 22; 4:6; 16:12)

			(Acts 20:31)	Paul may have lived with them during his 3-year residence in Ephesus
			Rom. 16:4 (?Acts 19:30)	Risked their lives for Paul
5	?55–60	Rome		(Returned to Rome after the death of Claudius) (autumn 54)
			Rom. 16:3–4	Received Paul's greetings; known to 'all the churches of the Gentiles'
			Rom. 16:5	Part of the church in Rome met in their home
				Not mentioned in greetings Paul conveys from Christians in Rome (60–61): Philem., Col., Eph., Phil.
6	60–?	Ephesus	2 Tim. 4:19	(Supported the timid Timothy [2 Tim. 1:7] in his work in the Ephesian church)

Acts 18:2 informs us that Aquila was a Jew and a native of Pontus (which was a Roman province situated on the southern side of the Black Sea and linked administratively with Bithynia). He had recently arrived from Rome with his wife Priscilla as a result of an edict of the emperor Claudius that expelled all the Jews from Rome.[20] Since Aquila is a Roman name (meaning 'eagle') and it was usual for an emancipated slave to assume the name of his master, it is just possible that Aquila had been a slave in Pontus, or that he had been emancipated prior to marrying the daughter of his master in Rome.[21]

[20] On this edict, see the discussion and bibliography of Bruce 1990: 390–391. Bruce dates the edict in AD 49 (see also Ollrog 1979: 25, 246).

[21] Sanday & Headlam 1902: 420, Lock 1924: 120 and Murphy-O'Connor 1992: 40

But against this must be set two facts: Jews outside Palestine not infrequently assumed Roman names; and the epigraphical evidence shows that 'Aquila' was not ordinarily a slave name.[22] Luke calls Aquila simply 'a certain Jew' (*tina Ioudaion*). But this is no indication that he was not yet a Christian when Paul 'found' (*heurōn*) him in Corinth (Acts 18:2), for Luke also describes Apollos, the Christian (Acts 18:25–28; *cf.* 1 Cor. 3:5–9), as 'a certain Jew' (*Ioudaios tis*) later in the same chapter (Acts 18:24). Now it is true that Luke mentions only identity of trade (tentmaking)[23] as drawing Paul to Aquila (Acts 18:3), but this does not exclude a spiritual affinity of Christian discipleship. Also, it seems unlikely, in the light of 2 Corinthians 6:14 ('Keep out of all incongruous ties with unbelievers', Moffatt), that Paul would enter a close business relationship with an unbeliever. If, as Acts 18:1–3 seems to imply, it was immediately on coming to Corinth that Paul 'came across' (v. 2a, Moffatt) Aquila, paid him and his wife a visit, and 'made his home with them' (v. 3a, NEB), we should assume that this couple were already believers when Paul fell in with Aquila (so Ollrog 1979: 25).[24] This refugee Jewish tentmaker may have come to faith in Christ in Pontus as a consequence of the witness of the Jewish pilgrims from Pontus present in Jerusalem on the day of Pentecost (Acts 2:9). Certainly there were Christians in Pontus when 1 Peter was written (1 Pet. 1:1), *viz.* about AD 63. Alternatively, it may have been at Rome that Aquila believed and was baptized.

In his three references to Aquila's wife (Acts 18:2; 18, 26), Luke uses the name Priscilla, the diminutive form of Prisca, in keeping with his preference for the language of conversation. Paul, on the other hand, always refers to her by her formal name, Prisca (Rom. 16:3; 1 Cor. 16:19; 2 Tim. 4:19). While there is no evidence that would link her with the Catacomb of Priscilla on the Via Salaria in Rome, it is certainly possible that she was related in some way to the

---

suggest that both Aquila and Priscilla were freed slaves of the Acilian family in Rome.

[22] For the latter point, see Lampe 1992a: 1. 319, citing Lampe 1989: 142, 151f.

[23] By etymology the term *skēnopoios* (Acts 18:3) means 'tentmaker', but it could also refer to the 'leather-worker'. Lampe, however, believes that 'contrary to the traditional view that both [Aquila and Paul] were leather-workers selling primarily to the military, they more likely sewed linen tents for private customers for use as tents on the beach, sunshades in the atrium, or market stalls' (1992a: 1. 319, citing Lampe 1987: 211–221). See further Murphy-O'Connor 1992: 44f.

[24] But for the view that Aquila and Priscilla became Christians through Paul in Corinth, see Meyer 1889: 346.

renowned Roman family, the *gens Prisca* (so Bruce 1985: 45f.). Since epigraphical data show that the name Prisca was not usually a slave name, we may fairly assume she was probably freeborn (Lampe 1992c: 467). That she was not a Jewess is probable (*pace* Ollrog 1979: 25 and n. 92), when we consider the fact that after referring to Aquila as a Jew, Luke adds that he had recently come from Italy 'with his wife Priscilla' (Acts 18:2). W. M. Ramsay (1920: 268f.) notes in this connection that 'it is characteristic of Luke to suggest by subtle arrangement of words a distinction which would need space to explain formally'.

Their devotion to one another[25]

There are, it appears, at least three indications of this couple's mutual commitment.

1. If we are right in assuming some familial connection between Prisca and the *gens Prisca*, it is significant that when Claudius's edict expelled the Jews from the capital, Prisca the Roman, under no compulsion by reason of race to leave Rome, accompanied her Jewish husband in his departure.

2. When Luke says that 'because he [Paul] was of the same trade he stayed with them (*par' autois*) and worked, for by trade they were (*ēsan*) leather-workers' (Acts 18:3), the plurals 'them' and 'they' both refer to Aquila and Priscilla. Whether or not Priscilla was a woman of high birth, the fact that she toiled at the same craft as her husband indicates the compatibility and co-operation between the pair, especially if she learned her craft from her husband after their marriage (although, of course, this cannot be demonstrated).

3. Aquila and Priscilla are mentioned six times in the New Testament – three times by Luke in the book of Acts and three times by Paul in his epistles. It is remarkable that they are always mentioned together, never separately. The invariable conjunction of their names reflects the inviolate unity of their lives. As we trace their movements, Rome–Corinth–Ephesus–Rome–Ephesus (see the chart above), they are always found side by side, toiling at their craft, adjusting to new situations, and creating new circles of friends, always in unison. For them, mutual love and respect as well as marital fidelity were corollaries of being enslaved by Christ.

There is another remarkable fact about the New Testament record

---

[25] The four headings that follow are drawn, with modifications, from Lees 1918: 50–65.

of this couple. On four occasions Priscilla is named before her husband, twice by Luke (Acts 18:18, 26)[26] and twice by Paul (Rom. 16:3; 2 Tim. 4:19). It was customary in first-century society for the wife to be mentioned after her husband. Why, then, this unusual reversal of order?[27] We can dismiss any suggestion that Priscilla was the more active in Christian work or showed a greater commitment to the Christian cause, and therefore was mentioned first. Scarcely more convincing are the explanations that it was a matter of Christian courtesy extended to a woman, or of gratitude on Paul's part (perhaps shared also by Luke) for Prisca's special role in providing him with hospitality.[28] Quite popular has been the proposal that Priscilla is named first because of her higher social status,[29] but Paul's order of names in Romans 16:21–23, with Erastus, the city treasurer, being named second to last, would count against this, while Luke's interest in the appeal of Christianity to women of high social standing (*e.g.*, Luke 8:3; Acts 16:14; 17:12) does not adequately explain his inversion. Perhaps the most satisfactory explanation is the simplest. Priscilla may have been better known or more prominent in the church, having greater visibility because her giftedness lay in the more public arena. We may compare the way in which British people used to refer to their earlier Prime Minister and her husband as 'Margaret and Denis Thatcher'. In a first-century setting, where it was customary for the husband to be mentioned before the wife, tension might easily have arisen between Priscilla and Aquila, if she was

---

[26] In the Western text (D it^{gig} syr cop^{sa} arm *al*) of Acts 18:26, the names are reversed (see further Metzger 1994: 413f.)

[27] If we ask, 'Why the two exceptions?', the answer must be conjectural. In the case of 1 Cor. 16:19 ('Aquila and Prisca, together with the church in their house, send you warm greetings in the Lord'), written from Ephesus, Paul 'may well have been in their home at the time, and as he wrote, or rather dictated, it is quite credible that Priscilla insisted that her husband's name be put first' (Bruce 1985: 45), or, alternatively, Knight (1992: 476) suggests that the mention of ' "the church in their house" may recall the leadership role of Aquila in the church', while Dunn (1988: 2. 892) points to the special situation at Corinth involving women (1 Cor. 14:33–36). As for Acts 18:2, it was necessary for Aquila to be mentioned first to explain how he, along with his wife, came to be in Corinth.

[28] These are tentative suggestions put forward by Knight 1992: 475–476.

[29] Thus Ramsay 1920: 268f., who, in Ramsay 1895: 1. 637 no. 530, cites a contemporary example (AD 70–80) of a lady, Julia Severa, whose name precedes that of her husband, Tyrronius Rapon, probably because of her superior rank. In Roman epitaphs commemorating the death of a child, the husband's name usually comes first. In the relatively few cases where a wife's name precedes her husband's, there was sometimes a desire to highlight in a public record as a mark of prestige the citizen status of the wife when the husband was a slave (Flory 1983: 216, 218f., 223).

more conspicuously gifted than he and was usually referred to first. But their constant association in the New Testament would suggest that relations between them were harmonious rather than strained.

Their devotion to Christian doctrine

When Paul left Corinth and travelled to Ephesus, Priscilla and Aquila accompanied him (Acts 18:18–19), perhaps to establish a new branch of their tentmaking business there and to afford Paul support for his pioneering evangelism in the city, where they hosted part of the infant church (1 Cor. 16:19). It was there in Ephesus that they met Apollos.

Acts 18:24 gives a fourfold description of Apollos. He was Jewish, an Alexandrian by birth, a learned (or, cultured; *logios*) man, and 'strong in his knowledge of the scriptures' (Moffatt). His knowledge of Jesus and the Jesus movement (*ta peri tou Iēsou*, Acts 18:25; *cf.* 28:31), incomplete as it was (18:25), may have been gained from his home city, Alexandria,[30] or possibly from John the Baptist's disciples. That he was already a Christian before meeting Priscilla and Aquila seems clear from Luke's statement that 'with burning zeal'[31] he used to speak and teach accurately about Jesus' (v. 25),[32] and from his later resounding refutation of the Corinthian Jews in public debate as he proved the messiahship of Jesus from the Scriptures (v. 28).

But in spite of the fact that 'he had been instructed in the way of the Lord', he 'knew of no baptism but John's' (v. 25, TCNT). When Priscilla and Aquila heard this learned professor skilfully debate with the Jews in the synagogue in Ephesus, they were evidently deeply impressed by his ability as an exponent and defender of the gospel. They noticed, however, that he lacked any knowledge of Christian baptism, baptism in the name of Jesus Christ. Instead of criticizing Apollos for his defective understanding of Christian doctrine, or comparing him unfavourably with their close friend Paul (*cf.* Lees 1918: 60), they apparently discussed the matter together and decided to invite him to their home so that the three of them could talk at length about 'the way of God' (v. 26). Luke's use of the compound

---

[30] The Western text adds *en tē patridi* ('in his home city') in v. 25a, probably on the basis of historical fact.

[31] The phrase *zeōn tō pneumati* (v. 25) may mean either 'being fervent in spirit' (RSV; or 'with burning zeal'), or 'glowing with the Spirit' (Goodspeed; *cf.* Rom. 12:11).

[32] The imperfects *elalei* and *edidasken* point to his habitual practice wherever he went. Verse 26 means that Apollos began to do in the Ephesian synagogue what he had been doing elsewhere, *viz.* speaking and teaching about the life of Jesus, and establishing from the Scriptures that the Messiah was Jesus (Acts 18:28).

verb *proslambanō* ('take aside') highlights the sensitivity and graciousness of this Christian pair. It was not in public, where Apollos might be embarrassed, that they supplemented his accurate knowledge about Jesus, but 'aside' or 'privately' (*pros-*; see BAGD 717 *s. v.*). The same verb is used in Matthew 16:22 and Mark 8:32 of Peter's action prior to his rebuking Jesus. Moreover, it is a tribute to the humility of this distinguished Jewish Christian scholar that he was willing to learn from a woman and her husband. Luke intends no distinction to be drawn between 'the way of the Lord' in verse 25 and 'the way of God' in verse 26. Rather, the contrast is between Apollos's accurate (*akribōs*) knowledge of the way and Priscilla and Aquila's exposition of it to Apollos 'more accurately' (*akribesteron*). Things that they had learned from fellow-believers in Rome and from Paul at Corinth, Apollos learned from them at Ephesus. This Christian couple were engaged in the process of the transmission of orthodoxy, the guarding and handing on of the apostolic deposit (*cf.* 2 Tim. 1:14; 2:2). Priscilla and Aquila were themselves so well versed in the (Old Testament) Scriptures and Christian tradition that they were able first to identify the deficiencies in Apollos's knowledge and then to rectify those deficiencies by convincing him of the truth of their teaching, especially about Christian baptism and what it signified.[33] Just as Luke's next episode (Acts 19:1–7) shows Paul's concern to bring certain Ephesian disciples (perhaps the nucleus of the church at Ephesus) into line with normative Christianity as represented by the Jerusalem church, so 18:24–26 illustrates Priscilla and Aquila's concern to ensure the orthodoxy of a man whom they recognized to be an outstanding apologist for the faith.

So from this episode Priscilla and Aquila are seen to be knowledgeable believers, gracious team-teachers and champions of orthodoxy. What was said of the early Christians in Jerusalem was also true of this couple in Ephesus: 'they devoted themselves to the apostles' teaching' (Acts 2:42).

---

[33] Nothing can be deduced with certainty from Luke's silence about any baptism of Apollos. If in fact he was not baptized in the name of Jesus, it would presumably have been on the principle – applicable also to the twelve apostles – that the baptism of John was regarded or credited retrospectively as equivalent to Christian baptism for those who had submitted to John's baptism of repentance for the remission of sins and had also believed in Jesus as Messiah (the latter apparently not being true of the twelve or so Ephesian disciples [19:7], who were accordingly baptized in the name of Jesus).

Their devotion to Christ's work

As Paul concludes his first canonical letter to the Corinthians, he sends various greetings in addition to his own. 'The churches in the province of Asia send you their greetings. Aquila and Prisca greet you warmly[34] in the Lord, and so does the church that meets in their home' (1 Cor. 16:19).

Paul wrote 1 Corinthians from Ephesus (*cf.* 1 Cor. 16:8), where he ministered for over three years (*cf.* Acts 20:31, possibly autumn AD 52 – spring 56). During this time he probably lived in the home of Aquila and Priscilla[35] and worked with them at tentmaking (*cf.* Acts 20:34), as he had done earlier in Corinth. So it was very natural for him to name them specifically – and only them – as he passed on greetings to the Christians in Corinth from 'the churches of Asia' (1 Cor. 16:19) in general and 'all the brothers and sisters' in Ephesus (1 Cor. 16:20) in particular, of whom the believers who met in the house of Aquila and Prisca formed a part. In keeping with the early Christian emphasis on the obligation and privilege of hospitality (*e.g.*, Rom. 12:13; 1 Pet. 4:9; Heb. 13:2), this couple shared with Paul the shelter and security of their home in both Corinth and Ephesus as he toiled manually and spiritually.

Clearly Aquila and Priscilla had dedicated their home as well as their lives to the work of Christ. Not only was it their place of business (tentmaking), a place where Christian teaching took place (Apollos), and a home open to entertain guests (Paul); it was also a centre for worship, for one of the household churches in Ephesus met there. And when later they moved to Rome, once more these tentmakers made their home a 'tent of meeting' for the Lord's people. 'Give my greetings also', says Paul, 'to the church that meets in their home' (Rom. 16:5).[36]

There is yet another way in which this dedicated pair furthered Christ's work. On at least three occasions they prepared the way for Paul's arrival. In this respect their relation to Paul mirrored that of

[34] The uncommon expression *aspazetai ... polla*, 'send ... hearty greetings' (RSV) points to an especially affectionate relationship between Aquila and Prisca and their friends in Corinth.

[35] At the end of 1 Cor. 16:19, Western textual witnesses D* F G it add the phrase 'with whom I am staying as a guest' in reference to Aquila and Prisca. This probably reflects the actual case.

[36] Murphy-O'Connor (1992: 48–50) suggests that those early Christians who met in the home of Prisca and Aquila in Ephesus (1 Cor. 16:19) and Rome (Rom. 16:5) may have occupied for their meetings the upper-level living quarters of this couple's shop.

John the Baptist to Jesus. Whatever their reasons for moving from Rome to Corinth (Acts 18:2), from Corinth to Ephesus (Acts 18:18–19), and from Ephesus to Rome (*cf.* Rom. 16:3), the ultimate result in the divine providence was that they paved the way for Paul's subsequent evangelistic and pastoral activity in Corinth (Acts 18:4–11, 18), Ephesus (Acts 19:1–20:1) and Rome (Acts 28:17–31).[37]

Their devotion to the fellow-slaves of Christ

A cautious reconstruction of circumstances enables us to infer that, like Barnabas (Acts 4:36; 11:22–23), Priscilla and Aquila were given to encouraging others in their following of the Way.

There had been a mixed reaction to Paul's preaching in Athens concerning the resurrection of the dead. Some had come to faith, while others had mocked or had expressed a desire to hear Paul again on the matter (Acts 17:32, 34). So it would have been with mixed feelings about his success in Athens that Paul arrived in Corinth (Acts 18:1), a time when he confessed to being 'weak, nervous, and shaking with fear' (1 Cor. 2:3, NEB). We may legitimately infer that his discovery of Aquila and Priscilla at precisely this time (Acts 18:1–3) enabled them to be a source of encouragement to him as he faced the rigours of his Corinthian ministry (Acts 18:6, 10). It was they with whom he lived and worked (Acts 18:3), it was they who accompanied him to Ephesus after his eighteen months in Corinth (Acts 18:11, 18–19). Having themselves come to Corinth from Rome, they undoubtedly confirmed Paul in his desire to visit Rome (*cf.* Rom. 1:13; 15:23), as well as informing him about some of the prominent members of that church (some of whom Paul probably met on his or their travels; *cf.* Rom. 16:1–15). And in a wider sense, this couple afforded Paul 'the twofold blessing of a woman's friendship and a man's comradeship, under conditions that were free from all misunderstanding' (Lees 1918: 48).

Apollos and Timothy also benefited from this couple's encour-

[37] With regard to their move from Rome to Corinth (Acts 18:2), we may fairly assume that either at the time or perhaps later, they would have traced the hand of divine providence in Claudius's edict that forced their departure from the capital. 'Just as the decree of Caesar Augustus had led Joseph and Mary to Bethlehem for the fulfilling of prophecy, so the edict of Claudius had sent them to Corinth for the furtherance of the Evangel!' (Seekings 1914: 100). And concerning their move from Ephesus back to Rome, Hiebert (1973: 43) writes: 'Their presence there would assure him [Paul] a ready acceptance by the church in Rome when he arrived, and would do much toward furthering the cooperation of the church in Paul's plans for missionary work in Spain (Ro. 15:22–24).'

agement. As those who had recognized the special giftedness of Apollos and had invested themselves in his future (Acts 18:26), Priscilla and Aquila would have figured prominently among the Ephesian believers (*hoi adelphoi*) who encouraged him in his intent to minister in Greece (Acts 18:27a), a ministry that proved to be eminently successful (Acts 18:27b–28; 1 Cor. 3:5–6). As for Timothy, when he was grappling with the challenges of the burgeoning church at Ephesus, particularly the delicate issues of the enrolment of widows (1 Tim. 5:3–15) and the qualification of deacons' wives or women deacons (1 Tim. 3:11), it doubtless proved invaluable for him to have the wise counsel of Priscilla (*cf.* 2 Tim. 4:19), particularly since he himself was by nature timid and diffident (1 Cor. 16:10–11; 2 Tim. 1:7).[38]

In Romans 16:3–16 Paul gives his greetings to no fewer than twenty-six named persons. But heading the list are Prisca and Aquila (v. 3), an indication (along with v. 4) of the depth of Paul's friendship with them and of their prominence in the church in Rome. Not only does he describe them as his 'fellow-workers in Christ Jesus'; he adds the tantalizingly vague comment, 'who once risked their necks for my life' (v. 4).[39] The expression 'risk the neck' (*ton trachēlon hypotithēmi*) refers literally to the exposing of the neck to the executioner's sword, and metaphorically (as here) to exposure to mortal danger. Precisely when Aquila and Prisca placed their lives on the line so that Paul's life might be preserved is not known. It may have been when Paul's life was at risk in Corinth (*cf.* Acts 18:10) or when he 'fought' with man-shaped beasts in Ephesus (1 Cor. 15:32; *cf.* 16:9; Acts 20:19) or in the course of the Demetrius riot at Ephesus (Acts 19:23–41).[40] Whenever it occurred, 'this great sacrificial act Paul could never forget. It set Aquila and Priscilla apart among Paul's friends. They were henceforth knit together by this blood bond. The fact that they escaped with their lives in no wise decreased Paul's

[38] Just as Paul could regard the mother of Rufus as his mother also (Rom. 16:13), so too, Timothy may well have followed Paul's injunction of 1 Tim. 5:2 and treated Priscilla as his mother, 'with all propriety'.

[39] Paul uses a similar expression in Phil. 2:30 in reference to Epaphroditus. 'It was because of his devotion to Christ's work that he was at the point of death, risking his life (*paraboleusamenos tē psychē*) in the effort to make good any deficiency there might be in your service to me.' In Rom. 16:4 the aorist *hypethēkan* ('risked') is constative, but, given the dramatic nature of the action, it is more likely to refer to a single occasion (hence 'once risked') than to a succession of occasions, on which life was threatened.

[40] Paul's 'affliction in Asia' (2 Cor. 1:8–10) probably involved the apostle alone (see especially 1:9; the plural should be seen as epistolary).

sense of obligation to them for their heroic deed. It was loyalty to the limit and Paul cherished the memory of their courage' (Robertson 1922: 67). It was not simply because of this magnanimous act, but also because of their devoted service to the church in Corinth, Ephesus, Rome and elsewhere, that Paul and 'all the churches of the Gentiles' expressed deep gratitude to Prisca and Aquila (Rom. 15:4).

This review of Priscilla and Aquila's total devotion – to each other, to Christian doctrine, to Christ's work, and to the fellow-slaves of Christ – justifies the assessment that, as a Christian wife and husband, theirs was a spiritual comradeship in slavery to Christ that was unsurpassed in the apostolic age.

Appendix 1

The use of *doulos* in the Septuagint

The principal uses of *doulos* in the LXX may be classified as follows and will be seen to represent in part the range of meaning of *'ebed* (which *doulos* regularly translates in the LXX).

A. Any person or group of persons in a temporary or permanent position of subservience to, dependence on, or inferiority to another person or group of persons:

1. a person performing menial tasks for another (Jos. 9:23, woodcutters and water carriers; 2 Kgdms 14:30, setting a field on fire) who owns and may sell him or her (Ps. 104:17, *eis doulon eprathē Iōsēph*);
2. a king's soldiers (4 Kgdms 5:6; *cf.* 5:1) or subjects (1 Kgdms 19:4; 22:14);
3. a prophet's suppliants (1 Kgdms 12:19);
4. one nation as subject to another (1 Kgdms 2:27, Israelites and Egyptians; 2 Kgdms 8:2, Moabites and Israelites).

B. The expression *doulos kyriou* or *douloi kyriou* (or equivalent, such as *ho doulos sou/autou*) is applied to:

1. the patriarchs: Abraham (Ps. 104:42), Isaac (Dan. 3:35), and Jacob (Ezek. 37:25);
2. national leaders, especially kings,
   a. by the Lord himself (4 Kgdms 20:6 and Ps. 88:4, 21, of David, as frequently; 4 Kgdms 21:8, of Moses);
   b. by others (Judg. 2:8, of Joshua; 4 Kgdms 8:19, of David; Ps. 104:26, of Moses);
   c. as a self-designation (1 Kgdms 14:41, Saul; 3 Kgdms 3:7, Solomon);
3. prophets, in particular (3 Kgdms 20:28, Elijah; Jon. 1:9, Jonah) or in general (*hoi douloi mou/autou hoi prophētai*, Jer. 7:25; Amos 3:7; Zech. 1:6);
4. Israel as a nation, as Yahweh's *doulos* (Ps. 79:5, MT *'am*), or

Israelites corporately as *douloi* (Deut. 32:36; Neh. 1:6; 2:20);

5. individual Israelites, as worshippers of Yahweh (Pss. 133:1; 134:1), as those who want to fear Yahweh's name (Neh. 1:11), or as those who are submissive before Yahweh (1 Kgdms 3:10–11; 3 Kgdms 8:23; Ps. 18:12), especially as humble suppliants (Pss. 18:14; 85:2, 4).

Observations

1. The term *doulos* is virtually absent from the Pentateuch (two instances in Lv. [25:44; 26:13], in a non-Israelite context; one in Deut. [32:36], in parallelism to *laos*), where *paides*, not *douloi*, is used of slaves. Roughly two-thirds of the LXX instances occur in the historical books (229 out of 378). Elsewhere the term is common only in the Psalms (55 instances), where it usually refers to the righteous Israelite who continues wholeheartedly in Yahweh's way (*cf.* 3 Kgdms 8:23).

2. A metaphorical use of *doulos* in reference to those enslaved to good or evil is never found. And only rarely do we find:

   a. the combination *doulos theou* (Ezra 5:11; Neh. 10:30; 2 Macc. 1:2);

   b. *doulos* used in a messianic context (Zech. 3:8; Is. 49:5; Ezek. 34:33; 37:24–25); or

   c. *doulos* associated specifically with suffering (Pss. 89:50; 118:84, 122; 142:12).

In the four Servant Songs of Isaiah, where *'ebed* is normally rendered by *pais* (*cf.* Acts 3:13, 26), *doulos* is found only in 49:3, 5.

3. When *doulos* is applied to individuals, it could denote:

   a. any one of the patriarchs (B. 1);

   b. a leader of God's people (B. 2);

   c. a prophet as God's messenger (B. 3);

   d. any person involved in the worship or service of God (B. 5).

4. This analysis of the range of use of *doulos* in the LXX makes it likely that this term is flexible in the New Testament, and renders it unlikely that a single figurative connotation attaches to the term in the New Testament. For example, although the expression 'my/his *douloi*, the prophets' is common in the LXX, it is improbable that this use alone is determinative for the New Testament, so that *ex hypothesi* only the apostles in their role as prophets were *douloi* or

that every *doulos* was a prophet. Nor does it follow that simply because leaders such as Moses and David were called *douloi*, those called *douloi* in the New Testament must occupy some leadership position in the church.

Appendix 2

New Testament terms denoting slavery

The majority of New Testament terms that denote slavery are related to four Greek roots.[1]

Doul-

This is the principal Greek stem that generates words denoting servitude. There are the nouns *doulos*, 'slave' (male or female); *doulē*, 'female slave'; *syndoulos*, 'fellow-slave'; and *douleia*, 'slavery'. The cognate adjective, *doulos* (= *doulikos* in Attic prose), means 'subservient to', 'in slavery to', 'controlled by' (only in Rom. 6:19, twice).

From this stem are formed four verbs: *douleuō*, 'be a slave', 'serve as a slave'; *douloō*, 'enslave'; *katadouloō*, 'reduce to slavery' (two figurative uses: 2 Cor. 11:20; Gal. 2:4); and *doulagōgeō*, 'take into slavery' (figurative) (1 Cor. 9:27 only).

The compound noun *ophthalmodoulia* (Eph. 6:6; Col. 3:22) means literally 'enslavement to the eye', that is, 'eye-service', service with a view to impressing others (LN, 461 §35. 29), external or outwardly proper service that is performed without heart and only to gain attention.

---

[1] The earliest general Greek word for 'slave' is *dmōs*, a term found especially in Homer and Hesiod, mostly in the plural. Formed from the verb *damaō* or *damazō* ('subdue, conquer'), the word originally referred to a slave captured in war and is not used after the early fourth century BC. The NT does not use all the Greek words that refer to slaves. As a distinguished Cambridge classicist observes, 'The Greek language had an astonishing range of vocabulary for slaves, unparalleled in my knowledge' (Finley 1974: 54). A famous passage in Philo (*Jos.* 219) illustrates the point. As he amplifies the details of the Joseph saga, the writer describes the reaction of Joseph's brothers after the silver cup had been discovered in Benjamin's sack and they had returned to Egypt. 'They gave themselves up to him [Joseph] and volunteered to submit to slavery (*douleia*). They called him their absolute master (*despotēs*), and spoke of themselves as foreign captives (*problētoi*), as slaves born and bred in the house (*oikotribes*), as slaves bought in the market (*argyrōnētoi*), omitting to mention no name indicative of slavery (*oiketika onomata*).'

Figurative uses of the Doul- root (literal uses in brackets)

Book[2]	Doulos (noun)	Doulē	Syndoulos	Douleia	Douleuō	Douloō
Whole NT	124x	3x	10x	5x	25x	8x
Matthew	1[3] (29)		(5)		1 (1)	
Mark	1[4] (4)					
Luke	1[5] (25)	2			2 (1)	
John	2[6] (9)				1	
Acts	3	1			1 (1)	(1)
Paul	16 (14)		2	4	15 (2)[7]	6
Peter	3					1
Hebrews				1		
James	1					
Jude	1					
Revelation	11 (3)[8]		3			

Observations

1. In the four gospels, with their constant reference to historical circumstances and their inclusion of many of Jesus' parables (that are usually drawn from everyday life), it is not surprising that the literal use of *doulos* is normative, the figurative use being exceptional (only five instances out of 67, of which three refer to Jesus' disciples).

2. In Paul's letters the literal and metaphorical uses of *doulos* (found side by side in 1 Cor. 7:22) are almost evenly balanced. He has the 'slave–free' antithesis four times (1 Cor. 12:13; Gal. 3:28; Eph. 6:8; Col. 3:11) and often addresses the situation of Christian slaves (nine examples).

3. The only non-figurative uses of *doulos* in Revelation occur in the 'slave–free' contrast (Rev. 6:15; 13:16; 19:18).

4. Six of the metaphorical uses of *doulos* are found in epistolary salutations (Rom. 1:1; Phil. 1:1; Titus 1:1; Jas. 1:1; 2 Pet. 1:1; Jude 1; *cf.* Rev. 1:1, twice).

[2] In this column 'Paul' includes the thirteen letters of the Pauline corpus; 'Peter' refers to 1 and 2 Peter; the *doul-* root does not occur in the three Johannine epistles.

[3] Matt. 20:27 (of Jesus' disciples).

[4] Mark 10:44 (of Jesus' disciples).

[5] Luke 2:29 (of Simeon).

[6] John 8:34 (of sinners); 15:15 (of Jesus' disciples).

[7] Rom. 9:12 (of Esau's domination by Jacob and Edomite subjugation by Israel); 1 Tim. 6:2 (of the Christian slave's service to his master).

[8] Rev. 6:15; 13:16; 19:18 (all three passages have the 'slave–free' antithesis).

5. When all the words drawn from the *doul-* stem are considered (180 in all), 64 (or 36%) occur in the Pauline epistles.

6. In Paul's usage, the figurative sense of the root predominates (48 out of 64 examples).

7. The only Pauline epistle to lack any example of a word from this group is 2 Thessalonians.

8. The two nouns *doulē* and *douleia*, the two verbs *katadouloō* and *doulagōgeō*, and the adjective *doulos*, all relatively rare in the New Testament, are always used figuratively.

There is a close association between the terms *doulos* and *diakonos* ('servant'). For instance, within one letter Paul calls his colleague Epaphras both 'a loyal servant of Christ' (*pistos ... diakonos tou Christou*, Col. 1:7) and 'a slave of Christ Jesus' (*doulos Christou Iēsou*, Col. 4:12). A *doulos* gives service (*diakonia*), as is illustrated by the sequence *doulon ... diakonei* in Luke 17:7–8. Yet not all those who give service are 'slaves'. The ruler who serves by exercising authority and wielding the sword is called God's servant (*diakonos*), not his slave (Rom. 13:3–4, 6). All *douloi* are *diakonoi*, but not all *diakonoi* are *douloi*; *diakonos* is the broader term. Another important difference between the two words is that a *diakonos* may render his service under a negotiated contract, whereas both the work and the person of a *doulos* belong to another. *Diakonos* points to a more elevated status. In this connection A. H. M'Neile (1915: 290) observes that Matthew 20:27 represents an intensificatoin of the previous verse: 'as *protos* ['first', v. 27] is higher than *megas* ['great', v. 26], so is *doulos* [v. 27] lower than *diakonos* [v. 26]'.

Oik-

This 'household' root (*oikia* means 'house') gives us *oiketēs*, the domestic slave, as opposed to the industrial slave; *oikonomos*, a slave in charge of an estate or a household; and *oiketeia*, the household of slaves. Like the *doulos*, the *oiketēs* renders service[9] – 'no household-slave (*oiketēs*) can serve (*douleuein*) two masters' (Luke 16:13) – but in this case the *kyrios* is distinctively the *oikodespotēs*, 'the master of the house'. Included within the *oiketai* would be 'professionals', such as teachers (*paidagōgoi*) and doctors (*iatroi*) who worked as members

---

[9] In the 'household tables' of the New Testament, Peter uses the term *oiketai* for 'slaves' (1 Pet. 2:18), Paul the term *douloi* (Eph. 6:5; Col. 3:22; 4:1; 1 Tim. 6:1; Titus 2:9).

of the master's 'family'. When the cognate adjective *oikeios* ('belonging to the household') is used as a noun, it denotes 'members of the same family: parents and close relatives' (Spicq 1969: 1. 385), indicating a narrower group than *hoi idioi* ('one's own') (see 1 Tim. 5:8). Figuratively, *hoi oikeioi* refers to members of God's 'household of faith' or 'family of believers' (Gal. 6:10; *cf.* Eph. 2:19). The noun *oikiakos* is found twice (in the plural; Matt. 10:25, 36) of 'members of a household', or possibly, 'relatives'.

Paid-

The noun *pais* ('child'), which may be masculine or feminine in gender, has a wide range of referents. As BAGD (604f.) indicates, when *pais* describes the relation of one human to another, it may mean 'boy' or 'girl' (from the viewpoint of age), 'son' (from the viewpoint of descent), or 'servant' or 'slave' (from the perspective of social status). In Matthew's account of the healing of a centurion's servant in Capernaum, the servant is called a *pais* (Matt. 8:6, 8, 13), whereas in Luke's version he is called both a *pais* (Luke 7:7) and a *doulos* (7:2–3, 10). Other New Testament terms derived from this root include *paidiskē*, a female slave; *paidagōgos*, the man (usually a slave) responsible for the general supervision and sometimes the tutoring of a boy; and *paideutēs*, the man (often a slave) responsible for the instruction and discipline of children or others.

Therap-

From this stem comes *therapōn*, a slave who is a personal attendant, but in the New Testament it is used only of Moses (Heb. 3:5, citing Num. 12:7) in his role as a person who served God with eager and spontaneous devotion (*cf.* Spicq 1978: 216). *Therapeia* can refer to a group of personal slaves (Luke 12:42).[10]

Sometimes a combination of several of these terms for slaves appears

---

[10] On one occasion, in a list of cargo (Rev. 18:13), the term *sōmata* (lit. 'bodies') signifies slaves (*cf.* the English expression 'body-count'), just as in the papyri passengers as entities paying fares are called *sōmata*. Significantly, in this verse *sōmatōn* is immediately followed by *kai psychas anthrōpōn*, 'that is, human souls' (RSV), or '– human beings!' (NIVI), which attenuates any pejorative sense of 'bodies' = 'slaves'. This use of *sōmata* to denote slaves is also found in the LXX: Gen. 34:29; 36:6; 47:18; Neh. 9:37; Tobit 10:10; 2 Macc. 8:11 – cited by Ziesler 1983: 135–138.

in a single passage. In Jesus' parable regarding watchfulness and faithfulness (Luke 12:42–48), the master had a steward or manager (*oikonomos*, v. 42), also called a slave (*doulos*, vv. 43, 45–47), who was responsible in his master's absence (v. 42) for allocating rations to other slaves in the household (*therapeia*), both male (*paides*) and female (*paidiskai*, v. 45) slaves.

Appendix 3

The translation of *doulos* in English versions of the New Testament

A strange phenomenon

In New Testament Greek there are at least six terms that are often translated or could be translated by the English word 'servant'.[1] But only one New Testament word – *doulos* – has the distinctive meaning of 'slave',[2] and this word occurs 124 times in the New Testament and its compound form *syndoulos* ('fellow-slave') ten times.

Yet in the history of the English Bible we find the strange but almost uniform tradition of generally avoiding the rendering 'slave' for *doulos*, unless literal slavery or slavery to something inanimate is in mind – as in the 'slave–free person' antithesis, in the household codes of conduct (commonly called *Haustafeln*, 'household tables'), or in reference to slavery to sin or depravity. An illustration of this remarkable fact and the dilemma faced by translators is afforded by Ephesians 6:5–6, where, in a single Greek sentence there are two instances of *douloi* (plural), one literal (*douloi* who have 'earthly masters', v. 5), and one figurative (*douloi* of Christ, v. 6). Some English versions, rightly I believe, have 'slaves … slaves',[3] but we also find 'servants … servants' (RV, Moffatt, Berkeley),[4] 'bondsmen … bondsmen' (Conybeare & Howson), and 'slaves … servants' (RSV, Cassirer)[5] or 'slaves … bondservants' (Weymouth).

---

[1] *Viz. diakonos, oiketēs, pais, hypēretēs, leitourgos, paidiskē*; and possibly *misthios, misthōtos* and *oiketeia*.

[2] The cognate noun *doulē* means 'female slave'. On the richness of the Greek language as a whole with regard to terms denoting slavery, see Appendix 2 n. 1 (p. 177).

[3] TCNT, Goodspeed, Montgomery, Williams, NEB, NASB, GNB, JB, NAB1, 2, NIV, NJB, REB, NRSV, CEV, NLT.

[4] RV has a footnote, 'Gr. *bondservants*', on the second *douloi*.

[5] RSV has a footnote, 'Or *slaves*', on the second *douloi*.

Reasons for this phenomenon

How are we to account for this reluctance to translate *doulos* by 'slave'? There may be three main reasons for this hesitation. First, the history of modern slavery in the West is a patent embarrassment to most people; painful historical memories would suggest that we should try to consign to oblivion the very concept of slavery. Why perpetuate those disconcerting memories by enshrining in the holy Scriptures an institution that has always deserved to be abhorred? Second, one task of the translator is to avoid, wherever possible, creating wrong impressions, to obviate misunderstandings. If *doulos* is rendered 'slave', there is the ever-present danger that readers will project their first-hand or second-hand knowledge of modern slavery back into the first century, when slavery had a considerably different complexion.[6] Such a retrojection produces a first-century slave in the image of Uncle Tom (of Harriet Beecher Stowe's *Uncle Tom's Cabin*) or Kunta Kinta (of Alex Haley's *Roots*). Perhaps awareness of this danger contributed to translators' reticence to use the term 'slave' except where it was virtually necessary (as in the 'slave–free' contrast).[7] Third, there are certain linguistic facts that partially explain the preference for 'servant' over 'slave'.

1. 'In the 14th and 15th c[enturies] [*servant* was] often used to render the L[atin] *servus* slave. In all the Bible translations from Wyclif to the Revised Version of 1880–4, the word very often represents the Heb. *ebed* or the Gk. *doulos*, which correspond to *slave*, though this term as applied to Israelitish conditions would perh[aps] be misleading' (*OED*, IX [Section S – Soldo], 508, 3. a).

2. The AV avoided the term 'slave' (except for Jer. 2:14; Rev. 18:13), perhaps because in Elizabethan English it denoted a captive in fetters or a prisoner in jail (so Yamauchi 1966: 40–43). At this point, and in a multitude of other cases, the AV has exercised a formative influence on subsequent translations.[8]

3. 'In the North American colonies in the 17–18th c[enturies], and

---

[6] On the differences between ancient and modern slavery, see chapter 2, pp. 44f.

[7] But even here the AV has 'bond ... free' (*e.g.*, Col. 3:11).

[8] One may compare the similar influence on the history of the German NT of Luther's uniform rendering of *doulos* by *Knecht*, not *Sklave*. Even in Rev. 18:13, the one place in the New Testament where the AV has 'slaves' (for *sōmata*, lit. 'bodies'), Luther has *Leiber* ('bodies').

subsequently in the United States, *servant* was the usual designation for a slave' (*OED*, IX, 508, 3. b).

A notable exception to the general practice

E. J. Goodspeed served for many years as Professor of Biblical and Patristic Greek at the University of Chicago, and from 1923 to 1937 he was head of the New Testament Department there. His pioneering work in the collection, deciphering and publishing of Greek papyri meant that he was eminently qualified to take up the challenge of faculty colleagues to prepare a translation of the New Testament free of archaisms and Britishisms, a readable translation in the everyday language of the American people. The result was the publication in 1923 by the University of Chicago Press of *The New Testament: An American Translation.*[9]

His is the only modern English translation that consistently renders *doulos* by 'slave'.[10] In defence of this policy he writes:

> English translators of the Bible almost without exception have avoided the distasteful word 'slave' in translating the Greek word *doulos*. Yet it means nothing else, and their fastidiousness has led readers of the King James, for example, far astray; modern political scientists have gained from it the impression that Paul says nothing at all about slaves and slavery and cared nothing about them (1945: 139).

And later:

> The consequence of this trifling with the plain meaning of the New Testament is that Paul and the early church generally are steadily represented as oblivious of what was, of course, the greatest wrong in the ancient world (140).[11]

[9] As with almost all translations when they first appear, Goodspeed's version met with vigorous opposition. In his autobiography (1953: 172), Goodspeed reminisces about the furor his work provoked and cites the eloquent outburst of a Dr Keene Ryan of Chicago: 'Theologians and laymen alike will await with awe for God to strike him dead for thus laying his calloused hands upon the Holy of Holies'!

[10] But there are surprising exceptions to Goodspeed's general procedure. For example, in a single parable (Luke 17:7–10), *doulos* is rendered 'servant' in v. 7 but 'slave' in vv. 9–10. And in Col. 4:7, 'fellow-servant' renders *syndoulos* but the same Greek word is represented by 'fellow-slave' in Col. 1:7.

[11] See further Goodspeed 1943: 169f.

A case study (the New International Version)

The NIV is, remarkably, the first version in 360 years to eclipse the AV in annual sales.[12] So an analysis of its treatment of the *doul-* root will give some general indication of the present state of the issues under consideration.

Five words formed from the *doul-* root are invariably translated by some form of the root 'slave' or its equivalent, but never by 'servant', 'serve', 'service':[13] *doulagōgeō* (1 NT use); *douleia* (5x) (but *cf. ophthalmodoulia*, Eph. 6:6; Col. 3:22); *doulos* (adjective) (2x); *douloō* (8x); *katadouloō* (2x).

The feminine noun *doulē* (3x) is always rendered 'servant' (Luke 1:38, 48; [Acts 2:18]).

The verb *douleuō* (25x) is rendered by 'serve' (16x), the 'slave' root (8x), or 'serve as slave' (1x).

The noun *doulos* (124x) is rendered by 'servant' (94x), 'slave' (29x), or 'slavery' (1x).

The *diakon-* root is never translated 'slave' (*diakoneō*, 37x; *diakonia*, 34x; *diakonos*, 29x).

Syndoulos (10x) is rendered 'fellow-servant' (9x) or 'other servant' (1x).

The word 'servant' is used to translate some ten different Greek terms: *doulos* (94x), *diakonos* (20x), *pais* (13x), *syndoulos* (10x), *paidiskē* (6x; 'servant girl', 'maidservant'), *hypēretēs* (4x), *doulē* (3x), *oiketēs* (3x), *leitourgos* (2x), *oiketeia* (1x; 'servant in the household').

An examination of these data shows that like most English versions, the NIV generally avoids the rendering 'slave' for *doulos* unless physical slavery or slavery to something impersonal is in view. Overall, 'servant' is used about three times more frequently than 'slave' to translate *doulos*. *Syndoulos* is never rendered 'fellow-slave'. With respect to the commonest verb formed from the *doul-* stem, *viz. douleuō*, the translation 'serve' is twice as frequent as a form using the term 'slave'.

---

[12] The NIV NT was first published in 1973 and the full Bible in 1978.

[13] The following data are drawn from Goodrick & Kohlenberger III 1990: 1701, 1705.

'Slave' and 'servant' in modern English

The three principal meanings of the noun 'slave' given in *OED*, IX (Section Si. –St.), 182 are:

1. One who is the property of, and entirely subject to, another person, whether by capture, purchase, or birth; a servant completely divested of freedom and personal rights.

2. a. *transf[erred]*. One who submits in a servile manner to the authority or dictation of another or others; a submissive or devoted servant.

   b. *fig[urative]*. One who is completely under the domination *of*, or subject *to*, a specified influence.

3. One whose condition in respect of toil is comparable to that of a slave.

In modern English, both the terms 'slave' and 'servant' may refer to a person who renders service to or labours for another. But whereas a slave belongs to another person as a chattel, a servant may be in the employ of another person as a wage-earner.[14] Every slave is a servant in that he or she is obligated to do the bidding of a superior; but not every servant is a slave, for a servant may be a paid employee (*e.g.*, a public servant is a person employed and paid by the government).

We may legitimately conclude that in modern English usage these two terms share some common conceptual territory, *viz.* service for another, but they differ in that the slave, being another person's property, does not have the servant's right to discontinue service. Hence our initial definition (p. 25) of a slave as 'someone whose person and service belong wholly to another', a definition that applies equally to ancient and modern slavery and equally to literal and figurative slavery.

A translation proposal

I do not advocate that *doulos* should invariably be rendered 'slave'. Just as the cognate verb *douleuō* may be appropriately translated by 'serve' as well as by 'be a slave' or 'act as a slave', so the New

---

[14] Goodspeed (1945: 139) defines a servant as 'an employed person, who could be discharged or resign'.

Testament translator may legitimately use 'servant' as an occasional rendering of *doulos*, especially in the narrative and parabolic sections of the gospels. After all, by definition a *doulos* was always a *diakonos*, 'one who serves'.

Translators should continue to use 'slave' for *doulos*, (a) in the 'slave–free' antithesis; (b) in the 'household tables', where masters and slaves are mentioned; and (c) when slavery is to something impersonal (such as sin, depravity or obedience).

But the area where translators need to be more courageous is in translating the terms *doulos* and *syndoulos* as 'slave' and 'fellow-slave' in reference to the Christian's relation (a) to Christ or God, and (b) to other believers (2 Cor. 4:5, where Goodspeed, NAB2, and NRSV already have 'slaves'). Under category (a), the following passages are relevant.

Reference	English versions reading 'slave(s)'
Matt. 10:24–25	Goodspeed, NASB, GNB, JB, NJB, NAB1, 2, NRSV, CEV, RSV (fn. 'Or *slave*')
Luke 17:7, 9–10	Weymouth (fn. 'Or *slave*', on vv. 7, 9), Goodspeed (vv. 9–10), NRSV, NASB
John 13:16	Goodspeed, RSV and NRSV (fn. '*slave(s)*'), NASB, GNB, NAB1, 2, Cassirer
John 15:15	Goodspeed, RSV and NRSV (fn. '*slaves ... slave*'), NASB, NAB1, 2
John 15:20	RSV and NRSV (fn. '*slave(s)*'), NASB, GNB, NAB1, 2, Goodspeed
Acts 4:29	RSV and NRSV (fn. '*slaves*'), Goodspeed
Acts 16:17	NRSV, NAB2, Goodspeed
Rom. 1:1	RSV and NRSV (fn. '*slave*'), Goodspeed, NAB2, NLT
1 Cor. 7:22	TCNT, Moffatt, Goodspeed, RSV, NEB, NASB, GNB, JB, NAB1, 2, NIV, NJB, NRSV, Cassirer, CEV, NLT
Gal. 1:10	RSV and NRSV (fn. '*slave*'), Goodspeed, NAB2, Cassirer
Eph. 6:6	TCNT, Goodspeed, NEB, NASB, GNB, JB, NAB1, 2, NIV, NJB, REB, NRSV, CEV, NLT
Phil. 1:1	RSV and NRSV (fn. '*slaves*'), Goodspeed, NLT
Phil. 2:7	NEB, REB, JB, NJB, RSV (fn. '*slave*'), NRSV, NAB1, 2, Goodspeed, Cassirer, CEV, NLT
Col. 1:7	Goodspeed, NRSV (fn. 'Gk *slave*'), NAB1, 2
Col. 4:7	NRSV (fn. 'Gk. *slave*'), NAB1, 2

Col. 4:12	RSV and NRSV (fn. '*slave*'), Goodspeed, NASB ('bondslave'), NAB2
2 Tim. 2:24	Goodspeed, NAB2, NRSV (fn. 'Gk *slave*')
Titus 1:1	RSV and NRSV (fn. '*slave*'), NAB2, Goodspeed, NLT
Jas. 1:1	NRSV (fn. 'Gk *slave*'), NAB2, Goodspeed, NLT
1 Pet. 2:16	NRSV (fn. 'Gk *slaves*'), NEB, REB, JB, NJB, NASB ('bondslave'), GNB, NAB2, Goodspeed, NLT
2 Pet. 1:1	NAB2, Goodspeed, NLT
Jude 1	NAB2, Goodspeed, NLT
Rev. 1:1	Goodspeed, NRSV (fn. 'Gk *slave(s)*')
Rev. 2:20	Goodspeed, NRSV (fn. 'Gk *slaves*')
Rev. 6:11	Goodspeed, NRSV (fn. 'Gk *slaves*')
Rev. 7:3	Goodspeed, NRSV (fn. 'Gk *slaves*')
Rev. 10:7	Goodspeed, NRSV (fn. 'Gk *slaves*')
Rev. 11:18	Goodspeed, NRSV (fn. 'Gk *slaves*')
Rev. 15:3	Goodspeed, NRSV (fn. 'Gk *slave*')
Rev. 19:2	Goodspeed, NRSV (fn. 'Gk *slaves*')
Rev. 19:5	Goodspeed, NRSV (fn. 'Gk *slaves*')
Rev. 19:10	Goodspeed, NRSV (fn. 'Gk *slave*')
Rev. 22:3	Goodspeed, NRSV (fn. 'Gk *slaves*')
Rev. 22:6	Goodspeed, NRSV (fn. 'Gk *slaves*')
Rev. 22:9	Goodspeed, NRSV (fn. 'Gk *slave*')

Support for such proposals

In the last forty years there has been a greater willingness shown in English translations to render *doulos* by 'slave'. This is particularly apparent in the rendering of Matthew 10:24–25 ('Students are not above their teachers, nor *slaves* above their masters. It is enough for students to be like their teachers, and the *slaves* like their masters'); Matthew 20:27 ('Whoever wants to be first must be your *slave*'; thus most modern translations, since v. 27 with *doulos* is an intensification of v. 26, where, in parallelism, *diakonos* ['servant'] is found); Romans 6:16 ('Don't you know that when you offer yourselves to someone as obedient *slaves* you are *slaves* of the one whom you obey – whether you are *slaves* of sin, which leads to death, or of obedience, which leads to righteousness?'); Philippians 2:7 ('[Christ Jesus ...] emptied himself by taking the form of a *slave*'); 1 Peter 2:16 ('Live as free persons, but do not use your freedom as a pretext for evil; live as *slaves* of God').

Specific evidence of this trend includes the following:

1. NASB has *doulos* = 'slave' (without a footnote) at six important places where RV had 'servant' (fn. 'Gr. *bondservant*'), *viz.* Matthew 10:24–25; 18:23; 20:27; Romans 6:16 (2x).

2. NRSV has *doulos* = 'slave' at six important places where RSV had 'servant' (sometimes with a footnote 'Or *slave*'), *viz.* Matthew 10:24–25; 18:23; Acts 16:17; 2 Corinthians 4:5; Philippians 2:7.

3. NAB2 (a more conservative rendering than NAB1) has *doulos* = 'slave' at twelve important places where the first edition had 'servant', *viz.* Acts 16:17; Romans 1:1; Philippians 1:1; Colossians 4:12; 2 Corinthians 4:5; Galatians 1:10; 2 Timothy 2:24; Titus 1:1; James 1:1; 1 Peter 2:16; 2 Peter 1:1; Jude 1).

4. NLT (1996) has *doulos* = 'slave' in at least nine important places, *viz.* Matthew 20:27; Romans 1:1; Philippians 1:1; 2:7; Titus 1:1; James 1:1; 1 Peter 2:16; 2 Peter 1:1; Jude 1.

It is of special significance that the strongest support for rendering *doulos* by 'slave' comes from lexicographers, who, while not translators, are not unaware of the need for sensitivity to the dominant connotations of a word in the 'receptor language'. The three most distinguished New Testament lexicographers of recent times are G. A. Deissmann, W. Bauer and C. Spicq.[15] Deissmann comments that 'the translation of *doulos* by "servant" rather than "slave" [led] to the total effacement of its ancient significance' (1965: 319). The standard lexicon for New Testament and early Christian Greek, now known as BAGD (Bauer–Arndt–Gingrich–Danker), is essentially the pioneering work of Bauer. This dictionary proposes 'slave' as the appropriate rendering of *doulos* everywhere in the New Testament, except for ten places in Matthew where 'minister' (of a king's official) is the suggested translation (205f. *s. v.*).[16] Finally, Spicq (1994: 1. 380) begins his treatment of *doulos* with the blunt affirmation, 'It is wrong to translate *doulos* as "servant", so obscuring its precise signification in the language of the first century.' Similar sentiments are expressed by S. S. Bartchy (1992: 6. 66), an authority on first-century slavery: 'In contrast to the Authorized Version's translation of the Gk term *doulos* as "servant", the word "slave" should be used in order to stress the legally regulated subordination of the person in slavery. Yet in contrast to present connotations of the term "slave" resulting from the specific racial, economic, educational, and political practices characteristic of slavery in the

---

[15] Deissmann and Spicq were also eminent papyrologists.

[16] The ten instances in Matthew are 18:23, 26–28, 32; 22:3–4, 6, 8, 10.

New World, the slaves and slavery mentioned in NT texts must be defined strictly in terms of the profoundly different legal-social contexts of the 1st century C. E.'

Bibliography

Allard, P. (1988). *Les esclaves chrétiens depuis les premiers temps de l'église jusqu'à la fin de la domination romaine en occident.* Evanston, IL: American Theological Library Association. (Paris: Lecoffre, 1876; 6th ed. 1914).

Balch, D. L. (1988). 'Household Codes'. In *Greco-Roman Literature and the New Testament*, ed. D. E. Aune, 25–50. Atlanta: Scholars.

Balsdon, J. P. V. D. (1969). *Life and Leisure in Ancient Rome.* London: The Bodley Head.

Barclay, J. M. G. (1991). 'Paul, Philemon and the Dilemma of Christian Slave-Ownership'. *NTS* 37: 161–186.

Barclay, W. (1958). *The Mind of St. Paul.* New York: Harper.

Barrow, R. H. (1968). *Slavery in the Roman Empire.* New York: Barnes and Noble. (London: Methuen; New York: Dial, 1928).

Bartchy, S. S. (1973). *Mallon Chrēsai: First-Century Slavery and the Interpretation of 1 Corinthians 7:21.* Missoula: Society of Biblical Literature.

——(1988). 'Slavery'. *ISBE*2 4. 543–546.

——(1992). 'Slavery: New Testament'. *ABD* 6. 65–73.

Barth, M. (1974). *Ephesians 1 – 3.* Garden City, NY: Doubleday.

Bauckham, R. J. (1983). *Jude, 2 Peter.* Waco, TX: Word.

Beare, F. W. (1959). *A Commentary on the Epistle to the Philippians.* San Francisco: Harper.

Beavis, M. A. (1992). 'Ancient Slavery as an Interpretive Context for the New Testament Servant Parables with Special Reference to the Unjust Steward (Luke 16:1–8)'. *JBL* 111: 37–54.

Beckwith, I. T. (1967). *The Apocalypse of St. John.* Grand Rapids: Baker. (London: Macmillan, 1919).

Beekman, J., & Callow, J. (1974). *Translating the Word of God.* Grand Rapids: Zondervan.

Bellen, H. (1971). *Studien zur Sklavenflucht im römischen Kaiserreich.* Wiesbaden: Steiner.

Bömer, F. (1957, 1960, 1962, 1963) *Untersuchungen über die Religion der Sklaven in Griechenland und Rom*, 4 vols. Wiesbaden: Steiner.

Bradley, K. R. (1987). *Slaves and Masters in the Roman Empire: A Study in Social Control.* New York: OUP. (First published Bruxelles: Latomus, 1984).

——(1994). *Slavery and Society at Rome.* Cambridge: CUP.

Bristol, L. O. (1958). 'A Servant of Jesus Christ'. *Foundations* 1: 79.

Bruce, F. F. (1977). *Paul: Apostle of the 'Free Spirit'.* Exeter: Paternoster. Published in the USA as *Paul: Apostle of the Heart Set Free.* Grand Rapids: Eerdmans.

——(1982). *The Epistle of Paul to the Galatians.* Exeter: Paternoster; Grand Rapids: Eerdmans.

——(1985). *The Pauline Circle.* Exeter: Paternoster; Grand Rapids: Eerdmans.

——(1988). *The Book of Acts*, rev. ed. Grand Rapids: Eerdmans.

——(1990). *The Acts of the Apostles: The Greek Text with Introduction and Commentary*, 3rd ed. Leicester: Apollos; Grand Rapids: Eerdmans.

Buckland, W. W. (1969). *The Roman Law of Slavery: The Condition of the Slave in Private Law from Augustus to Justinian.* New York: AMS Press. (Cambridge: CUP, 1908.)

Büchsel, F. (1964). '*agorazō*'. *TDNT* 1. 124–128.

Bultmann, R. (1955). *Theology of the New Testament* II. London: SCM.

——(1968). '*pisteuō*'. *TDNT* 6. 174–182.

Burton, E. de W. (1921). *The Epistle to the Galatians.* Edinburgh: Clark.

Caird, G. B. (1976). *Paul's Letters from Prison.* London: OUP.

Carcopino, J. (1940). *Daily Life in Ancient Rome: The People and the City at the Height of the Empire*, ed. H. T. Rowell, tr. E. O. Lorimer. New Haven and London: Yale University Press.

Chamblin, J. K. (1993). *Paul and the Self: Apostolic Teaching for Personal Wholeness.* Grand Rapids: Baker.

Coleman-Norton, P. R. (1951). 'The Apostle Paul and the Roman Law of Slavery'. In *Studies in Roman Economic and Social History in Honor of Allan Chester Johnson*, ed. P. R. Coleman-Norton, 155–177. Princeton: Princeton University Press.

Corcoran, G. (1980a, 1980b). 'Slavery in the New Testament', Part 1, *MS* 5: 1–40; Part 2, *MS* 6: 62–83.

Crabtree, H. (1991). *The Christian Life: Traditional Metaphors and Contemporary Theologies.* Minneapolis: Fortress.

Cranfield, C. E. B. (1975, 1979). *The Epistle to the Romans.* 2 vols. Edinburgh: Clark.

Crook, J. A. (1967). *Law and Life of Rome, 90 BC – AD 212.* Ithaca, NY: Cornell University Press.

Cruz, H. (1990). *Christological Motives and Motivated Actions in Pauline Paraenesis.* Frankfurt am Main: Lang.

Cupitt, D. (1972). *Crisis of Moral Authority: The Dethronement of Christianity.* London: Lutterworth.

Daube, D. (1959). 'Concessions to Sinfulness in Jewish Law'. *JJS* 10: 1–13.

Davies, M. (1995). 'Work and Slavery in the New Testament: Impoverishments of Traditions'. In *The Bible in Ethics: The Second Sheffield Colloquium*, ed. J. W. Rogerson *et al.*, 315–347. Sheffield: Sheffield Academic Press.

Davis, D. B. (1966). *The Problem of Slavery in Western Culture.* Ithaca, NY: Cornell University Press.

Deissmann, G. A. (1903). *Bible Studies.* 2nd ed. Tr. A. Grieve. Edinburgh: Clark.

——(1965). *Light from the Ancient East*, 2nd ed. Tr. L. R. M. Strachan from 4th German ed. (1922). Grand Rapids: Baker. (London: Hodder; New York: Doran, 1927.)

Dibelius, M. (1976). *A Commentary on the Epistle of James.* Philadelphia: Fortress.

Dodd, B. J. (1996). *The Problem with Paul.* Downers Grove, IL: IVP.

Duff, A. M. (1958). *Freedmen in the Early Roman Empire.* Cambridge: Heffer; Oxford: Clarendon. (Reprint of 1928 edition.)

Dunn, J. D. G. (1977). *Unity and Diversity in the New Testament.* London: SCM.

——(1988). *Romans 1 – 8, 9 – 16.* 2 vols. Dallas: Word.

——(1993a). *Christian Liberty: A New Testament Perspective.* Grand Rapids: Eerdmans.

——(1993b). *The Epistle to the Galatians.* London: Black; Peabody, MA: Hendrickson.

Elert, W. (1947). 'Redemptio ab Hostibus'. *TLZ* 72: 265–270.

Fee, G. D. (1987). *The First Epistle to the Corinthians.* Grand Rapids: Eerdmans.

Ferguson, E. (1987). *Backgrounds of Early Christianity.* Grand Rapids: Eerdmans.

Finley, M. I. (1974). 'Was Greek Civilization Based on Slave Labour?' In Finley, ed., 1974, 53–72. (= *Historia* 8 [1959]: 145–164.)

——(1976). 'A Peculiar Institution?' *TLS*, 2 July, 819–821.

——(1980). *Ancient Slavery and Modern Ideology.* London: Chatto & Windus; New York: Viking.

——(ed.) (1974). *Slavery in Classical Antiquity: Views and Controversy*. Cambridge: Heffer (1st ed. 1960).

——(ed.) (1987). *Classical Slavery*. London and Totowa, NJ: Cass.

Fisher, N. R. E. (1993). *Slavery in Classical Greece*. London: Bristol Classical Press.

Fitzmyer, J. A. (1989). *Paul and His Theology: A Brief Sketch*, Englewood Cliffs, NJ: Prentice Hall.

Flory, M. B. (1983). 'Where Women Precede Men: Factors Influencing the Order of Names in Roman Epitaphs'. *The Classical Journal* 79: 216–224.

Frank, T. *et al.* (eds.) (1933–1940). *An Economic Survey of Ancient Rome*. 6 vols. Baltimore: Johns Hopkins University Press.

Fung, R. Y. K. (1988). *The Epistle to the Galatians*, 2nd ed. Grand Rapids: Eerdmans.

Gale, H. M. (1964). *The Use of Analogy in the Letters of Paul*. Philadelphia: Westminster.

Garlan, Y. (1988). *Slavery in Ancient Greece*, rev. ed. London and Ithaca, NY: Cornell University Press.

Garnsey, P. (1982). 'Slaves in Business'. *Roma* 1: 105–108.

Giles, K. (1994). 'The Biblical Argument for Slavery: Can the Bible Mislead? A Case Study in Hermeneutics'. *EQ* 66: 3–17.

Goodrick, E. W., & Kohlenberger III, J. R. (1990) *The NIV Exhaustive Concordance*. Grand Rapids: Zondervan.

Goodspeed, E. J. (1943). 'Paul and Slavery'. *JBR* 11: 169–170.

——(1945). *Problems of New Testament Translation*. Chicago: University of Chicago Press.

——(1953). *As I Remember*. New York: Harper.

Gülzow, H. (1969). *Christentum und Sklaverei in den ersten drei Jahrhunderten*. Bonn: Habelt.

Gundry, R. H. (1982). *Matthew: A Commentary on his Literary and Theological Art*. Grand Rapids: Eerdmans.

Harrill, J. A. (1995). *The Manumission of Slaves in Early Christianity*. Tübingen: Mohr.

Harris, M. J. (1978). 'Prepositions and Theology in the Greek New Testament', in *NIDNTT* 3. 1171–1215.

——(1983). *Raised Immortal: Resurrection and Immortality in the New Testament*. London: Marshall; Grand Rapids: Eerdmans.

——(1986). 'Lord', in *ISBE*2 3. 157f.

——(1991). *Colossians and Philemon*. Grand Rapids: Eerdmans.

——(1992). *Jesus as God: The New Testament Use of Theos in Reference to Jesus*. Grand Rapids: Baker.

Heitmüller, W. (1903). *Im Namen Jesu: Eine sprach- und religions-geschichtliche Untersuchung zum Neuen Testament, speziell zur altchristliche Taufe.* Göttingen: Vandenhoeck & Ruprecht.

Hiebert, D. E. (1973). *Personalities Around Paul.* Chicago: Moody.

Hopkins, K. (1978). *Conquerors and Slaves.* Sociological Studies in Roman History 1. Cambridge: CUP.

Jacoby, F. (1926). *Die Fragmente der griechischen Historiker.* Berlin: Weidmann.

Jeremias, J. (1969). *Jerusalem in the Time of Jesus.* London: SCM.

Jones, A. H. M. (1974). 'Slavery in the Ancient World'. In Finley, ed., 1974, 1–15. (= *The Economic History Review*, 2nd series, 9 [1956]: 185–199.)

Kittel, G. (1964a). '*aichmalōtos*'. *TDNT* 1. 195–197.

——(1964b). '*desmos*'. *TDNT* 2. 43.

Kleinknecht, H. (1967). '*nomos*'. *TDNT* 4. 1022–1035.

Knight, G. W., III. (1992). *The Pastoral Epistles.* Carlisle: Paternoster; Grand Rapids: Eerdmans.

Kruse, C. (1992). 'Human Relationships in the Pauline Corpus'. In *In the Fullness of Time*, ed. D. Peterson and J. Pryor, 167–184. Homebush West, New South Wales: Anzea.

Lampe, P. (1985). 'Keine "Sklavenflucht" des Onesimus', *ZNW* 76: 135–137.

——(1987). 'Paulus – Zeltmacher'. *BZ* 31: 211–221.

——(1989). *Die stadtrömischen Christen in den ersten beiden Jahrhunderten*, 2nd ed. Tübingen: Mohr.

——(1992a). 'Aquila'. *ABD* 1. 319–320.

——(1992b). 'Onesimus'. *ABD* 5. 21–22.

——(1992c). 'Prisca'. *ABD* 5. 467–468.

LaSor, W. S. (1965). *Great Personalities of the Bible.* Westwood, NJ: Revell.

Lees, H. C. (1918). *St. Paul's Friends.* London: Religious Tract Society.

Lightfoot, J. B. (1900). *St. Paul's Epistles to the Colossians and to Philemon.* London: Macmillan.

Llewelyn, S. R (ed.). (1992). *New Documents Illustrating Early Christianity*, 6: *A Review of the Greek Inscriptions and Papyri Published in 1980–81.* North Ryde, New South Wales: Macquarie University Press.

Lock, W. (1924). *The Pastoral Epistles.* Edinburgh: Clark.

Longenecker, R. N. (1976). *Paul: Apostle of Liberty.* Grand Rapids: Baker. (New York: Harper, 1964.)

——(1990). *Galatians*. Dallas: Word.

Luther, M. *Christian Liberty* (1943). Philadelphia: Muhlenberg. (First published 1520.)

Lyall, F. (1970). 'Roman Law in the Writings of Paul – The Slave and the Freedman'. *NTS* 17: 73–79.

——(1984). *Slaves, Citizens, Sons: Legal Metaphors in the Epistles*. Grand Rapids: Zondervan.

M'Neile, A. H. (1915). *The Gospel According to St. Matthew*. London: Macmillan.

Marshall, I. H. (1974). 'The Development of the Concept of Redemption in the New Testament'. In *Reconciliation and Hope: New Testament Essays on Atonement and Eschatology Presented to L. L. Morris*, ed. R. Banks, 153–169. Exeter: Paternoster; Grand Rapids: Eerdmans.

Marshall, P. (1987). *Enmity in Corinth: Social Conventions in Paul's Relations with the Corinthians*. Tübingen: Mohr.

Martin, D. B. (1990). *Slavery as Salvation: The Metaphor of Slavery in Pauline Christianity*. New Haven: Yale University Press.

Mendelsohn, I. (1948). *Slavery in the Ancient Near East: A Comparative Study of Slavery in Babylonia, Assyria, Syria, and Palestine from the Middle of the Third Millennium to the End of the First Millennium*. Oxford: OUP. (New York: OUP, 1949.)

——(1962). 'Slavery in the OT'. *IDB* 4. 383–391.

Metzger, B. M. (1994). *A Textual Commentary on the Greek New Testament*, 2nd ed. New York: United Bible Societies.

Meyer, H. A. W. (1889). *The Acts of the Apostles*, 2nd ed. New York: Funk & Wagnalls.

Moffatt, J. (1970). 'The Revelation of St. John the Divine'. In *EGT* 5. 279–494.

Moo, D. J. (1996). *The Epistle to the Romans*. Grand Rapids: Eerdmans.

Moody, D. A. (1995). 'On the Road Again'. *RE* 92: 95–101.

Morris, L. (1996). *Galatians*. Leicester and Downers Grove, IL: IVP.

Moule, C. F. D. (1962). *The Birth of the New Testament*. London: Black.

Moule, H. C. G. (1896). *The Epistle to the Romans*. London: Pickering and Inglis.

Mueller, H. (1964). 'Morality of Slavery in Holy Scripture'. *AER* 151: 307–316.

Murphy-O'Connor, J. (1992). 'Prisca and Aquila'. *BR* 8: 40–51.

O'Brien, P. T. (1982). *Colossians, Philemon*. Waco, TX: Word.

——(1991). *The Epistle to the Philippians*. Grand Rapids: Eerdmans.

Ollrog, W. H. (1979). *Paulus und seiner Mitarbeiter*. Neukirchen-Vluyn: Neukirchener Verlag.

Oost, S. I. (1958). 'The Career of M. Antonius Pallas'. *AJP* 79: 113–139.

Osiek, C. (1984). 'Slavery in the New Testament World'. *BT* 22: 151–155.

Patterson, O. (1982). *Slavery and Social Death: A Comparative Study*. Cambridge, MA: Harvard University Press.

Petersen, N. R. (1985). *Rediscovering Paul: Philemon and the Sociology of Paul's Narrative World*. Philadelphia: Fortress.

Pritchard, J. B. (ed.) (1969). *Ancient Near Eastern Texts Relating to the Old Testament*, 3rd ed. Princeton: Princeton University Press.

Ramage, E. S., *et al.* (1974). *Roman Satirists and the Satire*. Park Ridge, NJ: Noyes.

Ramsay, W. M. (1895, 1897). *The Cities and Bishoprics of Phrygia*, 2 vols. Oxford: Clarendon.

——(1920). *St. Paul the Traveller and the Roman Citizen*, 14th ed. London: Hodder.

Rapske, B. M. (1991). 'The Prisoner Paul in the Eyes of Onesimus'. *NTS* 37: 187–203.

Rengstorf, K. H. (1964). '*doulos*'. *TDNT* 2. 261–280.

Richardson, A. (1958). *An Introduction to the Theology of the New Testament*. London: SCM.

Robertson, A. T. (1922). *Types of Preachers in the New Testament*. New York: Doran.

Rollins, W. G. (1976). 'Slavery in the NT'. *IDB* 5. 830–832.

——(1987). 'Greco-Roman Slave Terminology and Pauline Metaphors for Salvation'. *Society of Biblical Literature Seminar Papers 1987*, ed. K. H. Richards, 100–110. Atlanta: Scholars.

Rupprecht, A. A. (1974). 'Attitudes on Slavery among the Church Fathers.' In *New Dimensions in New Testament Study*, ed. R. N. Longenecker and M. C. Tenney, 261–277. Grand Rapids: Zondervan.

——(1975). 'Slave, Slavery.' *ZPEB* 5. 453–460.

Russell, K. C. (1968). *Slavery as Reality and Metaphor in the Pauline Letters*. Rome: Catholic Book Agency.

——(1972). 'Slavery as Reality and Metaphor in the Non-Pauline New Testament Books.' *Revue de l'Université d'Ottawa* 42: 439–469.

Sanday, W., & Headlam, A. C. (1902). *The Epistle to the Romans*, 5th ed. Edinburgh: Clark.

Sass, G. (1941). 'Zur Bedeutung von *doulos* bei Paulus'. *ZNW* 40: 24–32.

Schulz, S. (1972). *Gott ist kein Sklavenhalter*. Zürich and Hamburg: Flamberg.

Seekings, H. S. (1914). *The Men of the Pauline Circle*. London: Kelly.

Segal, E. (1987). *Roman Laughter: The Comedy of Plautus*, 2nd ed. Cambridge, MA: Harvard University Press.

Sevenster, J. N. (1961). *Paul and Seneca*. Leiden: Brill.

Sowell, T. (1994). *Race and Culture: A World View*. New York: Basic Books.

Spicq, C. (1969). *Les épîtres pastorales*, 2 vols. Paris: Gabalda.

——(1978). 'Le vocabulaire de l'esclavage dans le Nouveau Testament'. *RB* 85: 201–226.

——(1994). *Theological Lexicon of the New Testament*, 3 vols. Eng. tr. Peabody, MA: Hendrickson.

Stek, J. H. (1978). 'Salvation, Justice and Liberation in the Old Testament'. *CTJ* 13: 133–165.

Swete, H. B. (1909). *The Apocalypse of St. John*, 3rd. ed. London: Macmillan.

Szakats, A. (1975). 'Slavery as a Social and Economic Institution in Antiquity with Special Reference to Roman Law'. *Prudentia* 7: 33–45.

Theissen, G. (1982). *The Social Setting of Pauline Christianity*. Ed. and tr. by J. H. Schütz. Philadelphia: Fortress.

Tidball, D. (1984). *The Social Context of the New Testament: A Sociological Analysis*. Grand Rapids: Zondervan.

Tuente, R. (1978). '*doulos*'. *NIDNTT* 3. 592–598.

Vaux, R. de. (1965). *Ancient Israel: Its Life and Institutions*. Eng. tr., 2 vols., 2nd ed. London: Darton, Longman and Todd; New York: McGraw-Hill.

Visscher, F. de. (1946). 'De l'acquisition du droit de cité romaine par l'affranchissement'. *Studia et documenta historiae et iuris* 12: 69–85.

Vogt, J. (1972). *Sklaverei und Humanität: Studien zur antiken Sklaverei und ihrer Forschung*. Historia-Einzelschriften Heft 8, 2nd ed. Wiesbaden: Steiner.

Waldstein, W. (1986). *Operae Libertorum: Untersuchungen zur Dienstpflicht freigelassener*. Stuttgart: Steiner.

Wallon, H. (1879). *Historie de l'esclavage dans l'antiquité*, 3 vols., 3rd ed. Paris: Hachette.

Wansink, C. S. (1996). *Chained in Christ: The Experience and Rhetoric of Paul's Imprisonments*. Sheffield: JSOT.

Watson, A. (1987). *Roman Slave Law*. Baltimore: Johns Hopkins University Press.

Weaver, P. R. C. (1972). *Familia Caesaris: A Social Study of the Emperor's Freedmen and Slaves*. Cambridge: CUP.

Wenham, D. (1995). *Paul: Follower of Jesus or Founder of Christianity?* Grand Rapids: Eerdmans.

Westermann, W. L. (1938). 'Enslaved Persons Who Are Free'. *AJP* 59: 1–30.

——(1948). 'The Freedman and the Slaves of God'. *PAPS* 92: 55–64.

——(1955). *The Slave Systems of Greek and Roman Antiquity*. Philadelphia: American Philosophical Society.

——(1974). 'Slavery and the Elements of Freedom in Ancient Greece'. In Finley, ed., 1974, 17–32. (= *Quarterly Bulletin of the Polish Institute of Arts and Sciences in America* 1 [1943]: 332–347.)

Wiedemann, T. E. J. (1981). *Greek and Roman Slavery: A Source Book*. Baltimore: Johns Hopkins University Press.

——(1987). *Slavery*. Oxford: Clarendon.

Willink, M. D. R. (1928). 'Paul, a Slave of Jesus Christ'. *Theology* 16: 46–47.

Winer, G. B. (1872). *A Grammar of the Idiom of the New Testament*, 7th ed. enlarged by G. Lünemann. Andover: Draper; London: Trübner.

Yamauchi, E. (1966). 'Slaves of God'. *BETS* 9: 31–49.

Yavetz, Z. (1988). *Slaves and Slavery in Ancient Rome*. Oxford and New Brunswick: Transaction.

Zerwick, M. (1963). *Biblical Greek Illustrated by Examples*. Rome: Pontifical Biblical Institute.

——(1988). *A Grammatical Analysis of the Greek New Testament*, tr. and rev. by M. Grosvenor, 3rd ed. Rome: Pontifical Biblical Institute.

Ziesler, J. A. (1983). '*Sōma* in the Septuagint'. *NovT* 25: 133–145.

Index of authors

Index of subjects

Index of principal Greek and Latin terms and phrases

Greek

Latin

Index of Bible references

Detailed or important discussions are indicated by an asterisk.
References to the Septuagint are indicated by LXX.

Old Testament

New Testament

Index of other ancient authors and writings